A Child's History of France

NAPOLEON I

A CHILD'S HISTORY OF FRANCE

BY

JOHN BONNER

AUTHOR OF "A CHILD'S HISTORY OF ROME"
"A CHILD'S HISTORY OF GREECE" ETC.

ILLUSTRATED

NEW YORK
HARPER & BROTHERS PUBLISHERS
1893

TO

SEWALL BOARDMAN

IN THE HOPE THAT THIS LITTLE BOOK MAY TEMPT HIM TO
READ LARGER AND BETTER WORKS ON THE SUBJECT
THIS "CHILD'S HISTORY OF FRANCE" IS

Affectionately Inscribed

MANY years ago, when I wrote the Child's Histories of Rome and Greece, I resolved to attempt similar histories of modern nations. It has never been possible for me to write them till now.

They are based on the idea that young people will enjoy and remember histories which are mainly devoted to incident, drama, portrait, landscape, romance, and local color; and that in reading these they may wish to become acquainted with more serious works, containing expositions of political doctrine, and narratives of campaigns with maps and dates. In this "Child's History of France," and in the Child's Histories with which I hope to follow it, I try to tell a tale which the young will like and will not forget.

The title of "Child's History" is not exact. These histories are not intended exclusively for young children; it is hoped that they will commend themselves likewise to boys and girls who are ready to enter college.

J. B.

April, 1893.

CONTENTS

ILLUSTRATIONS

A CHILD'S HISTORY OF FRANCE

Chapter I

CLOVIS, FIRST KING OF FRANCE

A.D. 481–511

Fourteen or fifteen hundred years ago, there came paddling across the Rhine, in canoes and on rafts, bands of tall warriors, some of them with painted bodies and wild beasts' skins on their shoulders, others in gaudy woollen stuffs, some with iron breast-plates, many with gold chains round their necks, and all armed with either sword, axe, spear, mace, or pike. They were called Franks, and came from the forests of Germany, and the fens of the valley of the Danube. They were going to the country which was then called Gaul, and which after them was called France.

Gaul was at this time the home of a number of races which bore the names of Gauls, Celts, Belges, Goths, Visigoths, Bretons, Iberians, and Burgundians, spoke the same or nearly the same language, and were brave, fierce, and rough. Among them was a sprinkling of Romans, and some of the young men of the native races had been educated at Rome, spoke Latin, wore clothes cut in the Roman fashion, and were mannered like the Romans. Some five hundred years before, the country had been conquered by the Romans under their valiant general, Julius

Cæsar, and had become a Roman province. It was for the most part a wild country, with much thicket, forest, marsh, swamp, and bare rock; cold fogs were frequent in the north; there were but few roads or bridges; to go from place to place travellers had to ride or trudge over bridle paths, through thick woods which were infested by wolves and bears, as well as by robbers and murderers. But on the plains and in the river valleys, especially in the south, were vineyards, orchards, and fields of waving grain; and in the towns, of which there were quite a number, stood theatres, circuses, aqueducts, churches, and temples. For the Romans improved every country they conquered.

They had had desperate work to conquer the Gauls. Julius Cæsar, the greatest general they ever had, spent nine whole years in fighting them. It looked as if they *could not* be conquered. The work was not done till Cæsar had killed two millions of them, and till the rivers ran south to the Mediterranean and north to the British Channel red with blood. Even the women fought like men, and died by their husbands' sides. There is a place in France which bears the dreadful name of Pourrières; if you go to see it, you will be told that a whole tribe—men, women, and children—were there butchered by the Roman soldiers, and their bodies left to rot in the sun.

At last, when the best fighting-men of every tribe had been killed, and the chiefs—great, tall, splendid fellows, with blue eyes and tawny hair, and heads which towered above the Romans—had been sent to Rome to march in Cæsar's triumphal procession with their hands chained behind their backs, the Romans felt that Gaul was theirs. The fighting was indeed over; the Gauls submitted to be ruled by Roman governors, and began in a feeble way to call themselves Romans.

It was a bad time to become a Roman. Soon after then, the great Roman Empire began to fall into ruin. It was crumbling to bits. Barbarians were swooping down on its borders and sacking its cities. Savages were bursting into its palaces and robbing them of their riches. Roman armies had lost their pluck, and instead of beating the enemy back gave him money and jewels to go away. Province

A ROMAN AQUEDUCT

after province was starting for itself, and declaring that it was not Roman any more. Meanwhile, whether the Empire lived or died, the gay people who lived at Rome went on leading luxurious lives, keeping hundreds of slaves to wait on them, eating food and drinking wine which were brought from distant countries, wearing beautiful clothes, spending millions of money, and taxing the submissive provinces to get it. One of the most submissive and the most grievously taxed was Gaul.

Every acre of land was taxed, every tree, every vine, every house and cow and pig and sheep, every barn and cart and plough ; a man had to pay a tax for the wife he lived with, and a tax for every child she bore. Those who resisted the tax-gatherer were scourged with whips. The air echoed the groans and shrieks of women who were tortured to make them confess whether their husbands had property, and where it was hidden. After long endurance of this frightful oppression, the great heart of the Gauls broke. Cæsar had taught them that they could not fight Rome. They just stopped tilling their fields and pruning their vines. They left their houses, fled into the woods where the cruel tax-gatherer could not reach them, and fell to robbing travellers and towns to feed their children. If this state of things had gone on, Gaul would have become a wilderness, the abode of wild beasts and men as wild as they.

It was then that the Franks came sailing across the Rhine into Gaul. They were a fighting people, hating work and loving war. They elected their king by vote : the strongest and bravest warrior was chosen, and was carried round on a shield on the arms of soldiers, who paraded him before the tribe. You will find in the histories of the Franks the names of several kings who are said to have led the Franks to battle—Pharamond, Clodion, Merovée, Childeric, and others. But I cannot feel sure that they were real personages. I am afraid that some of them—Pharamond especially—were invented long afterward, when the descendants of the Franks, like some people in our own day, had a fancy to prove that they sprang from very ancient lineage indeed.

But there is no doubt of the reality of Clovis, or Chlodoveg as some of the old books call him. You may feel quite sure that he came paddling over the Rhine into Gaul at the head of a body of Franks in or about the year of Our Lord four hundred and eighty-one. The people were very glad to see him—all except the tax-gatherers. With these he had a short, sharp way of dealing. When a tax-gatherer got in his way, he sent one of his captains to argue with him; and it was noticed that after the argument the tax-gatherer had nothing more to say. The Frank had persuaded him with his axe.

A few friends of Rome tried in a feeble way to oppose the march of the Franks, but Clovis persuaded them, too, with pike and sword; and the poor people came out of their hiding-places, and wrung the hands of the strangers, and bade them welcome. Nothing that Clovis could do to them could be worse than the oppression

CLOVIS, KING OF THE FRANKS

they had endured from the Romans. They made no objection when Clovis proclaimed himself master of town after town, valley after valley, province after province. So, after a time, he came to rule over a larger country than any Gaulish chief had ever swayed—and it was a country which, now that the people ventured to go to work once more on their farms, was worth governing. He called himself King of the Franks, but I think you had better remember him by the title which fits him best—that of the First King of France.

In larger books than this you will find that the Gauls submitted to Clovis because of his religion. At that time, in Gaul the old, cruel religion of the Druids, who met in groves, and, I am afraid, sacrificed children on stone altars, had died out, except in the northwestern corner of the country. In the place of it, four religions existed. The Franks had a weird, mystical religion, with gods named Thor and Odin and a goddess named Freya. Some of the Romans, and the Gauls who had been to Rome, clung to their old heathen religion, with Jupiter, Mars, Apollo, Venus, and Juno. And there were two kinds of Christianity. One of these Clovis said he professed, and he also said that it was very superior to the other kind. I do not think, myself, that he troubled himself much about either, or that he lay awake nights thinking about religion in any shape.

But when he found that rich fields on the Loire were owned by a tribe which professed one kind of Christianity, I can quite understand why he adopted the other kind—because his conscience would not allow him to permit such very fine fields to remain in the possession of people who were no better than unbelievers. As a good churchman, he explained to himself that he was bound to turn out the wrong kind of Christians, and to put in their place the right kind, namely, his own friends and followers—which is precisely what he did.

Again, down in Languedoc, in southern France, there was a tribe of Visigoths who grew grapes and wheat on a

BURIAL OF A GAUL IN OLDEN TIME

lovely plain. They, too, were so stupid that they professed the wrong kind of Christianity. When Clovis proposed to go south to argue with them his soldiers hung back, for the Visigoths had the reputation of being fierce fighters. But Clovis had them attend church at Tours, and pay particular attention to the first words which they heard from the priest who was chanting psalms. Just as they entered the priest cried in a loud chant, "Thou hast given me the necks of mine enemies." The soldiers took the hint and marched, and the Visigoths lost their lands. Of course the priest had not been told to select that particular text.

No, no, nothing of the kind. But it happened to suit the king's purpose very nicely indeed.

There came a time when Clovis reigned over nearly all France, except a corner in the south where he permitted the remnant of the Visigoths to remain, a small corner in the northwest where the brave Bretons fought stoutly for their homes and beat back the Franks over and over again, and the great duchy of Burgundy in the Rhone valley, which was ruled by a duke whose daughter was Clovis's wife. From the Pyrenees to the Rhine the country was all his, and the fame of his power spread so far and wide that the Romans made him a consul—which was not in those days so much of an honor as it had once been.

But he was not satisfied. On the river Rhine there was a small kingdom round what is now the German city of Cologne. Clovis sent word to the king's son, "Thy father is old ; he halts with his lame foot. If he should die, thou shalt have his kingdom and my friendship." The prince understood—he murdered his father that night. Then said Clovis, "It is well. Show thy treasures to my envoys, and I will acknowledge thee king." The poor fool opened a chest full of gold-pieces, and, bending over, thrust his arm into it; whereupon one of the envoys standing behind him split his head open with an axe and carried off the treasure. The people of Cologne, who were worthy of such a prince, raised Clovis on a buckler and proclaimed him king; and a Church chronicler, Gregory of Tours, declared that he was "successful in all things, because his heart was right before God."

In those days Paris was a small town, of no particular beauty. Clovis chose Soissons to be his capital, and he surrounded himself with a joyous court. Many of his own people were rough barbarians, who gorged themselves with meat and drink, fought from morning to night, and thought nothing of knifing their right-hand neighbor at the dinner-table—monstrous fellows with long yellow hair and long arms and roaring voices. But at the court of Soissons there were also gentlemen of polish and learning from Rome, or from the French cities in which Roman fashions had been adopted; likewise priests who had been well educated, and whom Clovis loved to gather about him—I suspect because their presence gave respectability to his court.

That it certainly needed. He had taken possession of a fine old Roman palace at Soissons, and lived in it—generally sleeping on the bare boards with his dogs by his side.

A NEW KING OF THE FRANKS

At his dinner, a roasted ox, or wild boar, or two or three sheep were served whole; the guests cut off chunks of meat with their knives, and held them in their fingers while they gnawed them. Wine was plentiful, and boys went round with cups, out of which each drank in turn. It was the general custom to get drunk; and after the meal to swagger and boast, as drunken men will. The Gauls had a rule that the thigh-bone of the animal that was served for dinner was prize to the bravest man in the company—you may fancy how many fights grew out of this custom.

What a contrast between such a life and the polite, refined, and delightful manners of the French people in our day!

HEAD OF KING CLOVIS

Chapter II

BRUNEHAULT AND FREDEGONDE

A.D. 511–752

The four sons of Clovis were named Thierry, Clotaire, Childebert, and Chlodomir. They were jealous of each other; they felt that there was not room for all four in France; but, before they had time to quarrel, their grandfather, the Duke of Burgundy, was murdered by one Sigismund, who usurped his throne, and their mother called upon them to avenge his death. Clotaire and Chlodomir accordingly invaded Burgundy, fought Sigismund, took him prisoner, knocked him about a good deal, and at last flung him into a well, which they filled up with stones. On their way back, a son of the dead Sigismund lay in wait for them, caught Chlodomir unawares, and ran him through the body with a pike. So one of the four sons was out of the way.

He had left three little boys, who were being brought up by their grandmother. Said Childebert to Clotaire: "These children must be got out of the way, so we may divide the kingdom between us." And they sent to the grandmother a messenger who bore a sword in one hand and a pair of scissors in the other, and bade her choose whether her grandsons should be tonsured (which means being forced to enter the priesthood) or be killed. She replied she would rather they were dead than priests. Thereupon, Clotaire stabbed the eldest boy, who was ten, under the arm, and reached out his hand for the younger, who was seven.

The child clung to the knees of his uncle Childebert and begged his life piteously. Childebert turned to his brother and cried, "Grant me the child's life—I will pay thee what ransom thou wilt." But the bloody-minded Clotaire scoffed him; he stabbed the boy as he had stabbed his brother, and the two sons of Clovis mounted their horses and rode into the city, seeking the third child. He would have perished like his brothers, had he not escaped by turning monk; he gave his name to the monastery of St. Cloud, which the French afterward turned into a palace, and the Germans burned a few years ago.

Childebert died soon afterward—in his bed—and so another of the four brothers was got rid of. Presently Thierry was taken ill on a march he was making to rob northern Italy, and expired of a fever. So at last, of the four sons of Clovis, Clotaire was the only one left. He became King of France, as his father had been; but three years afterward he also died, leaving his kingdom, as his father had done, to be divided between his four sons. I should have supposed that he had seen enough of such divisions.

Of the four, one died soon after his father, and another, Gontran, got the Duchy of Burgundy, and lived there quietly. The other two are chiefly known as the husbands of two of the worst women in history.

The eldest, Sigebert, married a Spanish girl of great beauty and some education, named Brunehault. Her sister had married Sigebert's brother Chilperic; but Chilperic one day met a lovely girl named Fredegonde, who fascinated him and cast over him a spell which he could not resist. She first made him strangle his wife in her bed; then she married him.

Brunehault persuaded her husband to avenge her sister, and war broke out between the two brothers. It did not last long. Two of Fredegonde's men-at-arms gained admission to Sigebert to deliver a message and stabbed him with poisoned knives. Fredegonde, rejoicing over the murder, pushed on and caught Brunehault, whose chances of life would have been slim if her beauty had been less.

CLOTAIRE KILLS HIS NEPHEWS

CHLODOMIR'S SON SUBMITS TO TONSURE

As it was, she made a conquest of a prince, who helped her to escape.

For years the war raged between these two women. Both were beautiful and fascinating; they were said to be sorceresses, probably because they could turn any man's head and mould him to their will. The advantage was generally with Fredegonde. But one day a bishop saw, or said that he saw, the sword of God's wrath hanging over her house, and frightened her almost to death by telling her the story. Shortly afterward, her two sons died of a fever, and she felt sure that this was her punishment. Husband and wife fell to railing at each other for having brought down the wrath of Heaven upon them, and Fredegonde, in her fury, had her husband assassinated. So now both women were widows, and the only one of Clotaire's sons who still lived was Gontran, Duke of Burgundy.

To him, for the people were furious at her husband's murder, Fredegonde fled and sought protection for herself and her young son. Gontran, who was a silly sort of person, took her part, declared that she was a much-injured woman, and lent her an army. She won a battle, is it said, by moving her troops under cover of large branches of trees, which made it appear that a forest was in motion; but the excitement was too much for her: she fell ill and soon after died. Gontran was then dead; so were his brothers; alone of the bad lot that had fought for Clotaire's inheritance, Brunehault survived.

She was an old woman now, and had neither husband, lover, nor son. But she insisted on continuing to rule in the name of her grandson; and, in order that he should not interfere with her, she surrounded him with idle companions, male and female, and encouraged him to lead a life of dissipation. She was as imperious as ever; whatever she said was law; every one had to obey whomsoever she honored. She humbled the nobles, made enemies of the priests, and provoked the soldiers. So when the son of her old enemy Fredegonde led an army to attack her, she was unable to defend herself. People would not fight for her. There was a battle, but Brunehault's troops threw down their arms, and the old queen was captured. It was no use expecting pity in those cruel times. A rope was twisted in the gray hair of the old woman, and was twined round one wrist and one ankle. The other end was fastened to the tail of a wild horse, and he was lashed into a furious gallop over brake, brier, thorn, and boulder. The body of the poor old queen was literally torn in pieces. Before her death, her old rival's son had inflicted on her every form of insult and torture, and it is quite likely that death, however cruel it was, was not wholly unwelcome. It was said of her that she had killed ten kings, most of

DEATH OF BRUNEHAULT

whom were her own kith and kin; and in those days it was thought to be much more serious business to kill a king than a common man.

For nearly a hundred and twenty years after the death of Brunehault there was but one king of France—Dagobert—whom you would care to hear about. The others were "idle kings," as the people called them: they wore long hair and long beards and crowns, and lived in palaces, and on coronation day were taken to church in wagons drawn by bullocks, while the people cheered, and the boys and girls shouted for glee; but they had no power, did not try to interfere with public affairs, but spent their time in games with friends as idle as they. Dagobert did try to do his duty; he improved the laws and punished those who were guilty of crime; but he led a loose life, and enjoyed the society of the gay ladies of his court better than that of his counsellors. As for the others, they were simply nobodies. No one paid any attention to them—neither the officers of the army, nor the priests of the Church, nor the nobility, nor even the working people, nor the peasants.

You will wonder how France was governed at this time. There was an officer who was elected by the bishops and the nobles, and who was called the Mayor of the Palace. All power was confided to him—subject in some respects to the approval of the bishops. He collected the revenues and paid them out; he chose magistrates, judges, and generals; he directed the movements of the army; he treated with foreign nations; he altered the laws and had them carried out. The Church had by this time become so powerful in France that no one who was its enemy could stand long. Generally the mayors of the palace managed to keep on the right side of the bishops, and as long as they did so the Church did not interfere with them. Much of the best land in France was passing into the ownership of the Church, and the only great monuments that were being built were cathedrals, churches, monasteries, and convents. The common people reverenced the priests and obeyed them in all things. Only the army stood jealously aloof and hated them.

In the year 714, Pepin, the Mayor of the Palace, lay on his death-bed, with his son Grimoald, whom he had chosen as his successor, by his bedside. A murderer entered the room and strangled Grimoald, on the very bed on which his father lay. Pepin died of the shock, and the nobles elected another son of his—Charles—to be mayor in his stead. Now, the mother of Charles was not his father's wife.

The priests and bishops had spoken much ill of her in consequence; one bishop had said such bitter things that her brother had broken into the bishop's palace and stabbed him to death while he was at his prayers. You may imagine that there was no love lost between the priests and Charles. He no sooner became Mayor of the Palace than he took from the Church one rich piece of property after another and bestowed it on officers of the army. But the bishops had no time to show their resentment, for an enemy even more formidable than the new Mayor of the Palace was threatening them at that very moment.

Sweeping northward from Spain, which they had overrun from the Mediterranean to the Pyrenees, an army of Saracens or Moors, which is said to have numbered several hundred thousand, chiefly cavalry, had sallied forth from Narbonne, crossed the Garonne, and was striking for the valley of the Loire. They were Moslems, that is, followers of Mohammed, and wherever they went they put Christians to death, because of their faith, and stamped out Christianity. They had spread their empire all over Western Asia, all Northern Africa, and all Spain. A few more conquests would make them masters of all Europe as well. They were good fighters, frugal livers, brave soldiers; they feared nothing, and scoured the world like the wind on their swift chargers, ready to die without a murmur for their religion; up to that time no race or people had been able to hold their own against them. For help against these terrible invaders, a piteous cry came up to Charles from southern France.

He was the man for the hour. Gathering troops from far and wide, pressing every able-bodied man into the ranks and arming him as he could, calling upon Gaul and Frank and Goth and Roman to strike a blow for God and country, he inspired his people with his own tireless energy. He moved as swiftly as the Moors themselves, and in a plain near Tours fell upon them like a thunderbolt. The battle lasted only a few hours; the Moslem troops could not stand the mighty shock of the heavy Northern infantry; the light African horse reeled under the onset of the great Flemish chargers; when the next day dawned the white tents of the Arabs were found empty, great mounds of corpses strewed the plain, and clouds of dust

THRONE OF DAGOBERT

on the southern sky told a tale of retreat. The Moors fell back, and back, until they left the soil of France for a time.

For the heavy blows which Charles had dealt to the enemy in this battle the people gave him the name of Charles Martel, or Charles the Hammer; and by that name you will remember him. But for him all Europe might have been Mohammedan, and perhaps—who can say?—you might to this day, at sunset, have been praying to Allah on a carpet.

Charles the Hammer died in 752, and named his son Pepin as his successor in the office of mayor. But the Pope of Rome, who happened to be a man of a good deal of common-sense, declared that the kingly title should rest where the kingly power was, and sent a priest to crown Pepin King of France. It was a good arrangement, no doubt; but it had the inconvenience of establishing the rule that kings must be crowned by the pope, and this, you will find hereafter, led to a good deal of trouble.

Chapter III

PEPIN THE LITTLE

A.D. 752–771

There were two objections to Pepin's becoming King of France. First, there was a king already, whose name was Childeric, and who was living in a cloister, wearing the long beard and the crown of a king. He did not meddle with government, but he was rightful king for all that. Of him Pepin disposed by shutting him up in a convent at St. Omer, where he soon died. When kings are made captives they seldom live long.

Next, Pepin was a very short man, so short that he was called Pepin the Little. Now, among the Franks and the Northern races generally, kings and chiefs were always men of lofty stature. They were generally the tallest men of their tribes. Some of the Frank soldiers sneered at Pepin because they could look over his head. But if he was short, he was broad; and he had the strength of a giant and the spirit of a hero.

At a circus, where the people had assembled to see the games, there was a fight between a lion and a bull. The animals dashed at each other, and were soon in a death-grapple. The bull had gored the lion, but the latter had thrown its big enemy, and was tearing its neck and shoulders with its sharp claws. All at once Pepin cried,

"Is there any one here who dares to separate these two brutes?"

He glanced over at the benches where the great nobles and the tall warriors sat, but they all looked the other way and pretended not to have heard. Then Pepin, drawing his sword, leaped into the ring, and with a few sharp blows drove off the lion and cowed the bull. Then, turning to his nobles, he asked,

"Say, now, am I worthy to be your king?"

I need not tell you of the shout which arose in the circus, or of the shamefaced air of the warriors who had objected to Pepin because he was too little.

CHAPEL OF ST. JOHN AT POITIERS

Pepin reigned over France for sixteen years, and in that time conducted two great wars. The first was against a savage people who were called Lombards, from their long beards, and who had invaded Italy and settled in the northern part. As they were fonder of fighting than of work, they were often short of money, and when this happened they had a way of marching down to Rome and other rich Italian cities and demanding tribute. Where the demand was denied they would sack the city and go home laden with plunder. The Pope of Rome now sent to Paris, and asked Pepin would he drive out the Lombards for the sake of his love for the Church? If he would, the pope and the bishops would be his stanch friends forever.

Nothing suited the little king better. He led his fighting Franks and Gauls across the Alps, scattered the Lombards in short order, and took their lands and their cities. These he refused to keep, but gave them, one and all, to St. Peter and the pope. You will not be surprised to hear that after this Pepin was much thought of at Rome, and was blessed on high days and holy days by the pope. The priests in France received strict orders to teach their people that it was exceedingly impious to oppose him in any way.

Pepin's other war was with Aquitaine, the southwestern portion of France. This country was largely peopled by a sturdy and turbulent race, called Basques, who were at first shepherds in the Pyrenees. They were a short, black-haired, black-eyed race, bright, quick, brave, and passionate. When they swarmed down the wooded slopes of the mountains, in their red capes, with knives in their belts and woollen shoes on their feet, driving before them flocks of sheep and followed by their wives and children, it was not particularly safe to bar their way. The leader of these people, Duke Eudes of Aquitaine, formed an alliance with a Moorish emir named Munuza, and proposed to establish a great kingdom in southern France and northern Spain. Eudes was a Christian, and Munuza was a Moslem; but neither of them troubled himself much about religion. Eudes gave his daughter to wife to the Moslem, and they took the field with a great army.

But they were between two fires, and both were hot. The Moslem Caliph of Seville, in Spain, sent an army against Munuza, and besieged him in a fortress. He beleaguered the place so closely that not a man nor a pound of food could get in to the garrison, and Munuza, after holding out till his men were nearly starved and looked as if they would eat one another, threw himself head-downward from the topmost stone of the fort. His Christian wife was taken with the rest of the spoil, and was sent as a present to the Caliph of Damascus. The poor, pale girl cried her life out as a captive in an Arab's harem.

Then Pepin, who had settled his account with the Lombards, turned on Eudes, Duke of Aquitaine. This time he met a foe who could fight. The war lasted year in and year out. Battles were fought, and battles won and lost; but the fighting went on forever. In some strife, we hardly know where, Eudes was killed; but his sons, Hunald and Hatto, went on with the war. It was the old, sickening story of treachery, superstition, rapine, bloodshed, and murder. Hatto betrayed Hunald. Hunald caught him and tore his eyes out. Then, repenting, he sentenced himself to life-imprisonment in a monastery. But his son Guaifer took up the cause and went on butchering and ravaging.

With the help of Moorish allies, Guaifer captured a party of Goths and massacred them; the people of Narbonne rose one morning and slew every Moor in the place. Pepin and his Franks marched through Berry, Limousin, and Aquitaine, burning every house and every tree, and cutting down every vine. Guaifer was at last driven into the wild fastnesses of the mountains. One by one his friends left him; and at last a couple of villains—there were plenty of such in those days—crept up to him while he slept and put him to death, in order to curry favor with Pepin. So there was an end of the war at last.

In his last years Pepin became very pious indeed. The bishops persuaded him that it was better for the country to let them make the laws, and he agreed on condition that they should give him relics of the saints. Of these the supply was large—I believe it is not exhausted yet. He used to parade on solemn occasions with his shoulders and head covered with saints' bones and shreds of saints' clothing. I hope they did him good; but they did not keep him alive, nor make him friends when his time came. As it was, he left his kingdom to a monarch far greater than himself.

CHAPTER IV

CHARLEMAGNE

A.D. 771–814

CHARLES, the son of Pepin, was twenty-six years old when he succeeded his father as King of France. His life began with the usual family quarrels. He quarrelled with his brother and drove him into exile, where he soon died. And he quarrelled with his wife, the daughter of the King of Lombardy, and sent her back to her father. But he soon had graver concerns than home strife.

The King of Lombardy, enraged at having his daughter thrown back on his hands, declared war upon Charles, who accepted the challenge, overcame his enemy in short order, and made himself King of the Lombards as well as King of the Franks. He put the iron crown of Lombardy on his head and went to Rome, where the pope made much of him, gave him his blessing, and called him Charlemagne. Charles accepted the blessing gratefully, but, in order to prevent mistakes, observed to the pope that, while he was the best friend the Church had, he proposed henceforth to be master. If disputes arose the pope was to take his orders from him, not he from the pope. This made matters clearer than they had been in the later years of Pepin. The pope submitted, the less reluctantly because Charlemagne told him that he had resolved to undertake the conversion of the Saxons.

The Saxons—from whom in part the American people are descended—were then a tribe, or a band of tribes, settled in the country that is now northern Germany, between the Rhine and the Elbe, and stretching south as far as Bohemia. They lived either in woods so dense that it was said a squirrel could travel twenty miles, leaping from branch to branch, without touching the ground ; or in vast prairies which were often water-soaked in summer and frozen over in winter. They had never been conquered, and had never become Christians ; they were as brave and as fierce and as savage as they had been when they defied Cæsar to invade their country. From France mis-

A KING OF FRANCE TRAVELLING

sionaries had gone to convert them, and had barely escaped with their lives. These were the people whom Charlemagne had undertaken to convert and to subdue. To be near at hand for his work, he moved his court from Paris to Aix-la-Chapelle, which is near the Rhine in Germany.

As the Saxons were an unlettered people, while the priests among the Franks were educated, all the accounts which we have of the war are from Frankish sources, and some of them are very surprising indeed.

In Saxony there stood a statue, which represented a huge man with a balance in one hand and a flag in the other; on his arm hung a buckler, with a lion on it, lording it over other animals. The priests said that this was an idol which the Saxons worshipped, so Charlemagne's soldiers marched on it and broke it to pieces. Forthwith, by a miracle, a spring of fresh water gushed forth from the base of the statue to refresh the thirsty troops after their exertions. Whether the spring did or did not gush forth, there is no doubt that the destruction of the statue exasperated the Saxons and fired them to continue their resistance.

According to the priestly accounts, miracles were not uncommon in that war. There was a Christian church which a saint had built in Saxony. The Saxon chief ordered that it be burned, and a soldier was sent to set it on fire. But it had been foretold by the saint who built the church that it could never be consumed by fire, and as the soldier knelt down to apply his torch, two angels descended from heaven, all clad in white, extinguished the flame, and petrified the Saxon, so that he was found long afterward, turned to stone, in the attitude of kneeling, with his cheeks still puffed out in the act of blowing the embers.

The Franks were better trained to fighting than the Saxons, and they were more numerous. But after a battle the defeated Saxons would fly to their wooded hiding-places to gain breath, and would renew the war just when they were least expected. They had an exceedingly ingenious and brave chief named Witikind, who fought year after year, and was almost always beaten, yet was never conquered: Charlemagne no sooner felt that his work was done, and that the Saxons would give him no more trouble, than Witikind would loom up again, and swoop down upon the Franks, and sack their camps, and capture their supplies. Charlemagne tried every device of war with small success. Once, when the Saxon army retreated after a battle, leaving behind them some four thousand five hundred wounded or sick men who could not keep up with the flying army, the cruel Frank had them all beheaded to strike terror to their friends. Again, he would surround Saxon settlements and transplant every one—men, women, and children—to some distant part of France. But those who remained still continued to resist.

They did not object so much to baptism, the meaning of which they probably did not understand. Indeed, when the priests gave out that every one who was christened

BAPTIZING THE SAXONS

must wear a white robe, and that if he didn't own one the Church would supply it, vast numbers of Saxons presented themselves for baptism to get the white robe. They came to be baptized not once, but many times. Some of them were particular about the robe: one of them told Charlemagne that if the priest couldn't furnish him with a clean new linen robe, white as snow, he wouldn't be baptized any more. But the baptized Saxons fought as fiercely against the Franks as those who had not undergone the operation.

The war lasted thirty-three years. It was not till 805 that Charlemagne could say that it was positively ended, that the Saxons were finally subdued, and that his empire extended from the Atlantic Ocean to the Elbe and almost to the Oder.

While it was raging, Charlemagne undertook another war against the Basques and their friends in northern Spain. He was successful at first, but, meeting with reverses, he ordered a retreat, and his enemy caught his army in a pass of the Pyrenees, at Roncesvalles, rolled great stones and logs on them from the overhanging crags, and cut them off to a man. Not a Frank escaped, and the overwhelming disaster so preyed upon Charlemagne's mind that he never returned to Spain.

It was at Roncesvalles that he lost one of his best captains, the famous Roland the paladin, whose story used to be a favorite with the troubadour minstrels. Roland carried a sword of such extraordinary strength and keenness that with one blow of it he clove a pass through the mountain range of the Pyrenees; when he broke it at Roncesvalles, he seized his horn and blew a rescue call that was heard miles and miles away. So loud and so piercingly did he blow his horn that he burst the veins in his neck in the effort and died in consequence. It was a pity, for he was a good friend of the Church and a right valiant knight.

When Charlemagne had crushed the Saxons, he ruled over a kingdom which comprised all of modern France,

ROLAND THE PALADIN AT RONCESVALLES

half of modern Germany, four-fifths of modern Italy, and all of modern Switzerland. On the strength of this vast empire he claimed to be the Emperor of the West and the successor of the Cæsars of Rome, and the pope crowned him by that title. Though his proper title had been King of the Franks, he was a German like his father, and spoke German all his life. He lived in a German city, and his most trusted friends were Germans.

But he gathered round him in his palace at Aix-la-Chapelle men of education from all nations, and, first of all modern monarchs, he encouraged learning. In his day there was no learning outside the monasteries and convents and cathedrals. Nobles and soldiers thought it beneath them to read and write. Charlemagne himself learned to read late in life, but he never could be taught to write; it was with effort that he trained his hand to sign his name. In his palace he established a school, with great scholars at its head, and there, with as many noblemen's sons and other young men as chose to attend, he studied astronomy, theology, law, grammar, rhetoric, and music. He stinted his sleep to gain time to study. He taught himself to speak Latin and Greek; the Gaulish and Frankish languages he had acquired in his youth. When he found a young man of promise, he rewarded him by giving him a high office in the Church. In this way boys were sometimes made bishops before their beards had begun to grow.

His domestic life was not happy. He had had nine wives—sometimes, I am afraid, two at a time; and when he was quite an old man, he offered marriage to the Empress Irene of Constantinople, who was not a young woman. The empress had heard of his conversation with the pope, which I have related, and she replied that she preferred remaining a widow. One of his wives, Hildegarde, had a roaring voice, and bellowed at him when she spoke; when she died, he married Fastrade, who had a gentle voice, but a most ungentle temper. She bullied her old husband to such a degree that the nobles of his court took pity on him and plotted to get rid of her.

By these wives he had six sons and eight daughters. Among the former there was not one who could deny that he was a fool. The girls were beautiful, but their father refused to allow them to marry, and they were rather discontented with their lot in consequence. In the old storybooks of the times there are several tales of the merry adventures with which the young ladies amused themselves, and tried to beguile the dulness of spinsterhood; but their old father had lattices fitted into every room in the palace, so that he could see all that was going on, and he kept pretty close watch of his family. He had a sly way of dealing with a young man who gave him offence. He ordered him to go to a distant monastery in Italy to do penance; and it was curiously remarked that the people who went off on these journeys were never heard of again.

Once in a way, a young man got the best of the king. One of his daughters had a sweetheart named Eginhard, who wanted to marry her. Charlemagne forbade him to appear at the palace, but, like a gallant knight, he set the king's commands at defiance in order to see his true love. It was her custom, when bedtime came, to let him out by a side door, so that Charlemagne should not know he had called; but one evening, while he was in the palace, snow began to fall, and when the lovers went to the side door they saw that Eginhard's footsteps in the freshly fallen snow would reveal his visit. The young knight was dismayed; but the girl, who was stout and strong, bade him cheer up; and taking him on her shoulders, she carried him out of the palace grounds. Charlemagne saw her out of one of his lattices, and was so much touched by her devotion that he gave Eginhard a fine estate.

In his later years he bestowed more time on his study of the liturgy and of church-music than on the affairs of the Empire. Thus large parts of France which ought to have been bearing crops were left to pasture, and the price of bread rose very high. Six bushels of wheat were worth as much as an ox. This, of course, made free labor worth less than it should have been, and slaves increased in numbers. To the head of his school at Aix-la-Chapelle, Charlemagne gave a farm with twenty thousand slaves on it.

In his seventy-second year he was attacked by a fever which proved fatal. As long as he retained his senses, he continued to read a Latin copy of the Gospels, which he had been studying; when the end came he stretched forth his hands, cried "Into thy hands do I commend my spirit!" and expired.

By his special direction he was buried in the cathedral at Aix-la-Chapelle which he had built. He was buried seated on his throne, in his royal robes, with his crown on his head and his sword by his side; and so well was the work of the embalmer done that when his tomb was opened two centuries afterward, he still sat erect, and it is said that his features were easily recognized. The crown, which was of value, was taken to Vienna, where the other imperial treasures are; the throne you can still see at Aix-la-Chapelle; and once every seven years you can see in the famous cathedral of that place the collection of relics which were sent him by the pope.

But the work which he did crumbled into dust even before his bones. His endeavor to revive learning proved a failure through the stupidity of the nobility and the jealousy of the priests; his empire fell to pieces like a house of cards; and the two nations whom he united under his sway, and over which he dreamed that his successors would reign, have been quarrelling almost ever since, and are now bitter enemies, waiting an opportunity to fly at each other's throats.

Chapter V

LOUIS THE GENTLE

A.D. 814–843

The son and successor of Charlemagne was named Louis, and as it was the custom of the day to give every one a nickname, he was called the Gentle. He had been brought up by priests, and had become very pious indeed—so pious that one of his first acts as emperor was to insist on priests leading quiet lives, and ceasing to carry arms, or to wear spurs, or to ride on horseback with the soldiers. Two priests, who had contrived to gain a good deal of power under his father, Charlemagne, he sent to their monasteries, and ordered them to remain there. No poor man appealed to him for justice in vain: he heard every one patiently and righted all who had been wronged. So people began to think they had got a very good kind of emperor indeed.

But his troubles were to come—and from his own family. Charlemagne had had an older son than Louis—Pepin—who died before his father; his son Bernard had been set over the Kingdom of Italy. He now claimed the whole Empire and gathered an army to overthrow his uncle. But after it had marched some distance, most of the officers lost heart, and deserted, so that Louis easily captured his nephew and his remaining adherents. He was so good-natured that he was for forgiving them; but his generals would not consent to that, saying that death was the proper doom of traitors. So said Louis's wife, a violent woman named Hermengarde. Louis still refused to allow his nephew to be executed; but when Hermengarde said, "At least, the traitor's eyes must be put out," he, very reluctantly, consented. Bernard was handed over to his cruel aunt, who put his eyes out so roughly that he died three days afterward. She soon followed him to the grave.

After her death Louis married a beautiful and wicked woman, Judith of Bavaria. She despised her gentle husband and chose as her best friend another Bernard, whose

THE NORMANS ASCENDING A FRENCH RIVER

father was William the Short-nose. The pair led Louis a miserable life. He had other cares beside. A race of corsairs, who were called Northmen or Normans, began to prey on the coasts of Europe, from England as far round as Sicily. These sea-rovers came from Norway, Sweden, and Denmark, and in search of plunder sailed the stormiest seas fearlessly in open boats without decks. They were as valiant fighters as they were expert mariners. They would land near a sea-coast town, rob it of everything that was worth taking, and scamper off to sea with their booty.

One branch of them, who came from Denmark, actually conquered England and held it for many years. Another branch is supposed to have landed in New England five hundred years before Columbus discovered America; but, as they did not find anything there that was worth stealing, they did not stay. Yet a third band swooped down on the coast of France and ravaged it far and wide; they captured many prisoners, but afterward they got so much booty that it filled their ships, and they had to release their prisoners to make room for it.

The story of their ravages filled Louis's tender heart with anguish. He was distressed beyond measure, too, over the memory of the death of his poor nephew. He could not forgive himself for having allowed his cruel wife to put the poor boy's eyes out, and that so brutally that he died of the operation. He brooded over these things till he brought himself to believe that he should do public penance.

He entered a church, walked up the main aisle, went down on his knees, and confessed himself a sinner in the presence of the whole congregation, while the bishops and priests, in their robes, stood in front, frowning sternly at him.

The priests must have been secretly pleased at his submission to the Church, but the nobles and soldiers did not like it at all. They said that a king who had done penance was degraded, and was not fit to lead armies. And they fell to plotting his overthrow. Of all men in France, they chose as their leaders in the conspiracy the king's own sons—Lothair, who was backed by the pope, and Pepin, who was induced to join by Bernard, the son of Short-nose. The rebels met the king, their father, on the plains of Alsace. During the night, the pope went over into the king's camp, for the purpose, as he said, of trying to settle the dispute, but the effect of his meddling was the desertion of a large part of the king's army next morning. As gentle as ever, Louis declared that he would have no man lose his life on his account, and walked over and surrendered to his son Lothair.

Lothair was quite capable of killing his father. He had thrust a lady with whom he quarrelled into a wine-cask and drowned her in a river. But he was afraid of the people, and he called a council of bishops to try the king. Before them the royal prisoner was accused of a long list of crimes, foremost among which was the murder of the nephew whom he had tried to save. This charge was followed by others equally false and equally absurd. But the poor, weak king made no defence. He would deny nothing—would do nothing but cry, and moan that he was a miserable sinner.

In the church of St. Medard at Soissons—you may see parts of it to-day—he was found guilty of the preposterous crimes with which he was charged. Archbishop Nebo, his foster-brother, tore his baldric from his shoulders and flung a shirt of sackcloth over his head. His son Lothair stripped him of belt and sword, and held him down at the altar with his gray hairs sweeping the floor, while the fierce priests pronounced sentence. Lothair then led him to the cathedral at Aix-la-Chapelle, which his father Charlemagne had built; there he stood at the door, in the wind and rain, with bare feet and ashes strewn over his head, making confession to all the people of crimes which he had not committed, and begging the pious to pray for him, a miserable sinner.

But the wicked princes and priests overshot their mark. From the vast crowd which had assembled to see the king humbled, a piteous groan of shame and sorrow rose to heaven. Every Frank felt that he had been insulted in the person of the king. Next morning the people, with the nobles at their head, took up arms, and the tables were suddenly turned. The bad son Lothair fled on a swift horse and took no rest till he reached Italy. The vile Archbishop Nebo, stripped of his rank and wealth, hid himself in a distant convent and was never heard of more.

A NOBLE'S CASTLE, WITH TOWN AT ITS BASE

Every bishop who had served on that council was sent into exile and deprived of his property. An extraordinary mortality broke out among the leaders of Lothair's army—scores of them died within the year. And once more Louis the Gentle was set on his throne. But his peace was not to last.

Another son of his, Louis of Bavaria, clamored for more land to govern, and, the king refusing, took up arms. The father was then sixty-three years of age and much broken by the sorrows of his life, but he sallied forth at the head of his armies to meet his rebellious son and got as far as the bank of the Rhine. His fatigue and vexation there overcame him, and he was carried to an island in the river, near Mentz, where he died. From his death-bed he sent his son this message: "I forgive Louis; but let him look to himself, who, despising God's command, has brought his father's gray hairs with sorrow to the grave."

Louis was a well-meaning man, but, as you will see as you read this history, something more than good intention is required of a king to make his country happy. Under his reign the best part of France fell into the hands of the Church and the nobles. There were no towns of any size except those which grew up around abbeys, bishop's palaces, or baronial castles. Nobles and churchmen cultivated their lands with slaves. The greatest men in the kingdom were the Archbishop of Rheims, the Bishop of St. Martin at Tours, the Bishop of St. Hilary at Poitiers, the Abbot of St. Medard at Soissons, the Abbot of St. Denis near Paris. They were lordly personages, with mitres on their heads, and crooks like shepherdesses in their hands; richer and more powerful than the dukes and counts, for they not only had armies at their command, but they could terrify ignorant people by threatening them with all sorts of horrible tortures in the world to come. When Lothair marched against his father, he took with him a pope who threatened those who refused to join the rebels that neither they nor any of their kith or kin should ever be married by a priest, or their children baptized, or their dead buried with the rites of the Church. And in those days this was considered an awful doom.

We shall have occasion before we come to the end of this history to speak of some bishops and priests whose memory you can reverence. But in these old, old days the clergy were not a success as managers of public affairs.

CHAPTER VI

HINCKMAR THE ARCHBISHOP

A.D. 843-987

LOUIS THE GENTLE left three sons: two by the cruel Hermengarde—Lothair, the son who had humbled him, and Louis of Bavaria—and one, Charles, by Judith. They at first divided the Empire; then fought for it; and at last it fell into the possession of Charles, who was the youngest and was bald.

The real ruler during the reign of Charles was Hinckmar, Archbishop of Rheims. Charles was a poor-spirited creature, who crouched and cowered when this angry priest lifted his finger and thundered at him; and really, of the two, the priest was more of a man than the king. Anything in the shape of a priest or a bishop made Charles's knees knock together.

A priest named Venillo, whom Charles had made an archbishop, deserted him to join his enemy Louis; whereupon Charles wrote a whining letter to the council of bishops, complaining that it was mean of Venillo to have left him after having made him king, anointed him with the sacred oil, handed him the royal sceptre, and crowned him with the royal diadem. He asked the council had he not always been obedient to the Church? Had he ever refused to bow down at the feet of the bishops and submit to their fatherly correction?

Hinckmar took away from the king the right of trying criminals in his courts; the proper persons to hold courts, he said, were the priests. And when the king wanted soldiers for his wars, Hinckmar required him to get them through the bishops—which, I think, was a queer business for a servant of Christ to engage in. In return, Hinckmar promised Charles the support of the Church whenever he needed it. After a battle, the monks of St. Medard came forth to him and loaded him with relics, which he bore on his shoulders to the cathedral at Rheims, greatly to the edification of the people. And when Louis of Germany quarrelled with Charles, Hinckmar went to see Louis and took a very high tone indeed. "As regards myself," said the haughty churchman, "I do pardon you. But as to your offences against the Church which is intrusted to my keeping, I can only offer you my advice, which is to obtain absolution."

Hinckmar ruled his Church with an iron hand. There was a priest named Gotteschalk, who had opinions on religion which Hinckmar did not like. The archbishop sent a band of soldiers to seize Gotteschalk, questioned him, and, finding his answers not satisfactory, had him soundly beaten with whips and locked up in an underground dungeon with the bats and rats. Gotteschalk offered to prove the truth of his faith, by stepping successively into three barrels filled with boiling water, boiling tar, and boiling pitch. But it did not serve. Hinckmar sent him back into the dungeon. It was not particularly safe, at that time, in France, for a man to have opinions on any subject, no matter how he offered to prove their truth.

But it was a much easier thing to shut up a priest in a dungeon than to shut up the Northern pirates in their country. Hinckmar found this job beyond his power. Every year, as soon as the spring-birds began to sing, these sea-rovers came swooping down upon the coasts of France, landing in some sheltered cove, seizing money, jewels, food, cattle, and young girls, and dashing off to sea again with their booty. By and by, they were not content with the sea-coast. They sailed up the rivers, in their broad boats, with ribs of iron, and with great beaks of bronze and ivory, fashioned in the shape of a serpent or a bird of prey. Back of this beak stood a warrior, shouting, singing, and

THE NORMANS ATTACKING THE CITY OF PARIS

gesticulating, to strike terror into the hearts of those who saw him : he was called a Berserkir, which in the Norman tongue meant a madman. Along the bank of the river ran other warriors, blowing horns and bellowing war-cries. When the poor French peasants saw a fleet of these boats come sweeping round the hill, dashing the foam from their bows, and heard the horn yonder on the beach, they fled, as swiftly as they could, with wives and children, and, if they had time, with such scraps of their belongings as they could pick up, to the nearest castle or monastery. Sometimes the count or the abbot was strong enough to give battle to the pirates ; but this did not often happen ; convents, churches, and castles were often pretty thoroughly robbed, and their owners killed under their own roofs. The only sure way to get rid of the Northmen was to buy them off. One year, Charles paid them four thousand pounds of silver ; the next year he paid them five thousand ; the year after that they insisted on getting six thousand—and they got them. The abbot of the rich abbey of St. Denys paid them a sum of money equal to three hundred thousand of our dollars.

These sea-rovers were not all Northmen. Many of them were vagabonds of other races, who joined the Northmen for plunder. One of the most famous, named Hastings, was a French peasant.

Hearing stories of the rich plunder which these Northmen got in the North, the Moors of Spain thought they would do a little robbing on their own account in the South, and marched one day upon the Archbishop of Arles, who was very rich. He gave them battle at the head of his soldiers, but three hundred of the latter were killed, and the archbishop himself was taken. His people sent a messenger to bargain for his release, and actually paid the Moors a hundred and fifty pounds of silver, a hundred and fifty cloaks, a hundred and fifty swords, and a hundred and fifty slaves. This was on account. The rest of the ransom was to be paid as soon as the people of Arles could raise it.

Meanwhile, the archbishop, who was a prisoner in chains on a Moorish vessel, suddenly died. The cunning Moors concealed the fact of his death, and kept telling the Arlesians that they would not wait much longer for the rest of their ransom, but would cut off the archbishop's head if it were not forthcoming soon; whereupon the money was made up and sent to the Moorish chief. When it was received, the Moors set the archbishop in his chair, clad in his priestly robes, carried him on shore, dead as he was, and sailed away.

Things had got to such a dreadful pass that Hinckmar himself was forced to confess that he had undertaken to do more than he could. He wrote a rather manly letter to the pope, telling him that neither he nor the king was able to take care of France, and would His Holiness appoint some one who could? Several members of the family of Charles the Bald undertook the task; one of them, a nephew of Charles, raised an army in Italy for the purpose. Charles marched to meet him, and got as far as the Alps. There, being suddenly taken ill, near Mont Cenis, he was carried to the hut of a goatherd. He had with him a Jew physician, named Zedekias; this man is said to have poisoned him. However this may be, he died, and with him the Empire which Charlemagne had built up dissolved into air.

After him one of his sons, who was called Louis the Stammerer, pretended to be emperor and king for a few months, but nobody minded him, either while he lived or when he died. Two sons of his also played at being kings for a little while, but soon gave up the game; and then a son of one of them—who was called Charles the Fat—pretended to succeed. He was too fat to move around. The Normans besieged him in his own city of Paris, and captured every fertile valley from the mouth of the Seine to the mouth of the Garonne. He finally died of corpulence, in the year 877, just one hundred and nine years after Charlemagne had founded the Empire of the West.

Then followed another century of such horrible confusion

CHARLES THE BALD AND HIS PRIESTS

that I do not know how I can describe it to you. There were a number of real or pretended descendants of Charlemagne, each of whom, in his turn, claimed to be king or emperor, but could not keep the peace in his own backyard, much less protect his subjects. In the north, bands of Northmen, in the south, bands of Moors, in the southeast, bands of Hungarians, whose faces had been slashed by their fathers to make them more hideous, marched into the country at harvest-time, and carried off the ripe crops, adding to them any trifle of silver, any good weapon, any silk or linen garment, or any pretty girl they found. To resist the robbers, the peasants armed themselves, picked out their bravest men to lead them, and did their little best —they could not do much; these leaders became known as counts and barons and dukes, and the peasants were quite willing that they should take pay in land for the work they did. But there was no settled order or authority anywhere.

There was a Count of Paris named Eudes, who was a gallant soldier, and was very powerful for ten years; there was a king called Charles the Simple, who is said to have had quite a long reign. There was a brave and good leader of the people whose name was Duke Robert of Paris; he had a good and brave son called Hugh the White; father and son were for many years more powerful than any king or noble in France. There was another dreary descendant of Charlemagne named Louis, who was called the Foreigner, because he had been brought up in England; he was sometimes in prison and sometimes on the throne —but always in misery. And there was another Lothair, who is chiefly remembered as the monarch who agreed that Alsace and Lorraine should belong to Germany and not to France. But greater and abler than all of these was the son of Hugh the White, who is known in history as Hugh Capet, and was chosen by a national assembly of bishops and nobles at Rheims, in the year 987, to be King of France.

Chapter VII

THE FEUDAL SYSTEM

A.D. 950–987

In all the miserable old days of confusion and war and pillage, the one who suffered most was the peasant. Everybody robbed him. He was lucky, where a body of armed men passed his way, if they did not force him to join them, and go out a-warring for a cause which was not his, leaving his wife and children to starve. As to his crops, he had to harvest them by stealth, and hide them when they were harvested, to save them from being stolen by some rough-rider. After a time his hardships at the hands of rival kings of his own race, or Northmen in the North, or Moors in the South, became so unbearable that he was of necessity driven to unite with his neighbors for common defence; and out of this union grew the system called the feudal system, of which you must understand something, if you wish to know French history. The way of it was this:

After a smiling valley or pleasant village had been raided by fighters or robbers, the people would meet together and agree with each other that henceforth they would stand shoulder to shoulder, and give manful battle to the next robber who came their way; they would choose the bravest and wisest among them to be their leader. In order to distinguish him from the rest, he should be called lord, or seigneur, duke, count, or baron. In order that he should stand loyally by the peasants, and not betray them or divide their substance with raiders, it was agreed all the land should be his, and that the peasant should hold it on lease from him. But the rent was to be merely nominal—

A NOBLE'S CASTLE IN THE MOUNTAINS

as, for instance, a quart of grain, a sucking pig, or a fat goose once a year for a field or an acre; there was very little money at that time in the country parts of France. Furthermore, it was agreed that whenever the lord called upon these tenants of his to turn out and fight, they were bound to do so; and whenever they called upon him to protect them against robbers, or rough-riders, or Northmen, or Moors, he was bound to do so. This was the feudal system, which, though it was greatly abused in later years, was an admirable contrivance at the time it was invented, and gave France many years of peace, wealth, and power. The land which was owned by the feudal lords and leased to their tenants was called a fief, and the tenants were called vassals. Of these fiefs there were one hundred and fifty in the time of Hugh Capet; indeed, there was very little land in the kingdom which was not included in some fief, and the plan struck those smart robbers, the Northmen, as so good that they adopted it, and established fiefs of their own, with robber chiefs as feudal lords over them. One of these lords called himself Duke of Normandy; you will often hear of his descendants in the course of this history.

In course of time, and by degrees, these feudal lords came to be kings in fact, if not in name, in their respective fiefs. They had their own armies, their own courts, their own mints, their own system of taxes, their own laws—quite independent of the king at Paris; they were, it is true, required to pay homage to the king, which consisted in holding his stirrup when he went riding, or some such idle formality; but practically the king had no authority over them at all. The peasants knew no superior but their own feudal lord.

The kingdom which Hugh Capet was called upon to reign over was thus cut down to a small piece of the Empire which Charlemagne had ruled, and only a small bit of modern France. It took in the valleys of the Seine and the Loire, but not Rouen or Nantes, or anything east of the Rhine, or south of the Loire, or west of the Mayenne. The Duke of Aquitaine, who was a feudal lord, ruled a much larger country, and so did the Duke of Burgundy, who was another.

The system suited neither the king nor the Church. Hugh Capet constantly found himself crossed by feudal lords as powerful as he and very jealous of their power. As for the Church, it had gone out of politics, and the

DEFENDING A BATTLEMENT

priests were minding their proper business of preaching and praying. A bishop was no better than any one else. Except that he could still refuse to baptize a child, or to marry a young couple, or to bury the dead, and that he still claimed to be able to sentence his enemies to millions of years of torment in another world, he was not of as much consequence as a valiant man-at-arms. So the priests looked sourly on the feudal lords, and as for Hugh Capet, he could hardly keep his hands off them.

Neither could do much, however. A feudal count or baron thought nothing of locking up a bishop for a dozen years in an underground dungeon and appointing his butler to take his place; and as for the king, when he ventured to take a feudal lord to task, the reply came quick, "Pray, who made you king?"

But the king and the priests became fast friends. When a Prince of Lorraine came to Rheims with his young wife, to see if there was any chance of getting a crown in France, the priests sent secret information to Hugh, who seized the prince and his wife while they were praying in the cathedral during Holy Week, and had them carried off to Orleans, where the prince soon died.

And, in order to show the people how much he thought of the Church, Hugh Capet would never wear kingly robes, but always appeared in public in the gown of an abbot, having been at one time Abbot of St. Martin at Tours. His last injunction to his son on his death-bed was to stand by the Church, and never to allow the nobles to despoil it; for, he said, no matter how well these feudal lords may get on at first, you may depend upon it that the Church will win in the end.

We shall see, as this history goes on, how near this prophecy came to the truth.

CHAPTER VIII

THE END OF THE WORLD

A.D. 996–1000

IN the year of Our Lord 996, Hugh Capet died, and his son Robert succeeded him. Now, it was the belief of good Christians that the world was to come to an end, and that the Day of Judgment was to come in the year 1000. This curious notion had been formed by putting on certain texts in the Bible a meaning which they cannot bear; the delusion had lasted so long that it was deeply rooted, and a man who doubted it was set down as no better than an infidel. In every church throughout Christendom priests preached about the end of the world as a thing fixed and settled, and in view of which devout Christians should put their souls in order against the coming of the Lord.

As if this was not enough to make people downhearted, famines and epidemic diseases broke out in many places. You know very well that famines are caused by crop failures, and that when laborers are taken from their farms to become soldiers crops are apt to fail. You also know that famines, when people have not enough to eat or when they have to eat poor food, are almost sure to be followed by outbreaks of disease, especially in places where the drainage is bad. So you can account for the famines and the pestilences in a very simple way. But nine hundred years ago people did not know as much as you do, and they ignorantly supposed that famine and pestilence were the works of an angry God. The priesthood proclaimed that they were a warning from God to prepare for the end of the world.

I suppose that there never was a time in the history of

France when the people were more miserable than they were then. Starving people ate rats, roots and bark of trees, grass, and human bodies. Little children were lured into lonely places, killed, and eaten. A butcher in a small town offered human flesh for sale on his stall. The judge had him arrested—he was sentenced to be burned to death. On the night of his burial his roasted body was dug up and was eaten by a hungry man, who was caught at it and was burned to death too. One man, who kept an inn in a forest, killed and ate his guests—forty-eight skulls were found in his cellar. Everybody was lean and hungry but the wolves—they grew fat.

When the pestilence broke out, no one knew how to cure it. The doctors were as ignorant as the rest. The only remedy that was advised was to go on a pilgrimage to a church and do penance. Thousands of poor stricken creatures, and other thousands who were still well but in dread of the disease, took the advice and crowded the churches and the graveyards round them. At Limoges the crowd grew so dense that those who were well took the disease from those who were sick, and they died together in heaps, poisoning the air. The priests did what they could: they brought out their best relics, from all parts of France, and waved them over the sufferers, trying to drive the disease away. But I need not tell you that the poor sick people went on dying as before.

Then men and women believed that the end of the world was coming in reality. Those who were in business shut up their shops. Those who had farms gave them to the Church. Those who had money laid it on the shrine of some saint, as though they could buy a place in heaven as you buy a place at the theatre. Every one spent his days in prayer—in a church if he could get in, and when the churches were all filled on the open roadside. It was not the poor and ignorant only who gave way to terrors. The Duke of Normandy got a friar's robe and insisted on becoming a monk. The Duke of Burgundy would have done the like, but was forbidden by the pope. The Emperor Henry went to the abbey at Verdun, and was actually admitted as a monk; but the abbot, who was a man of common-sense, set him the penance of going home and attending to his business as emperor.

I must say that the priests behaved very well at this trying time. They believed—as other people did—that the end of the world was at hand, but they faithfully and intrepidly attended to their work, and when people confessed to them with open and contrite hearts they insisted that their penitents should forswear quarrelling and fighting, stealing, drinking, and riotous behavior in future. They got a great deal of land through the ignorant terrors of the people; but, as it turned out, they did a great deal of good in return for it.

And the year 1000 came, and throughout every week and every month of it men looked to the sky for the coming of the angel of the Lord. But I need not tell you that the sky was just as serene as ever, nor were there any unusual storms or strange appearances. And when October and November and December passed, and yet the world stood where it was, and no fire nor flood from heaven marked the beginning of the end, the priests took courage to say that by reason of the penitence of the people a merciful God had stayed his hand, and that the world might endure a little longer. Many centuries had to elapse before people knew that the planets which have been planted in this universe are born, and flourish, and die in obedience to fixed laws of which we cannot measure the duration or the working. But in 1001 mankind breathed more freely when they found that the sun rose and set, and the winds blew, and the rains fell, and the earth continued to yield her increase, just as all these things had occurred throughout the memory of man.

Chapter IX

KING AND POPE

A.D. 996–1031

Robert, King of France, son of Hugh Capet, had been educated by the Archbishop of Rheims—who afterward became pope—and was, for that day, a learned and refined man. He was an excellent musician and a good architect. He knew so much of mechanics that he was suspected of being a sorcerer, as the archbishop his teacher had been when he made a clock for his cathedral. He was devout, kind, just, and gentle, the first king of France, I think, whom you can really like.

But his life was a sad one. Before he became king he married Bertha, who was daughter of the Duke of Burgundy and widow of the Count of Blois—a lovely woman to whom he was tenderly attached. Now Bertha was Robert's fourth cousin, and had besides been godmother to a child whose godfather Robert was. The Emperor of Germany objected to the marriage, because he feared it would lead to a union between France and Burgundy, and would defeat schemes he had himself laid to get hold of the duchy. So he persuaded the pope to declare the marriage null and void, on the ground that Robert and Bertha were too closely related to marry. Robert flatly refused to part with his dear wife.

On this the pope issued a decree ordering Robert to renounce his wife and do penance for seven years. "If he refuse to obey," said the decree, "let him be anathema."

Robert did refuse. Nothing, he said, should part him from the woman he loved.

Then the pope laid his kingdom under an interdict. All

the churches were closed and the bells muffled. The pictures of the Crucifixion and of the saints were taken down and wrapped in canvas. The statues were laid on beds of thorns and ashes. A couple of young lovers, coming hand in hand to the priest to be married, were driven roughly away. A mother, bringing her infant to be baptized, was not allowed to approach the font, and was ordered out of the church. The relations of a dead person could not in any way induce a priest to say a prayer over the body as it was lowered into the grave. All this because the Pope of Rome wanted to help the Emperor of Germany in his designs on the Duchy of Burgundy.

The interdict lay more heavily on the king than any one else. He was pronounced to be anathema—an accursed thing. No one could talk to him or keep his company. The clothes he had worn, the dishes out of which he had eaten, the cups out of which he had drunk, were thrown into the fire and burned. If any one touched him in passing he had to go home and wash all over. When people saw him coming they ran away.

You may fancy how this dreadful curse of the pope's distressed the ignorant people of France. They were intensely religious, and they believed that an unbaptized person who died without the sacrament, or had no prayers said at his funeral, would endure everlasting torment in the world to come, in lakes of fire and brimstone. They loved their king, and they stood by him in his resolve to keep his wife; but the interdict laid upon them more than they could bear. They flocked to the king, and besought him to relieve them of a hardship which made their lives a burden and a curse.

Robert would have fought the pope to the end, but he could not resist his people. He put away his wife. And not only that. At the earnest demand of the French, who wanted an heir to the throne so as to avoid civil war hereafter, he married another—a dreadful woman named Constance. But his heart was always faithful to the wife of

SWEARING ON RELICS

his youth, and when he died, thirty years afterward, her name was on his lips.

After his surrender to the Church he was in high favor with the priests, and according to the church chronicles many miracles were wrought in his honor. New churches were built all over the country, and old ones restored; and in many cases the finishing touches to these buildings were given by angels, who came down from heaven for the purpose, I suppose, with paint-pots under their wings. Of course the priests, among whom were good architects, clever painters, and gifted sculptors, had nothing to do with them. At least, they said they had not. In odd places queer old bones were dug up, which the bishops at once recognized as relics of saints who had died hundreds of years before; angels again—what would they have done without angels?—confidentially told the bishops that these relics had been kept hid for all these years on purpose that they should be discovered in the reign of Robert, who was so good a churchman.

He was besieging a castle which held out with courage and baffled his best efforts. On a certain day during the siege he left his camp, entered the church of St. Denis, and led the choir in singing a hymn. At the very moment the hymn ended the walls of the castle fell down, and he quietly walked in when the service was over.

Robert's heart was so full of kindness that he couldn't punish a thief if he was poor. When a ragged beggar was caught stealing some silver from the royal lance, he thrust the silver hastily into the thief's wallet and bade him begone, lest the queen should find him; and when she asked what had become of the silver, he answered, with a vacant look, that he really could not tell.

A monk stole a silver candlestick from an altar, and the king saw him. When the queen heard of it, she flew into a passion and swore that she would have the eyes torn out of the keepers' heads if they did not discover the thief. On this Robert went to the monk saying, "Haste thee hence, my friend, lest my Constance eat thee up." And he gave him money to take him home.

A rascal once crept under the table where he was dining and cut off a gold ornament which hung from his belt. The queen missed the ornament and asked, "What enemy of God has dishonored your gold-adorned robe?"

The king laughed and replied, "Probably some one

who wanted the ornament more than I did; with God to aid, it will be of more service to him than it was to me."

Like most religious men in his day, he thought that an oath taken on a relic was more sacred than a common oath. It was the custom to make the nobles of his court take an oath of allegiance on a box in which there was a relic of great power. Robert noticed how many of these oaths were broken. To save the nobles from committing mortal sin, he took the relic out and put an egg in its place. Now, said he, they can forswear themselves without dooming their souls to eternal damnation. As though a false oath sworn over an egg was less wicked than a false oath sworn over a dead man's finger-bone!

All this while Robert was unhappy with his wife. She was a Southern woman, fond of gayety and dancing and frolic, which the king abhorred. She had brought with her from the South a number of gentlemen and ladies who, like her, wanted to lead merry lives. They got up revel after revel, and laughed at Robert because he refused to take part in them. Their appearance was strange to the Parisians. The men shaved their chins, cut their hair short, and wore boots which turned up at the toes; they affected to be dandies, and sneered at the rough manners of the Northern friends of Robert. The king would have sent them home, but the queen, whom Robert called "my Constance," had a way of flying into rages, when every one, including her husband, made haste to get out of her reach; and so her Southern court remained to the end.

She was so violent a woman that when two priests were accused of being heretics, because they differed from their bishops on points of doctrine, and were sentenced to be burned at the stake, she insisted on going out of her palace to see them pass by. One of them was known to the queen; at sight of him she flew into a rage, and, seizing an iron-tipped stick from the hand of an attendant, she knocked the poor priest's eye out with a blow.

Toward the end of his reign, the brutal temper of this

QUEEN CONSTANCE STRIKES OUT A PRIEST'S EYE

woman and the growing impudence of the feudal lords made life bitter to the king. He could do nothing for himself, for the queen ruled him as if he had been a child; and he could do little for the people, for the feudal lords would have no interference with their vassals. So perhaps he was not sorry when the end came, after he had reigned over France for thirty-five years.

Chapter X

ROBERT THE DEVIL

A.D. 1031-1060

The most powerful feudal lord in France at this time was the Duke of Normandy. His name was Robert. He was the second son of his father, and therefore would not naturally have succeeded to the duchy; but he invited his elder brother and several other friends to a banquet, and next morning they were all found dead in their beds. For this dreadful deed the Normans gave him the name of Robert the Devil. His story inspired one of the greatest composers of modern times with the idea of an opera which I dare say you have seen.

When King Robert of France died in the year 1031—as I told you in the last chapter—he left two sons: Henry, who was the eldest, and Robert. Their mother, the bad Queen Constance, insisted that Robert should succeed, because he was her favorite. Henry appealed to the pope, who answered that he was the rightful heir. But Constance and Robert took the field at the head of the army and set Henry and his friend the pope at defiance. Then Henry sent to Robert the Devil, who was never so happy as when he was fighting, and asked him whether he would help him.

Robert the Devil replied, "With all my heart."

For he had set his heart on a corner of France which he thought would fit nicely into Normandy; and he had resolved to make this corner, which was called the Vezin, the price of his services.

He kept his word. Robert the Devil met Robert the Prince in three battles and utterly defeated him. His mother, wicked Constance, flew into such rages at being baffled in her object—she had not often been crossed in her angry life—that she went home and died. Her son Robert disappeared, Henry was acknowledged by every one as lawful king of France under the name of Henry the First, and the Duke of Normandy got the Vezin country which he had coveted.

But just then there broke out another of those dreadful famines which were always befalling France, partly because the peasants, under their feudal lords, would go on fighting, although they had promised the priests they would do so no more. When they neglected to plough and manure their fields the crops were sure to be short. There was no grain anywhere, and in whole districts people starved to death. So many unburied corpses lay by the road-side that the wolves feasted on human flesh ; and having acquired the taste of it, began to attack the living. The feudal lords had to turn out at the head of their soldiers to fight the ferocious beasts.

The bishops declared that the famine was a visitation from God to punish the people for their wickedness. They were brave enough to tell the Duke of Normandy to his face that it was God's punishment for the crimes which had won him the name of Robert the Devil. He was terribly frightened. His conscience smote him and told him that the bishops were probably right. So he humbled himself and besought them to tell him how he could make atonement before God.

"You must go on foot," said the bishops, "to the tomb of Christ in the country of Palestine and there do penance for your sins."

You will probably think that it was an excellent idea to have him do penance—he had sins enough, in all conscience, to repent of—but why the penance and repentance could not have been done at home, where they might have served as an example to others, it is not so easy to see. But the bishops insisted on Palestine, and to Palestine he went.

It is a long walk from Normandy to Palestine, and Robert the Devil had to find his way over river, mountain, bog, and wild, besides escaping the clutches of fierce races which regarded strangers as natural prey. But Robert overcame or eluded them all, and in due time found him self at the place where Christ had been buried over a thousand years before. It was a barren, sandy spot, with a few valleys in which vines grew and slopes on which olives still spread their twisted branches to the sky. Here and there were square forts, with loop-holes out of which bowmen shot arrows, and flat roofs on which the soldiers slept in the cool night breezes. The country was owned by the Moors or Saracens, who were followers of Mohammed and did not believe in Christianity.

When Robert asked them could he do penance on the tomb of Christ, they answered, "Why not?"

And he said all the prayers and made all the confessions he wanted without hindrance, the Moors sitting silently by and gravely watching him.

Then he turned his face homeward, but before he could get back into Europe he fell ill and died. So there was an end of his history.

But he left behind him a son who became more famous than he, both in France and in England. This was William, who is called William the Conqueror, because he conquered England in the year 1066. His mother was a poor tanner's daughter, with whom Robert had fallen in love as he watched her washing clothes in a brook. She never became Robert's wife, nor is there much said of her in the histories of her famous son. William not only conquered England and made it Norman, setting up Norman lords to govern the English, and the Norman tongue in the place of the Anglo-Saxon tongue which the people then spoke, but he became more powerful in France than the king, and his history is, perhaps, better entitled to be considered the history of France in his day than is the history of Henry the First, Regent Baldwin, and Philip the First, who were the nominal rulers of the kingdom during his time.

Chapter XI

PHILIP THE FIRST

A.D. 1060–1108

When Henry the First died, his son and successor, Philip the First, was only eight years old, but his father had chosen Baldwin of Flanders to be his guardian; and, as he was a prudent man, no serious trouble befell France while Philip was growing up. But when he grew to manhood he met with trouble enough.

William, the son of Robert the Devil, had become King of England as well as Duke of Normandy, and with him Philip picked a quarrel. His choice of an enemy was unlucky: William fought him time and again, and the King of France was always beaten. After one of these defeats Philip made some coarse joke about William's size: he was fat, and his stomach was prodigious. The joke was repeated to William, who flew into a rage, invaded Philip's dominions, and took and burned the town of Nantes. You will perceive that whenever these kings or dukes quarrelled, it was their subjects who paid the penalty. As he rode over the burning ruins of Nantes, William's horse trod on a hot cinder and started, throwing his rider on the pommel of the saddle. William was carried into a house and died of the injury. So Philip was rid of his worst enemy.

But another soon took his place. The pope of that day is called in history Gregory the Seventh. But he is best known by the name he bore before he became pope—which was Hildebrand. He was imperious and domineering and really believed that he was head not only of the Church, but also of the world. He led a pure life himself and insisted that all others should do the like. Unfaithful bishops and priests he punished without mercy. It was he who put a stop to the marriage of priests. He resolved to set the popes above all the kings of the earth, and he very nearly succeeded. He quarrelled with the kings of Hungary, Poland, and Spain, and insulted them—daring them to resent the insult. He defied the Emperor of Germany and kept up the defiance till he died. He turned on Philip of France and bullied him, threatening him with all the curses of the Church, which at that time was rich in curses.

Philip most certainly deserved to be bullied. He was a poor weak creature, who was always doing wrong, begging pardon for it, promising not to do so any more, and then straightway repeating the offence. He had a good wife, Bertha of Flanders, who had born him several children; he put her away and locked her up in a castle at Montreuil. Then he fell in love with another man's wife—Bertrade of Anjou—and persuaded her to elope with him. She, being proud, insisted on being married to the king. He issued his orders to the bishops, and they performed the ceremony, though Philip's wife was still living in her lonesome prison.

On this the pope boldly excommunicated both the king and the lady. Philip cringed and crawled in his usual mean way: he laid down his crown and sceptre, and promised to give up Bertrade, on which the pope withdrew his excommunication. But it was no sooner withdrawn than Philip took Bertrade back and went on governing as before.

A great council was held at Clermont, about a matter of which I shall tell you in the next chapter. All the clergy were present, including the pope. It was not Hildebrand—who had been driven out of Italy by the Emperor of Germany and had died a fugitive, saying with his last breath, "I have loved righteousness and hated iniquity, and therefore I die in exile"—but his successor Urban. This pope again excommunicated Philip and declared that any place that harbored him or Bertrade should be laid under an interdict; whereupon Philip made a great show of putting her away, but when the pope's back was turned he went to live with her as before and had her formally crowned as queen.

People despised him so much that they had ceased to pay attention to him, when his poor deserted wife Bertha died in her prison. Many angry words were then spoken, and it might have gone ill with the king if the French had not had something else to think of at that time. As it was, he idled his life in feasting and hunting with his fair Bertrade, and paid not the least attention to the affairs of the kingdom, when one day he was seized with an agonizing disease. The doctors, who in those days did not know much about disease, pronounced that this one must be mortal. And they bade the poor shuffling king prepare for death.

He cowered and shivered, and finding that he could not be cured, he bethought himself of his soul, and once more sent abject letters of entreaty to the pope for relief from excommunication—for he had been excommunicated again. Once more the pope revoked his decree, on the condition that Philip should do penance. The king promised, and this time he kept his word—perhaps the more willingly because the pope allowed Bertrade to remain with him to nurse him. As he grew worse he laid down his kingly power, became a Benedictine monk, and spent his days in prayer and humiliation. He used to go about in sackcloth and ashes, and to beg people, with tears in his eyes, to pray for him. For once his contrition was sincere. As his end approached he gave orders that his body be not laid beside the other kings of France; he said he was not worthy to rest in such company—in which opinion I think you will agree with him.

Chapter XII

THE FIRST CRUSADE

A.D. 1094–1137

In the year 1094, a poor French priest, named Peter, who, as was a common custom in those days, had been on a pilgrimage to Jerusalem, returned to France with his heart full of rage and grief at the sufferings which pilgrims like himself had to endure. The Holy Land was in the possession of followers of Mohammed—Arabs and Turks, who in that day were often called Moors or Moslems or Saracens. They hated Christianity, and when they found that Christian pilgrims made long journeys to pray on the Saviour's tomb, they sometimes required them to spit on it before they would allow them to kneel. If the pilgrims carried anything worth stealing, the Moslems stole it; if they were empty-handed, the Moslems often killed them. That such a people should own the land where Christ had lived and died seemed to Father Peter and to other devout Christians an unbearable outrage. Peter came back from the Holy Land burning with zeal to wrest Jerusalem out of the hands of the infidels.

He found Pope Urban quite of his mind. A great meeting was held at Clermont, in France, at which four hundred bishops and mitred abbots, as many feudal lords, and thousands of the common people were present. Pope and pilgrim called upon everybody to enlist in the war for the cross, or, as it was then called, the Crusade.

The idea took like wildfire. Almost every one pinned on his right shoulder a cross of red or white stuff. Feudal lords sold lands and jewels, and pledged what they could not sell for loans of money to outfit themselves and their vassals. Common people gave up their trade and their work to enlist in the Crusading army. Nobody thought of anything but Jerusalem. Men left their homes and their wives and their children to march under the banner of some fighting baron. People ran through the streets shouting, "It is the will of God! It is the will of God!"

Very few people knew how far Jerusalem was, or how they were to get there. Nobody knew how many Turks or Moslems they would have to fight. Hardly any one had any fixed plan as to how they were to get home. They were simply wild to drive the infidels out of the Holy Land and to place the tomb of Christ in Christian hands. The wildness was so general that, according to the histories of the times, nearly nine hundred thousand men started for the Holy Land. I think myself that the figure is large.

There is no doubt that all through the summer of 1096 armies set out for Jerusalem. One of these, in front of which Peter the Hermit marched, in a brown woollen gown with a cord round his waist, is said to have been one hundred thousand strong when it set out, but by the time it reached Asia, disease, hunger, hardship, and battle had so thinned its ranks that there were only three thousand left.

The great army, which was led by Godfrey of Bouillon, started in August, 1096. It marched into Germany, followed the valley of the Danube to the country which was then the Empire of the East, made some stay at its capital—Constantinople—crossed the Bosphorus, worked its way south through Asia Minor, and finally appeared before Jerusalem in July, 1099, having been nearly three years on the way. Throughout this weary journey the Crusaders had fought every inch of their way, for they had to steal the food on which they lived, and in every country they traversed the people rose up in arms. To get victuals they had to rob town and country; thus every man's hand was against them, and when they reached Constantinople their own was literally dripping with blood.

Constantinople, which had formerly been known as By-

PETER THE HERMIT PREACHING A CRUSADE

zantium, was the capital of the Eastern Empire. It was the most splendid city in Europe, perhaps more splendid than Rome had ever been. It was full of fine churches, noble palaces, marble houses, beautiful statues, and gilded domes. Rows of stores displayed rich stuffs, jewels, and arms, such as the men of France had never conceived. To these jewels and stuffs, and especially to the arms, the Crusaders began to help themselves. Some robbed the palaces and the churches. Many thought Constantinople would be as good a stopping-place as Jerusalem. But the Byzantines were cunning and tricky.

When the emperor, whose name was Alexius, asked Godfrey what he wanted, and was answered that he wanted ships and boats to ferry his army over into Asia, a fleet quite large enough for the purpose was ready next day.

And when the Crusaders lingered, having never seen so much plunder before in one spot, a curious disease broke out among them, and they began to die in prodigious numbers. It is said that the wells and the bread had been poisoned. Then the survivors embarked for Asia, not however till they had killed the emperor's pet lion, and taken the lead from the roofs of the churches to barter for food on their coming journey.

Down south, over parched plains, sandy wastes, and hills on which no herb grew, with clouds of Arab horsemen circling round them, and cutting off every one who strayed from the main body, the Crusaders marched, their number growing less day by day. At one spot five hundred men died of thirst. At another a squadron of Turkish troopers swooped down on a tired regiment and sabred every one. There was a little comfort when Antioch was reached—Antioch, the gay and rich city, with its three hundred and sixty churches and its four hundred and fifty towers—but when the starving Crusaders found themselves once more in a land of plenty they ate so ravenously that disease again broke out among them, and the generals ordered the march to go on. This time the men refused. They lay down on the floors of houses where they had taken shelter, and the houses had to be fired to get them out. Then a trooper declared that by digging in a certain spot the very lance which had pierced our Saviour's side could be found, pointing to Jerusalem. And he offered to make good his assertion by submitting to the ordeal of fire. He did, in fact, enter the flames and was duly burned, as might have been expected. But the lance was found for all that, and on the army marched. At last, when patience and courage were both nearly exhausted, on a sultry day in July, through the hot, palpitating air of the desert, over a plain where a few tufts of grass peered through clefts in the rocks, the flat roofs of Jerusalem were seen.

How many of the Crusaders were left at that time it is hard to say. One account says sixty thousand, another

ATTACKING THE SARACENS IN THEIR MOSQUE

only twenty-five—in either case a small remnant of those who had set out from France with the red-and-white cross on their right shoulders. A movable tower was built to overtop the walls of the city, and when it was nearly finished the Crusaders marched round the walls, barefoot and waving crosses. This they kept up for eight days. Then the tower was run up to the city gate, the Crusaders poured out, opened the gate, Jerusalem was taken, and every living creature in the place was killed. At last the Crusaders declared that their work was accomplished. They left Godfrey of Bouillon with three hundred knights to rule the conquered city and returned home.

Many of them died by the way. Those who lived to see their homes again found France much changed. The king was called Louis the Fat. He may have been fat, but he was wise and wary as well.

At the time he came to the throne the feudal lords had become so overbearing that, except in a few cities, the king was only king in name. They led expeditions to pillage their neighbors. They built towers by the road-side and would let no one pass till he paid toll. No man's house, nor his purse, nor his daughter, was safe from them. And the king was helpless. But when most of these lords had gone off to the Crusade at the head of their marauding vassals, the king took advantage of their absence to pull down some of their towers, to put his own men into some of their castles, and to punish very thoroughly the robbers and murderers without asking leave of their lords.

There was one impudent baron named Montlery, who had built a castle on the Orleans Road and took toll from passers-by. He went to the Crusade, and while he was away the king tore his castle down. There was a Count of Anjou who was constantly making war against his neighbors on his own account. He was a vain man, and once asked the king if he might have the sole right of laying the royal dinner-table?

Louis the Fat replied: Yes, he might lay the dishes on the table and no one else should.

Whereupon the Count of Anjou became a good friend to the king and undertook no more private wars.

In this way Louis the Fat so managed matters that he was able to go from Paris to Orleans or Rheims without having an army at his back, and it was actually said that a merchant could cross the forest of Montmorency without

THE FIRST CRUSADE LED BY PETER THE HERMIT

having a man-at-arms in front of him with lance in rest. Strange times, when such signs of order were thought wonderful proofs of progress.

The last years of Louis the Fat were unhappy. His heart was wrapped up in his son Philip, who was to succeed him, but one day, as the youth rode through the streets of Paris, a pig got between his horse's feet, the animal threw him heavily to the ground, and he died that night. His father almost went mad with grief. His second son, Louis, was consecrated as his heir; the sacred oil was poured on his head by the pope himself; but the father never ceased to mourn his eldest born, and was a sad man to the day of his death.

He died in 1137, after a reign of twenty-nine years. You will remember him as one of the good kings of France. There was more rest and safety among the poor peasantry under his reign than there had been for many years before; he taught the feudal barons that there was a power greater than theirs, and that laws were made for the strong as well as for the weak. He owed much throughout his life to the counsels of a good and wise priest named the Abbot Suger.

This abbot built a splendid monastery at St. Denis and lived in it, occupying one room fifteen feet long by ten wide; he slept on a bed of straw, covered with a single woollen counterpane. In that room he governed France, in the king's name, for years; he was never guilty of injustice to any man, nor did he ever excuse wrong or fear earthly power. Ah! if there had been in those days more abbots like him!

CHAPTER XIII

A TALE OF TWO FAIR WOMEN

A. D. 1137–1180

LOUIS THE SEVENTH, who is called in French history Louis the Young, was eighteen when he became king. He had been educated by the good Abbot Suger, who, you may be sure, taught him nothing but what a king should know. But he had the ill-fortune to marry the wrong woman, and she proved his evil genius.

This woman was Eleanor of Aquitaine, a beautiful, witty, spoiled child of the South. From her childhood she had been petted and flattered; poets had written sonnets about her; gay gallants had ridden by her side, telling her that she was the most bewitching and delightful and ravishing creature the world had ever seen. She grew up believing this flattery, as I believe girls sometimes do even in our time; and she became an imperious, self-willed young lady, so fond of pleasure and music and merriment that she thought of nothing else. When she married the heir to the crown of France, who was only eighteen, she felt that she was going to lead a joyous life; and she quite declined to take advice from good Abbot Suger, who was a serious man, and did not like frivolities.

Not long after her marriage she got Louis into trouble. The pope appointed an archbishop of Bourges in Aquitaine. Eleanor said that Bourges was her city, and that the pope had no right to give its archbishopric away. She ordered that a new archbishop should be chosen, and her husband said she was quite right. Then the pope excommunicated Louis.

Just before that he had excommunicated a sister of

A MINSTREL SINGING TO THE COURT OF ELEANOR OF AQUITAINE

Eleanor's for marrying a man who had a wife already. To avenge her sister, Eleanor persuaded Louis to invade Champagne, which was full of the pope's friends, and in the course of the march the king's troops set fire to the town of Vitry. A large number of the people of Vitry—about thirteen hundred, men, women, and children—took refuge in the cathedral. The flames reached the building, and, the doors having got jammed, every one of the thirteen hundred was burned to death. The king, who rode up as the church was burning, heard their dying shrieks and groans. He was not a bad young man. He was filled with horror at the wrong he had done. He begged pardon of God and the pope and offered to perform any penance that might be set him.

Just then came news from the Holy Land that the Saracens had gathered a great force and marched upon the city of Edessa, where many Christians lived, and had massacred every one. The pope declared that the time had come for a new Crusade—as though the result of the last one had been so satisfactory. Louis was not in favor of it, and the Abbot Suger was quite opposed to the scheme. He told the king that his first duty was to his own people. But Eleanor was frantic to lead a Crusade, and everybody gave way to her imperious will.

On Easter Day another great national council was held, this time on the slope of a hill overlooking the town of Vezelai in Burgundy. Scores of counts, and barons, and bishops, and abbots, all with their men-at-arms by their sides, their banners waving in the air, and thousands of the common people gathered on the hill, while above them, on a raised platform, sat the king and the proud and beautiful Queen Eleanor, and beside them a thin, pale-faced monk with burning eyes. When all were silent, this pale monk—his name was Bernard—rose and poured out a torrent of fiery words about the shame and disgrace of allowing the Holy Land to remain in the hands of infidels. As had happened just fifty years before, the people went mad over his words. Cries of "Crosses!" "Crosses!" rose on all sides. Queen Eleanor seized Bernard's hand, kissed it before all the people, and pinned a cross on her own right shoulder. The king followed her example, and the priests and monks tore up red and white stuff they had brought, and their very garments, to supply the people with Crusaders' badges.

It was the same old sickening story over again. The Crusaders—or as many as survived of the hundred thousand who set out—found their way into Asia, but there the Sara-

CRUSADERS FORDING A RIVER

cens fell upon them and defeated them over and over again. By paying money out of his own pocket, Louis got some help from the Emperor of the East; but the tricky Greek betrayed him to the Turks, who fell upon the remnant of his army as they were sleeping. The slaughter that ensued was so frightful that the Turks in pity stayed their hand at last, and nursed the wounded, while the Greeks sent their prisoners to Constantinople to be sold as slaves. Of the whole army, only Louis, Eleanor, the Emperor Conrad, and about two hundred and fifty knights reached Jerusalem. Louis hastened home, for at Antioch he learned that he had lost the love of his faithless wife.

As soon as he reached Paris the king told the Abbot

Suger that he could live with his wife no more. The wise and good priest tried to dissuade him, saying that it was his duty to forgive a weak woman ; but when the abbot visited the weak woman he did not find her quite as weak as he had expected.

"I have married a monk," she said, "not a king. I will live with him no more."

After this, of course, there was nothing to be done but to arrange the divorce.

You will like to hear what became of this proud and wicked woman. When she was divorced from Louis she took back the duchy of Aquitaine which she had brought him in marriage, and at the age of thirty she married Henry Plantagenet, who afterward became King of England, and brought him a dowry which, with his own dukedom of Normandy, made him ruler of two thirds of France. But she could live at peace with no husband. She quarrelled with Henry and incited his sons to rebel against him, whereupon he seized her and locked her up in prison for sixteen years. She lived to see two of her sons—Richard and John—crowned kings of England, and died at the age of eighty-one.

There lived at this period in France another lady whose life was very different from hers, and who I think will be remembered when Eleanor, with all her beauty and all her pride, has been quite forgotten. This was Héloïse. She was the niece of a canon named Fulbert, and was young, lovely, and gifted. Few of the learned men of the day knew as much as this young girl. She fell in love with her teacher Abelard, who, I think, was unworthy of such a love, though he was famous and much thought of everywhere. But he had no more heart than a brickbat, while Héloïse overflowed with love and tenderness and passionate affection. They ran away. He became a Benedictine monk, and she, by his orders, became the abbess of a convent, where she taught religion, Greek, Latin, and Hebrew. He spent his life in arguing questions with the other monks of the day, and was quite often locked up in jail for knowing more than other people—which I believe has happened since then. She was appointed by the pope the head of an order of nuns, and spent her life in doing good, teaching the ignorant, tending the sick, and always thinking of the one undying love of her young heart. When you go to Paris you will see in the eastern cemetery a monument which covers the remains of Hèloïse and Abelard; many years ago their bones were dug from the graves where they had been laid side by side, and were brought to Paris, so that these two who were parted in life might at last be united in death.

After his divorce from Eleanor, King Louis married again; and his wife dying, he took a third, who became the mother of the son I shall speak of in the next chapter. When the boy was fifteen years old, his father had a stroke of paralysis, and the doctors warned him to prepare for death.

You will form an idea of the manners and customs of that day from King Louis's preparations for his death. The usage was that whenever the king came to Paris after a journey or residence elsewhere, his servants could enter any house in the city and lay hands upon such articles of clothing and such living utensils as he might want. It was taken for granted that the good citizens of Paris would be only too glad to let their king have a pair of trousers or a hair-brush, or a kettle, or a pair of boots—if he needed such things. In this way the king's rooms were generally pretty well furnished and supplied. King Louis now ordered all his boxes to be emptied, his drawers ransacked, and their contents laid upon a table. He put his money in one heap, his jewels in another, and his clothes in a third. Then he summoned all the poor people who lived near the palace and divided his belongings among them, so that every one got something, and at the close of the day the king had nothing left but the clothes he wore. Then he turned his face to the wall and died.

CHAPTER XIV

PHILIP AUGUSTUS

A.D. 1180–1223

AFTER Louis's death another boy prince—Philip Augustus—succeeded to the throne. He reigned forty-three years, and he managed, by successful wars, by the aid of the Church, and by cunning politics, to take from the King of England and from the French feudal lords so much of the territory they held in France that he was able to leave a considerable kingdom to his heir. Personally, however, he does not cut a very large figure in the history of his reign.

He began badly. There was a hermit who lived in a cell in the woods near Paris, and who was supposed to be a very holy man. Whether he was holy or not, he was a cruel and bigoted fanatic ; for he persuaded the king that it would be agreeable in the eyes of the Lord to expel the Jews from France. A decree to that effect was issued and executed ; the poor Jews, with their wives and children, were torn from their homes and driven out of the king's dominions. People who owed them money were released from paying, on condition that they handed over to the king one fifth of what they owed.

This inhuman edict had no sooner been carried out than news came that Saladin, the chief of the Saracens, had retaken Jerusalem, and was meting out to the Christians the measure they had meted to the Jews. Nothing would serve but another Crusade. But this was to be the greatest of all Crusades. Three monarchs—King Richard of England, King Philip of France, and the Emperor of Germany, whose name was Redbeard—took the lead ; and with them were dukes, counts, barons, knights, archbishops, bishops, and men-at-arms from Italy, Belgium, Denmark, as well as England, France, and Germany—to the number, it is said, of six hundred thousand, all trained soldiers. Most of them went in sailing craft by way of the Mediterranean. They stopped for a while at Sicily, where Richard of England—who was always quarrelling with some one—fell out with Philip of France, and nearly put an end to the expedition; but the dispute was finally settled, the great fleet made a landing on the coast of Palestine near Acre, and proceeded to besiege the place.

FIGHTING THE SARACENS

The siege was long and bloody. The Crusaders built towers which they ran up to the walls, and from which men-at-arms poured burning arrows, fire-balls made of sulphur and pitch, and great stones upon the garrison; and, in return, the Turks kept up an incessant fire of darts and arrows upon the assailants. At one fight so many arrows hit King Richard that his body was said to be like a pincushion stuck full of needles. But at last the place was taken, and Saladin refusing to make satisfactory arrangements about the prisoners the English had taken, their throats were all cut in his presence.

This Saladin, the chief and general of the Saracens, is one of the few figures in the story of the Crusades whom you can remember with pleasure. He was a brave soldier who led his troopers to battle intrepidly, and when the battle was over he was merciful and generous to his fallen foes. He sent fruits and cooling drinks to the fevered Crusaders, and rather than have his prisoners taken to Constantinople, to be sold as slaves, he and his brother ransomed them with their own money and set them free. It seems to me that this Moslem's soul was imbued with a more Christian spirit than that of many of his Christian foes.

Acre captured, Richard, who could not remain quiet, quarrelled with his allies. King Philip, who had slept in the same bed with him, eaten from the same plate, and drunk from the same cup, accused him of having tried to poison him, took ship, and went home. The Duke of Austria had raised his banner on a corner of the wall; Richard tore it down, and threw it into the ditch; whereupon he broke camp and departed. Richard so grossly insulted the Duke of Burgundy that he also withdrew his forces, and left the King of England to go on with the Crusade. You will not be surprised to hear that this brawling king gave up the game himself at last, tried to find his way home in disguise, but was betrayed by his wearing court gloves, and was thrown into jail by the very duke whose banner he had flung into the ditch.

But though the Crusades did not place Jerusalem in Christian hands, they accustomed the people of that day to the idea of fighting for religion. You know that you cannot change men's religious faith by making war upon them; our Saviour never told his disciples to make war on those who differed from them—his religion was a religion of peace. But seven centuries ago a notion prevailed that it was right and proper to stab, and rob, and wound, and kill people because they held religious opinions which did not agree with those of the stabbers and the robbers and the killers. This was the reason why the Pope of Rome, having failed to wipe the followers of Mohammed off the face of the earth, began to look nearer home for a people which had religious opinions to which he objected. And he found such a people in beautiful, sunny, smiling Languedoc.

They were the brightest people in France. They had ideas of their own and plenty of them. And one of those ideas was that they were quite as well able to think for themselves on religion as the pope was to think for them. They had always raged at the power which the pope held in France. They called themselves Albigenses and said they were independent of Rome. At this particular moment their wrath was kindled by a new attempt of the pope to plunge the French people into misery because the king would not obey him.

Philip had married a princess of Denmark. From the first hour he saw her he hated her, and shortly after the marriage he divorced her and married a lovely girl from Tyrol, named Agnes of Méranie. The pope ordered him to put away Agnes and to take back the Dane under penalty of an interdict. He refused. After waiting three years the pope's legate or messenger summoned a council of bishops to meet in the cathedral at Dijon; they discussed the matter for a week, and on the seventh day, at midnight, an interdict was laid upon the kingdom. Each priest held a burning torch to light up the gloom of the church, and all chanted the prayers for the dead. Black crape was laid on the altar, the holy relics were laid away in tombs, and at a signal the torches were dashed to the ground, the cathedral was wrapped in gloom, and the whole of France was laid under a curse. For eight months there were no church services, no baptisms, no marriages, no burial services in France. Then the king yielded.

But the people of Languedoc were not in a yielding mood. They declared that so domineering a Church was not for them. The Christianity which they proposed to follow must be of a gentler type. And numbers of them, under the lead of the gallant Raymond, Count of Toulouse, began to say openly that they had no orders to take from the pope. A messenger, whom the pope sent to rebuke Raymond, and who was haughty and insolent, was followed to the Rhone by an Albigensian and stabbed to death; but Raymond's heart misgave him after this—he did penance and was openly scourged by the priests in the church.

His people were of sterner stuff. They shut themselves up in the town of Beziers and prepared for battle. The fighting men of the Church came on in overwhelming numbers under the lead of Simon of Montfort, an old Crusader and a bitter fighter, and the Abbot of Citeaux. The pope had offered every volunteer who joined the army full pardon for his sins, and it appeared that there were a good many sinners just then. The town was soon taken. When the soldiers asked how they should distinguish rebels from churchmen among the citizens, the Abbot of Citeaux solved the difficulty very simply. "Kill them all," said this gentle priest; "the Lord will know his own."

In the great church of St. Nazaire some priest set the bell tolling when the soldiers broke in; it never stopped tolling till there was not a living creature in the place outside of the attacking army. The Abbot of Citeaux wrote to the pope that he had done his best, but he was afraid he had not killed over twenty thousand. The town was then fired and burned to the ground; you can see part of the ruins to this day.

Other places shared the fate of Beziers. Ten thousand persons were executed at Toulouse. Simon of Montfort and the equally savage Abbot of Citeaux rode over the lovely plains of Languedoc, slaying, burning, ravaging, and giving up pleasant towns to be sacked by their ruffianly camp-followers. One castle which held out for a while was taken, it is said, by the help of a machine of war invented by the Archdeacon of Paris, of all people in the world. When the work was done, Languedoc was a desert waste. Simon of Montfort continued for several years to hunt down scattered fugitives, until one day, when he was riding past the walls of Toulouse, a heavy stone flung from the ramparts by a woman struck him on the head and dashed his brains out.

Philip had taken no very active part in the persecution of the Southern people. He had business of his own in the North. He wrested Normandy out of the hands of the English and fought a battle with the German emperor, in which the latter was badly beaten. He got Flanders too, and part of the country we call Belgium. Judged by the rules of that day, which measured kings by the extent of their dominions, no matter how the dominions were acquired or governed, he was a great monarch. Perhaps one of the most creditable works he did during his reign was to pave the city of Paris.

Chapter XV

FRANCE SIX HUNDRED AND SEVENTY YEARS AGO

A.D. 1223–1226

The successor of Philip Augustus was a young man to whom people gave the name of Louis the Lion, though in his brief three years' reign he was as unlike a lion as anything you can imagine. He had a fine coronation. Long tables were set in the streets of Paris and laden with food for the poor to eat; minstrels sang songs all day in honor of the lion king; and everybody who could afford it illuminated his house. Louis fought the English for a year or two, as the custom was; then he turned on the people of Languedoc, and was going to fight them too, but a fever broke out in his army and carried off twenty thousand men, the king among the number.

You would take less interest in the doings of this not very famous king than in the story of Jeanne of Flanders. Jeanne was the daughter of Baldwin, who in 1204 became Emperor of the East, when Constantinople was taken by an army of Venetians and Crusaders combined. He had barely got settled on his throne when he was obliged to march out to fight the Bulgarians and was taken prisoner. Word came to his daughter Jeanne, who was reigning in his stead in Flanders, that he was in prison in Bulgaria, and would his dear good daughter send money to ransom her father?

Jeanne replied that she had no money for any such purpose.

Nearly twenty years afterward an old man, bowed, gray, and wrinkled, appeared before Jeanne, and said that he was her father, and that he had escaped from his prison in Bulgaria.

Jeanne replied that she did not believe him, and that he was an impostor. She referred to King Louis of France, and he too, being a very close friend to Jeanne, doubted the old man. The pope sent a legate to look into the case, and he also, after some consultation with Jeanne, declared that he was unable to make up his mind. While they were debating, Jeanne got the old man into her hands, imprisoned him, tortured him cruelly, and put him to death.

The Flemish people were indignant, and accused Jeanne of being the murderess of her father. She answered them that Count Baldwin had died in his prison in Bulgaria, and she offered to prove it. She did, in effect, send a trusty officer of hers to that distant principality on the Danube, and he returned, saying that Baldwin had really died there, as Jeanne had said; that he had seen his grave, and he knew it was the count's, because a miraculous flame played round it—which ended the matter, and Jeanne reigned over Flanders in peace.

Perhaps it may help you to understand this child's history of France if you know something of the way in which the French lived at this time—six hundred and seventy years ago, about two hundred and seventy years before Columbus discovered America, and nearly four hundred years before the Puritans landed on Plymouth Rock.

The country parts of France were fertile, as they are now, and grew wheat, barley, rye, vines, fruit, vegetables—but not potatoes—and hay for cattle; in the south corn was raised, and on the hill-sides and in the meadows near by cattle were pastured—horned beasts, horses, mules, asses, sheep, goats, and pigs. If you had lived in those days you might have seen in the farm-yards the same poultry as we have now, except turkeys, and the woods were full of deer, wild boars, and many kind of birds that were good eating. The streams and ponds were full of fish.

There were a number of towns, but they were small.

The only fine buildings in them were the churches, monasteries, convents, and abbeys; the houses of the people were built of sun-dried brick or wood and thatched with straw; they were set endwise to the street; the window-panes were small; except in Paris the streets were not paved, and there were no sidewalks anywhere. A few old Roman roads from city to city were still in order; but few of the other roads were mended, and in rainy weather they were full of ruts and mud. There were no public vehicles to carry people or goods from place to place. Travellers went on foot or on horseback or in carts without springs; merchants carried their wares in packs on the backs of mules. There were no hotels or lodging-houses for travellers. When people went on a journey, they slept and got their meals at a feudal lord's castle or at a monastery. The monks lodged and fed all comers; the guests paid if they could; if they had no money they did some work for the monastery. Rooms were warmed with wood burned in open hearths, or with hot embers in braziers which could be carried from room to room. There was no coal yet.

In the castles of the feudal lords a long dining-table was set for twelve-o'clock dinner. The lord and the lady sat at the head in their best clothes, and their children, relations, and guests lower down the table; then came a huge salt-cellar, and below the salt-cellar sat the servants and travellers who had come in for a meal. There was no carpet on the floor. Even in the king's palace floors were strewed with rushes, and at meals bones were picked clean and thrown on the floor. People ate with their knives—there were no table forks. Boys who were called pages went round from guest to guest with tall tankards of silver or pewter, full of wine or beer. There was no tea nor coffee nor sugar in those days; drinks were sweetened with honey.

The lord and his lady slept in a chamber of state, in a huge bedstead, on a mattress of wool or straw or feathers;

counterpanes, often richly embroidered, were their covering; they used no sheets. The ladies of the family had rooms by themselves, and one or two men-at-arms slept outside their doors. The servants and guests slept as often on the floor as elsewhere. Among the people, houses were generally divided into an attic, where the whole family slept, and a downstairs room, where meals were cooked and eaten, and the man of the house carried on his business.

All classes wore woollen cloth. Cotton cloth was in use in the Eastern Empire, and fabrics of silk were worn there and in Italy and Spain; but both were very scarce and dear in France. The coats of the common people were often made of leather. No one wore stockings—not even the ladies. When the knights and feudal lords went into battle they thrust their bare feet into their boots and covered their body and legs with coats of mail or iron, which were sometimes so heavy that when the wearer of one of them was knocked down he could not get up again without help. Lords and men-at-arms wore on their heads helmets made wholly or partly of iron. The common people wore woollen hoods called chaperons.

Printing was not invented till over two hundred years after this time. There were thus no books, but in the monasteries and convents copies of the Bible, of the writings of the saints, and of a few Latin and Greek authors, written by hand on parchment and often richly decorated, were carefully preserved. Hardly any one knew how to read and write except the priests. Some of these could read not only their own but foreign languages; but the feudal counts and barons affected to believe that reading and writing were beneath a nobleman or a man-at-arms, and they boasted of their ignorance. Many a feudal noble who could put fifty thousand men into the field could not write his own name, but signed leases and treaties by stamping a seal with the hilt of his sword. As for the common people, they never had a chance to learn, and it was not considered the thing for a lady to be reading manuscripts. It was thought she should spend her time in playing the lute or working embroidery. In the South love songs and romances were handed down from minstrel to minstrel, and were sung or spoken at feasts, and in parts of the North there were schools where nice questions of philosophy and theology were discussed. But there were no real schools in France.

Nobody knew anything about medicine. Wounds were generally dressed by women, a few of whom learned something about the effect of herbs. As for the men-doctors, they either gave doses of medicine which were as likely to kill as to cure, or burned their patients with red-hot irons, or they bled them, as though any good could be done by weakening a man who was weak enough before.

If you ask me if the French were a happy people at this time, I must say that I do not know, though they had much to make them otherwise. The main business of France, as you have perceived already, was war. Every year some war raged, some poor fellows were killed in other people's quarrels, some honest peasants' farms were pillaged by soldiers, and some women and children were thrown out into the wide world to starve. Neither life nor property was safe, and the people of France had little or nothing to say about their government.

In some towns people had clubbed together and paid their feudal lord a sum of money in return for his promise not to interfere with them; and now and then these cities fought fiercely for the liberties they had thus gained. All the people were pious, and they took a great deal of comfort out of their religion, especially when the priests were wise and kind, which I think was generally the case. Then as now, I make no doubt but, when the enemy was not in sight, the French were often gay and cheerful, as they are to-day, and I dare say they sometimes thought their lives were not so wretched after all.

MINIATURE PORTRAIT OF KING LOUIS IX

Chapter XVI

SAINT-LOUIS

A.D. 1226–1270

The last king of France—Louis the Lion—was Louis the Eighth; his successor, who was Louis the Ninth, is better known as Saint-Louis, because he was so good that he was canonized as a saint. He was indeed wise, gentle, kind, generous, merciful, and great-hearted. During the first years of his reign his mother, Blanche of Castile, ruled the kingdom for him, and on the whole ruled it prudently.

Almost her first act was to put an end to the war at the South by adding Languedoc and the county of Toulouse to her son's realm. Raymond, Count of Narbonne, who had kept up the war and had been excommunicated in consequence, made his peace with France and the pope. On a day set he appeared in the cathedral of Notre Dame at Paris, bare from shoulders to waist. As he walked up the main aisle of the church the pope's legate walked behind him, scourging him with a whip. When he reached the altar and knelt in contrition, the legate cried,

"Count of Narbonne, I absolve thee from thy excommunication."

To which the count answered, "Amen!"

CASTLE OF ANGERS, BUILT BY SAINT-LOUIS

When Louis was twenty, he married a princess named Marguerite of Provence, who was only fourteen. The wedding-feast was one of the grandest banquets ever seen in France. The king wore a coat of cloth of gold and a scarlet mantle of the same stuff trimmed with ermine. His brother waited upon him and carved the meat. The feast was given in a cloister of the Cistercian monks; the king's table was at one end of the cloister, and at the

ISABELLA SENDS TWO RUFFIANS TO KILL THE KING

other were the kitchens, pantries, and offices, from which the meat, wine, and bread were brought. In the other aisles of the cloister and in the space in the middle were tables at which no less than three thousand knights banquetted, all in their armor and their suits of cloth of gold and rich stuffs.

Everything passed off pleasantly, which was not always the case when the king met his subjects. When the king and queen went to Poitiers, Isabella of Angouleme visited them. The king sat on one side of his bed and the queen, with two of her ladies, on the other, and they never rose from their seats when Isabella entered the room or when she went out. Her proud spirit could not brook the affront, and she called on her husband to avenge her.

At first he did not seem hungry to fight the king, but he said,

"Madame, I will do all that I can."

"If you do not," replied his wife, "you shall never enter my presence again."

As he made little progress Isabella sent two of her vassals to poison the king. She gave them poison which they were to mix in his wine. They were caught and hanged, and Isabella's husband nearly lost his life and his lands. To please his wife he had sworn that he would never have his hair or his beard cut till he had humbled the king, but when Louis drew near with his army he sent for the barber directly.

Then the old dreadful subject of the Crusades came up again.

Tribes of fierce Tartars came swooping down from Central Asia and proved far more savage than the Turks. The Emperor of the East had tried to pacify them by swearing friendship to one of the tribes on the body of a dead dog, but neither the oath nor the dead dog served him. He had to beg for help from King Louis, and to win his favor he sent him the true crown of thorns with which our Saviour had been crowned over twelve hundred years before, and the king walked barefoot as far as Vincennes to receive it. Still Louis, who was in many things wise as well as good, did not accept the emperor's invitation.

While he was pondering he fell ill—so ill that he became speechless; and a nurse pulled a cloth over his face, believing that he was dead. But he suddenly recovered his speech and cried,

"The cross! the cross!"

They laid the Crusader's badge on his heart; he got well and called his men-at-arms to prepare for one more Crusade.

The army assembled at a seaport on the Mediterranean, called Aigues Mortes. On a bright August day, when all had embarked on board ship, the chief captain said to the king,

"Sire, call up your priests, for the weather is fine, and we must weigh anchor."

"Sing, in the name of God!" called the king; and one after another every ship's crew took up a pious chant, and the whole fleet put to sea.

Ten months afterward they cast anchor off the port of Damietta, in Egypt, King Louis having resolved to attack the Egyptians, whose sultan had conquered the Holy Land. King Louis was the first to leap ashore in water up to his waist. There was a battle fought at a place called Mansourah, where both sides claimed the victory, but the French lost many of their best fighting-men. The Saracens threw fire-balls which stuck to the bodies of the French and burned fiercely; water would not put them out. After the battle disease broke out among the French, and they died by hundreds. Those who touched the dead bodies took the disease themselves; thus many corpses were left unburied. King Louis dug trenches with his own hands and carried the bodies to them, but he could not put spirit into his followers. The French tried to retreat, but the Saracens followed them, and in the end they were obliged to surrender, King Louis becoming a prisoner.

While the Saracens were discussing his ransom, forty Mamelukes, who were the best fighters in the Saracen army, appeared before him, and one of them, drawing out of a bloody cloth the head of a freshly killed man, cried,

"There, King, is your enemy, the Sultan of Egypt, who would have killed you! What will you give me for having slain him?"

The king turned his head away in disgust and dismissed the murderers.

He was ransomed after a time and spent four years in Palestine, caring for the Christians. Then, on the death of his mother, who had ruled France during his absence, he returned home.

For fourteen years he ruled France so wisely and so well that I do not know where to find an equal to him in the whole list of French kings. He neither wronged any man himself nor allowed any man to be wronged by others. When the feudal lords oppressed their vassals, he called them to account, and punished them severely if they persisted in the wrong. He compelled them to have the roads through their fiefs guarded so that travellers should not be robbed in broad daylight as they had been. When the priests went to him and complained that people were getting not to mind being excommunicated, and that they refused to ask for absolution, which was rather an expensive luxury, he sent them off with the sharp reproof: "It is contrary to God and common-sense to compel people to seek absolution when the priests have done them wrong."

Near the church at Vincennes, which he attended, stood an old oak-tree with spreading branches, under which the king used to sit on a rug to hear the complaints of his people. Every one was free to tell his story. When he sat down he called,

"Is there any one who has a suit?" And when some one rose he continued,

"Now, silence all! Then speak one after the other."

His judgment was so clear that he hardly ever decided a case wrong.

But news kept coming of the dreadful persecutions of the Christians in Asia. Louis felt that he could not go to his last rest without one more effort to stop them. Once more he raised the cross in the great hall of the Louvre. But people had learned wisdom in the last hundred years. Everybody was opposed to another Crusade. The pope was against it; so were the bishops; so were the priests; so were the people. However, Louis was firm, and his

SAINT-LOUIS HOLDING COURT IN THE WOODS

barons could not let him go alone. Nor could the kings of Navarre, Castile, Aragon, nor the sons of the King of England. Poor Louis was nearly dead. He could neither sit on a horse nor ride in a wagon. He had to be carried in a litter. But his spirit was as undaunted as ever.

The Crusaders landed near Carthage. The plague broke out among them, and King Louis was one of the first attacked. He lost his best-loved son in a skirmish in landing. He turned to his daughter Isabella and said,

"Most dear daughter, many persons go to bed full of vain and sinful thoughts, and in the morning are found dead. The true way of loving God is to love him with our whole heart."

In the night he rose in bed several times, crying, "Jerusalem! Jerusalem!" Then he bade his attendants lay him on a coarse sack covered with ashes. The cross was raised before him, and with the words, "I will enter into thy house, O Lord!" he peacefully expired.

I think you will agree that if any one of whom I have told you is entitled to the name of saint, he is the man.

Chapter XVII

THE SICILIAN VESPERS

A.D. 1270–1285

After Saint-Louis, the next in the line of French kings is Philip the Third, called Philip the Bold, I suppose because he was timid and henpecked. The most interesting person in his reign was his uncle—Charles of Anjou—who commanded the French at Carthage after the death of Saint-Louis. This Charles of Anjou had a thrilling history.

Eight years before Saint Louis's death—that is to say, in the year 1262—the pope offered Charles the throne of Naples and Sicily. The throne did not belong to the pope to give, nor was it becoming in Charles to accept it—but he did. The true heir to the throne was a boy of fifteen, named Conradine. Him Charles caught, as he appeared at Naples to demand his rights, and thrust into a dungeon. What was to be done with him?

"Try him for high treason," whispered the pope.

They tried him, though the charge was so absurd that all the judges save one objected to find a verdict, and Charles's own son-in-law afterward slew that one with a blow of his sword; but the verdict was found, a scaffold was erected in the public square of Naples, and there on the 26th of October, 1269, young Conradine had his head chopped off, his last words being, "My mother, my mother, how thou wilt grieve over the news they will bring thee!"

But there was a man who swore a great oath that he would avenge him. This man's name was John of Procida, his calling that of a doctor, his country Italy. He took no man into his counsel, but went over into Spain and asked the King of Aragon would he make war upon Charles of

Anjou and become King of Naples and Sicily? Don Pedro of Aragon would have liked nothing better, but Charles of Anjou, with France to back him, was too strong, and he refused. Then John of Procida sold his house and all that he had, and disappeared so completely that no one could tell what had become of him. In fact, he had put on the robe of a begging monk, and was wandering through the world in that disguise, begging his bread from place to place.

He went to the Emperor of the East, and offered him Sicily if he would send an army against Charles. The emperor was not loath, but he also was afraid. Then Procida went to the pope: he hated Charles and desired his ruin; but he died, and Charles made a trembling monk of Tours, whom he owned body and soul, pope in his place. Then John of Procida went to the feudal lords of Sicily, and they neither died nor were afraid; but said that whenever Procida gave the word they would rise against Charles at the head of their vassals. The Sicilians were all boiling with rage against the tyrant, who ground them with such cruel taxation that the goat-herd, and the shepherd, and the cow-herd, and the bee-keeper, and the fruit-grower did not know where to turn to get bread for their families. There was such a mutinous look in their eyes that Charles forbade the Sicilians to carry arms and ordered his officers to carry out the law strictly.

In the afternoon of the Easter Monday of the year 1282, through green fields and gardens bursting with flowers, the people of Palermo, in their best clothes, walked up the hill to Monreale to hear vespers. Among them was a beautiful girl of high degree, on the arm of her betrothed and surrounded by her family. An officer of Charles, named Brouet, stopped the men, examined them for concealed weapons, and then grossly insulted the young lady. Her betrothed struck the brute dead with his own sword. Instantly the cry arose, "Death to the French!" and wherever a Frenchman was found he was slain. Procida had laid his plans so well that people had their arms in readiness, and ran out of their houses prepared for battle. But there was no resistance. The cry was "Kill!" "Kill!" and the sun of that Easter Monday went down in blood. The terrible massacre is known in history as the Sicilian Vespers.

Then the King of Aragon took courage, sent a fleet to Sicily, and landed an army. Charles would not fight him; he drew off his ships, and the Spanish vessels, though far inferior in numbers, went in chase of them. They were many days absent.

At last one morning before daybreak a fleet was seen from the light-house at Messina. The Sicilians felt sure that these were the ships of Charles of Anjou, and that they had captured or destroyed the Spanish fleet. They roused Don Pedro, who mounted a horse and rode down to the sea-shore in the gray morning; he found all the people weeping and wailing. He looked warily out to sea and called aloud, "Good people, be of good cheer; those are our galleys which are bringing in Charles's fleet."

Just then an armed vessel, bearing the flag of Aragon, detached itself from the fleet and steered for the golden fountain behind which King Pedro sat on his horse, with his banner borne by a body of cavalry. When the vessel touched shore the captain landed and said to the king,

"Lord, behold your galleys; they bring you those of your enemies."

At these words the king dismounted and fell on his knees. Soldiers and people followed his example, and all sang a hymn of praise to God. The Sicilians knew that they had regained their liberties, and never did any one see such joy as theirs.

Charles of Anjou was crazed by his defeat. He offered to settle the dispute with Don Pedro by a duel, and actually went to Bordeaux to meet him, but the King of Aragon was not foolish enough to indulge in such silly business; he rode into Bordeaux and rode out again so swiftly that he was gone before Charles knew that he had arrived.

Then Charles sent a fleet under a lame son of his to defy the Aragonese fleet in the Bay of Naples. The lame prince had forty-five galleys, the Spanish captain only thirty-five; but the Spaniards accepted battle and defeated the French fleet, taking the lame prince prisoner. When the news of his son's capture was brought to his father, he cried,

"Why is he not dead?"

Death soon overtook, not his lame son, but himself. His friend the pope took up his cause and gave the kingdom of Aragon—which did not belong to him—to a French prince, the son of Philip the Bold. But he could not deliver the kingdom—he could only cause more long and fruitless wars which left things as they were.

Philip the Bold was ruled by his wife, Mary of Brabant, who was beautiful and cunning. Before her marriage Philip had been ruled by a barber-surgeon whose name was Brosse. Brosse, jealous of the new queen, accused her of all manner of crimes; she denied everything and accused the barber-surgeon of crimes fully as black. King Philip referred the case to a fortune-teller, who decided that the queen was innocent and Brosse guilty. Whereupon the barber-surgeon was hanged, and the queen went on ruling her husband until he died of a fever on an expedition to capture Aragon for his son.

Chapter XVIII

PHILIP THE HANDSOME

A.D. 1285–1314

The successor of Philip the Bold was his son Philip the Fourth, who was nicknamed Philip the Handsome. His reign was exciting.

He made in the laws a great number of changes which were on the whole improvements. He would not allow any one but himself to rob the Jews. He would not allow priests to try cases in court, or to sit in Parliament, or to hold civil office. He stopped legacies of property to the Church. He provided that persons could buy and own land without being feudal lords. He founded colleges. He stopped the absurd fashion of trial by battle. He established custom-houses and laid duties on foreign goods imported into France. With these sensible changes, he made others which were not so sensible. He coined money of less than the lawful weight and made it a crime to weigh his coins. He fixed by law the clothing which people should wear and the food which they should eat. They could not have more than one soup and two meat dishes at dinner at half-past eleven, and not more than one kind of meat should be served in each dish. If he had done nothing worse than meddle with people's dinners, you would have thought better of him than I am afraid you can. But he was the greediest thief in France.

He had the usual war with England; it broke out this time from a fight between English and Norman sailors, in which the Normans hung an English sea-captain to his own yard-arm with a dead dog tied to his feet. A more serious war was with Flanders, which Philip seized and annexed to France on the pretence that the Flemish lords had been untrue to him—in reality because Flanders was rich, and he was always in need of money. He sent a body of troops into the country, under trusty officers, and bade them bleed the Flemings till their fat bodies ran with coin. They were not men to stand that kind of bleeding.

On the 21st of March, 1302, after night had fallen, every iron caldron in Bruges was brought out into the street, and people began to beat them with iron hammers. Everybody knew what this meant. A little one-eyed fellow named King, who was the leader of the workmen, had settled upon the signal. Instantly a butcher, meeting a Frenchman, struck him dead with his cleaver. The whole city burst forth in the black night, and wherever a Frenchman was met he was killed, the women taking great delight in throwing the fugitives out of windows. The bloody work went on next day and the day after, and what was done at Bruges was also done at Ypres, Gravelines, and other towns. So the French were wiped off the face of Flanders, as they had been wiped off the face of Sicily.

Up came French armies to avenge their countrymen, and opposite them in bold array stood the Flemings, drawn up behind a deep ditch, each man with a pike shod with iron stuck in the ground before him. The French could not see the ditch, and when they charged, with a furious rush, they rolled into it one on top of the other, the knights lying helpless in their heavy armor; the Flemings beat their brains out with iron or leaden mauls, and in a very little while the battle was over, and the remains of the French army marched back home.

But this was nothing to the war between Philip and the pope. The latter was a fighting priest, by name Boniface; he invited the whole world to visit Rome on the occasion of the centennial anniversary of the Church, in the year of our Lord 1300, and to those who came with full pockets and open hands he promised remission of their

THE TEMPLE

sins. They came in such crowds that they slept in tents or under awnings in the streets, and they laid so much money on the altars that priests raked it up with rakes without counting it. Now there was one thing which Philip loved above everything else—that was money.

It enraged him to see archbishops and bishops, canons and monks, all round and sleek, rolling in wealth and feeding on the fat of the earth. He established a new tax, the maltote, which required citizens to pay one fiftieth of their substance to the king, and he ordered that priests should pay like other people. The pope retorted with a bull, excommunicating priests who paid money to the king without the permission of the Church. Philip struck back by forbidding the export of gold or silver, which cut off the pope's supply of Peter's pence from France. The pope sent a legate into Languedoc to stir up the people against the king; the king caught the legate and condemned him to death. The pope issued a bull against the king, warning him against the danger of rebelling against his spiritual superior; the bull was burned in a public square in Paris, in the presence of nobles, soldiers, and people. The pope summoned the French clergy to meet him at Rome; the king forbade them to leave France.

I suppose the quarrel had become so bitter that it could not go on without an outbreak. So thought Novaret, a Gascon, and Sciarra Colonna, an Italian, both friends of Philip's and with Philip's money in their pockets. They started for Anagni, where the pope was staying, and tore into the town at the head of a body of cavalry. A few cardinals, who were in attendance on the pope, jumped out of a window and hid in country-houses. Sciarra Colonna broke open the doors of the house where the pope was, troopers dashed through the windows, and they burst into the pope's room. He was seated on his throne, with his pope's robe on, the papal tiara on his head, a crucifix in one hand and his keys in the other. He was silent for a moment; then he spoke,

"Here is my head! Here is my throat!"

Sciarra Colonna struck the old man—he was eighty-six—on his cheek with his mailed hand.

For three days they kept him prisoner, the Gascon Novaret not daring to kill him. Then the people of Anagni rose and rescued him, driving Philip's friends out of the place.

They bore him into the public square, crying like a child. "Good people," he stammered, "I thank you. I have had nothing to eat or drink for three days; if there be any good woman who will bestow on me a little bread and wine, or water if she have no wine, I will give her God's blessing and mine. Whoever will bring me the least thing to relieve my wants, I will give him absolution for all his sins."

They took him to Rome, where his mind gave way under the shock he had endured, and he died without having received the sacrament—as if to confirm the prophecy of a bitter enemy, who had said long before that, as "he had climbed like a fox, and reigned like a lion, he would die like a dog."

From the first to the last King Philip had but one thought — money. He had taken from the Church in France all the money he could find, and now he turned on the Knights Templar, who were known to be immensely rich. They were a body of fighting monks, who had at first banded themselves together to fight on the side of the Crusaders. When the Crusades were over they became soldiers of fortune, who fought for any one who would pay them, and, as they were brave and skilful, their services were in great request. They lived without women, attended no church but their own, wore armor at all times, and looked fierce enough with their cropped hair and their dark, frowning, weather-beaten faces. They had gradually acquired a vast quantity of property. It is said that they owned ten thousand estates, besides castles and strong places; but their principal home was in that part of Paris which was called, after them, the Temple, and which has given its name to one of the finest boulevards in the gay city. When they had built their house in this quarter they moved their treasure into it; it consisted of a hundred and fifty thousand florins of gold and ten mule-loads of silver. Philip declared that he would have that money.

He instigated all sorts of improbable and indeed absurd charges against the knights, and on them he had the Grand Master, Jacques Molay, and a hundred and forty knights arrested at Paris. Other arrests followed all over the kingdom. The attack on the knights was so unreasonable that the pope protested, whereupon Philip extorted from a hundred knights by the most frightful tortures—in which both fire and steel were used—confessions of hideous crimes. And in the meantime, to prevent interference, he made the pope himself a prisoner at Avignon in France.

Then followed a trial which lasted four years. In the intervals of the sittings of the court, torture was constantly applied to the prisoners to make them confess. Of those who did—and you may fancy how they were driven to confess when I tell you that the feet of one knight were held before a fire until the bones of his heel cracked off, while a third was three times stretched on the rack and was then kept for thirty-six weeks in a noisome pit on bread and water—fifty-four recanted their confessions when they were well enough to speak.

They were forthwith taken out and burned to death.

The Grand Master, Jacques Molay, made a sort of half confession, which in reality was only a submission to the Church. He was taken back to his dungeon; whether he had been or was tortured I do not know. But his manhood came back to him. He stood up bravely before his judges and declared that neither he nor his order had done anything that was contrary to religion or to the Church—that he had nothing to confess.

They took him back to his dungeon and sentenced him and three other knights, who had also recanted, to be burned alive. Two of the three recanted their recantation and were kept in prison for life. In the gray twilight of a March evening, in the year 1314, Molay and the other were ferried to an island in the Seine, on which two stakes had been set. When the knights were chained to the stakes a quantity of green branches and wet firewood was piled around their legs and feet, and it was set on fire. The damp logs and twigs burned slowly; the flames curled round the knights' bodies, inflicting excruciating agony without causing death. For an hour the voices of the dying men were heard through the thick smoke, protesting that their order was innocent of crime. Then a silence fell, and the wood began to burn up briskly.

On a log near by sat the King of France, listening to the crackling of the flames with no more expression on his face than you could have seen on the bark of the log on which he sat.

Chapter XIX

SORCERY AND DELUSION

A.D. 1314–1328

During the fourteen years which followed the death of Philip the Handsome—who was killed by a fall from his horse—three sons of his reigned in France: Louis the Tenth, who reigned two years; Philip the Fifth, who reigned six; and Charles the Fourth, who reigned six.

The events of their reigns were so unimportant that you would hardly care to hear of them. They were of no consequence while they lived, and their memory was of no interest when they were dead. All three met with sudden deaths. Louis the Tenth died from drinking mulled wine after a game at tennis; and Philip and Charles perished of diseases which no one could explain, but which carried them off very rapidly. You will not be surprised to hear that it was suspected they were poisoned. There were a good many people who had grudges against the posterity of Philip the Handsome.

It will interest you more to hear something of the strange delusions which pervaded the world, and France especially, during their time. People all seemed to have gone mad on some crotchet or other. In every country of the world, at all times, ignorant people have believed things which were contrary to reason; the propensity is liable to break out with virulence at odd intervals, and the fourteenth century saw one of the outbreaks. In that century people went positively crazy on the subjects of witchcraft, sorcery, religious enthusiasm, and race prejudice. This was in large part due to the misery of the common people. When Philip the Handsome robbed the feudal lords, the lords turned round and robbed their vassals; and these last, in their dreadful misery, lost their heads altogether.

Many thousands of them met in the fields near Paris and said they were going to the Holy Land, where they would find rest. They had no money; they had to steal food when they could not beg it; one town passed them on to another to get rid of them until they reached Toulouse. There troops were called out, and the miserable vagabonds were hanged in batches of twenty till they scattered.

The Jews were always being driven out of France and were always coming back, as if they enjoyed being robbed. The peasants now accused them of having plotted with lepers—that is, persons afflicted with the horrible disease of leprosy—to poison the wells. A miserable leper confessed that he had got money from a Jew for throwing into a well a package containing an adder's head, the legs of a frog, and a woman's hair, the whole mixed with human blood; and, the pretext serving, Jews and lepers were murdered whenever they were found. At Chinon a big pit was dug and the bottom covered with burning firewood. Into this pit a hundred and fifty Jews—men, women, and children—were compelled to leap at the end of a pitchfork.

Forty Jews agreed to die together at the top of a high house, and chose of their number an old and a young man to kill the other thirty-eight. When the work was done, and only the two remained, they drew lots which should kill the other; the young man drew the long straw, and he stabbed the old man, promising to meet him presently in the next world. But when he found himself alone he changed his mind and resolved to live. He stripped the thirty-nine corpses of purses, money, and jewels, and let himself down by a rope; but the rope was too short, he fell, was taken, and burned.

When you remember that there was no drainage anywhere in France, that heaps of rotting garbage seethed in the Southern sun, and that the common people were always ill-fed when they were fed at all, you will not be surprised to hear that disease never stayed its hand. There was an awful plague in this fourteenth century, which was called the Black Death. I suppose it was a malignant fever with blood-poisoning. It was always breaking out, destroying thousands of lives; then subsiding for a while; then breaking out again. After one terrible outbreak, in which some of the best people of the day were carried off, a lot of cranks declared that the wrath of God must be appeased by penance. They formed themselves into processions — men, women, and children — and marched through Europe in long files, whipping each other on the bare back. They were called Flagellants or Whippers; and it is said—I do not know how true it may be—that there were at one time nine hundred thousand of them, all lashing each others' raw backs till the blood poured down.

Everybody at that time believed in sorcery. Generally speaking, all science which ignorant people could not understand was called sorcery; thus you heard that in Charlemagne's time a bishop was supposed to practise sorcery because he had made a clock, and in this fourteenth century a monk was accused of sorcery because he had a bottle of phosphorus which shone in the dark. A great many people were supposed to be sorcerers, and to have the power of inflicting disease, or of paralyzing the tongue or the limbs of an enemy, or of causing death by means of enchantments. There were many ways in which these things could be done. A very superior kind of sorcerer could do a man to death with a few words whispered, in a foreign tongue, over the bed in which he was to lie. But legitimate sorcery was done with wax figures.

If you had lived in those days, and had been as bad as I hope you are good, and had wanted to put your enemy out of the way, you would have made a little wax image of him a few inches high. Into this you would have stuck needles. If your sorcery was the genuine article, each needle gave the real man exquisite pain, and eventually

HANGING A SORCERER IN THE MIDDLE AGES

laid him up in bed. Then you went on sticking more needles into the wax figure, and the man went on getting worse; until at last, when you were tired of playing with him, you set your figure before a hot fire, the wax melted, and the man died. This may strike you as something like what you have read in fairy tales. But in those ignorant old times lots of people lost their lives on charges of having caused death by the use of wax figures.

Jeanne, the wife of Philip the Handsome, bore a grudge against Gruilhard, Bishop of Troyes, in Champagne. The bishop went to a sorceress and gave her money to soothe the queen's temper. The sorceress failing to make the queen better disposed to the bishop, the latter went to a sorcerer and got from him a little waxen image of the queen, christened it in regular style, with godfather and godmothers, and stuck it full of needles. The queen remaining in good health, the sorcerer got frightened and confessed. Gruilhard was arrested, and it would have gone hard with him if, just then, Jeanne had not died. As it was, he spent the rest of his life in prison.

Marigny, the counsellor of Philip the Handsome, did not fare so well. It was charged against him that his wife had made a wax statue of Philip, and had set it before a fire just before the king's death. People were found to swear to the fact, and Marigny was hanged and his wife imprisoned for life.

Under the reign of Philip the Fifth, laws were made providing severe punishments for workmen who shut up evil spirits in looking-glasses, bracelets, and rings; and the king himself wore a ring which belonged to Margaret of Foix, in which a good spirit was said to live. So long as he wore that ring the king felt he was safe. But it did not prevent his dying at the age of thirty.

Chapter XX

FRANCE HUMBLED

A.D. 1328–1350

After the death of Charles the Fourth, in 1328, the crown of France fell to a cousin of his, Philip of Valois, who became Philip the Sixth. His history is a story of defeat in war and of social triumphs at the royal court.

It seemed that the English and French never could agree. The King of England, Edward the Third, had some claim to the throne of France, and his pretension was supported by a French noble who had been exiled from France. He did not at first put forth his claims, but finding a war raging—it raged off and on for a century or more—between the French and the people of Flanders, he sent the Flemings a fleet of war-ships to help them. Philip also fitted out war-ships, and the two fleets met off Helvetsluys, at the mouth of the Scheldt. Most of Philip's ships were hired from the Genoese, who were famous sailors in those days. But the Genoese sailor who commanded on this occasion did not know his business. He kept his ships moored close together in the port, and the English ships, sailing down upon them with a free wind, captured the *Christopher*, which was the flag-ship, and sank so many other vessels that the Genoese hoisted the white flag, after losing thirty thousand men.

The Flemish leader at this time was Jacob Van Artevelde, a brewer from Ghent, and a man of courage and common-sense. So long as he ruled Flanders it prospered, but one day the people grew tired of him and accused him of having stolen the public money.

"Gentlemen," said Artevelde, standing at an open window, while the mob stood below, "I have not taken a farthing."

But the mob roared that they did not believe him, and that he must come down to them.

He, knowing what that meant, fled to a church for refuge, but was caught on the steps and struck dead by a blow from a weaver's knife.

The war was transferred to the other side of the country, namely to Brittany. Here Charles of Blois claimed to be duke, and on his side was Philip of France; John of Montford also claimed to be duke, and on his side was Edward of England. Charles, who was such a saint that he walked barefoot through the snow to hear mass, put pebbles in his shoes, and wore a tightly knotted cord round his bare waist, caught John at Nantes and sent him prisoner to Paris. John's wife Jeanne, who was at Rennes, summoned her fighting-men together, showed them her little son, and made them swear to stand by this dear little boy to the bitter end. She shut herself up in a fort, which Charles besieged. At the head of her Bretons she sallied forth and drove him back time and again, but still he kept a close siege. Jeanne's provisions became low, her fighting-men grew discouraged, but her own intrepid soul never quailed. She told her soldiers that, sooner or later, the English would come to her relief. And sure enough, just as despair was settling on the garrison, the lookout on the topmost tower saw the banner of Walter Manny waving in the distant sunlight and creeping and creeping nearer and nearer over the plain, until he and his knights rode up furiously and cut their way through the besiegers' lines into the castle. Beautiful and brave Jeanne of Montford came down to meet them, leading her little son by the hand, and kissed every man of them.

Both the King of England and the King of France must then have felt that it was time to fight it out between them. The two armies met at a place called Creci, in Picardy. The English king had about thirty-two thou-

ASSAULT ON A WALLED TOWN

sand men, of whom eighteen thousand were Welsh and Irish—barefoot, ignorant, half savage, and armed with pike and knife. He had no cavalry, but he had a body of English archers, and, what was far better, a body of gunners with cannon—which for the first time in history were then used in battle. The French had more men, but of these many were hired Genoese archers, who, on the excuse that their bowstrings were wet, took but little part in the battle, and ran away as soon as they could. Among the rest were the flower of the chivalry of France—princes, dukes, counts, barons, and knights—with their men-at-arms, all heavily encumbered with steel armor. The French had plenty of cavalry, but no artillery.

Under the shower of English arrows, which fell like snow, the French nobles went down, horses and men together; where they fell they lay, and the Welsh and Irish despatched them with their knives. Wherever they were thickest, cannon-balls rolled in, felling a score of men-at-arms at a shot. The feudal lords fought splendidly. They charged again and again into the English infantry, plying their battle-axes; but whenever they were thrown, that was the end of them. They could not get up.

The old blind king of Bohemia, hearing shouts which to his trained ear seemed to mean defeat, called to two of his knights,

"Gentlemen, as I am blind, I must request you to lead me so far into the battle that I may this day strike one stroke with my sword."

They tied the reins of his horse to theirs, and together rode furiously into the English ranks. Next day all three were found dead side by side.

The battle was lost. Philip, with a few faithful knights, rode from the field and did not draw rein till he reached the gate of Amiens. When the warder answered his knock,

"Who seeks entrance at this hour?"

"It is," said Philip, "the fortunes of France."

Edward moved swiftly to Calais and laid siege to the place. He built a wooden town round it, with streets and a market-place. Very soon hunger began to be felt in the town. Four hundred infirm old men, women, and children were turned out because there was no food to give them. Edward let them die between his lines and the walls. The

CHARGE OF THE FRENCH KNIGHTS

garrison ate dogs, cats, and rats; they chewed leather boots; they made soup of weeds and the scrapings of old barrels in which meat and flour had been stored; they grew so thin that many could hardly stand; but not till the last ration had been eaten did they consent to surrender.

Then Eustache de Saint-Pierre, with five others, bareheaded, barefooted, and with ropes around their necks, bore to the king the keys of Calais. Edward ordered them to immediate execution, as the custom of that day was; but his queen, Philippa, and his bravest knights begged him on their knees to spare the old men, and after a time he yielded. But many a long year passed before Calais again became a French town.

You might fancy that a king who had endured so crushing a defeat as Creci, and who had lost Calais to France, would have spent his last years in sorrow and despair. But from his coronation to his death, in victory or defeat, Philip was always gay, splendid, magnificent, a reveller in polished and joyous society. He set the fashion of building gorgeous palaces in Paris, and made it then—what it is now—the finest city in Europe. After a terrible epidemic of the Black Death, when every family was in mourning, and he was fifty-eight years of age, he invited all the fashion of France to witness his marriage to a beautiful girl of eighteen, who had come to Paris to become the wife of his son.

His favorite home was at Vincennes, where in the middle of a glorious forest of oaks he had built a castle with towers and donjon, and drawbridges and lakes, and shrubberies and shady bridle paths, and leafy lanes for lovers. Here he feasted the feudal nobles, with their daughters and fair ladies, and gave deer-hunts and tournaments, at which the most lovely women in France figured in turn as Queen of Beauty. He insisted that every one should be splendidly dressed. The men wore piebald suits of silk, fitting closely to their figures, and with enormous sleeves; the hair was done up in a queue, and beards were trimmed fan-shape; the points of men's boots were fastened to their belts with thongs, and the heel ended in a sort of claw. On the heads of the ladies were tall hats, not unlike the mitres which bishops wore, and from these long ribbons dangled and floated in the wind. On each side of the hat the hair was dressed into the shape of a horn, and below the horn it was the fashion to wear false ears of prodigious size. Altogether, the ladies' heads must have looked like heads of cows. Their skirts were plaited and quilted and were often covered with rich embroideries. By this time stockings had come in ; they were of silk and clocked. Every lady wore a belt, to which a bag for money or keys was attached, and in the belt was stuck a dagger. Reading had become almost common among the ladies ; they were fond of Italian romances.

Chapter XXI

ROBBERS REIGN

A.D. 1350–1364

John, the son of Philip the Sixth, found the treasury empty when he came to the throne, and proceeded to try to fill it by imposing a tax which was called the gabelle. This tax Charles of Navarre refused to pay on his lands in France; he said that no gatherer of that tax should ever leave his fief alive.

King John took horse and rode thirty hours without stopping, from Orleans to Rouen, where Charles of Navarre was feasting with John's son, who, being heir to the throne, was called the dauphin. On arrival the king strode into the banquet-hall, preceded by a squire who cried,

"Let no man stir, under pain of death!"

Then, seizing the King of Navarre by the throat, King John exclaimed,

"Traitor! thou art not worthy to sit at my son's table. I will neither eat nor drink while thou livest."

The dauphin threw himself at his father's feet and besought him to remember that Charles was his guest. But the angry king bade his men bind the guest and three other guests; the first was thrown into a dungeon, the other three were beheaded on the spot. It was a bad beginning for a miserable reign.

A large part of France, as you know, was held by the English. A party of English troops, under Edward the Black Prince, were at Bordeaux. He had four thousand English archers and four thousand Gascons, half of whom were mere robbers who fought for the plunder they could get. The King of France, with fifty thousand men, includ-

ARREST OF CHARLES OF NAVARRE AT ROUEN

ing twenty-six dukes and a hundred and forty knights, marched out to fight him near a place called Poitiers. But as at Creci, the French were badly handled. They were brave enough, but they could not resist the shock of the English, who charged down a hill, threw the front ranks into confusion, and backed them upon the rear ranks; so the larger army lost the day. King John himself fought courageously. His youngest son was by his side, calling to him,

"Father! guard your right! Father! guard your left!"

Then, in the turmoil of battle, the king was surrounded, and a knight, cleaving his way through the press by sheer strength and thrusting aside the weapons with his hand, demanded his surrender. He became a prisoner in England, and never again, except on one short visit, did he tread the soil of France.

Then followed eight years of the most dreadful confusion you ever read of. The king's son, the dauphin, a poor, pale, consumptive boy of nineteen, was unable to keep order or exert authority. There was a meeting of the States-General, which was an apology for a congress, but it could say nothing except that France had been shamefully robbed and was greatly to be pitied. The English released their prisoners on condition that they should pay ransom, and the barons and knights squeezed their vassals so cruelly to raise it that the poor peasants starved. What the barons and knights left them, disbanded soldiers took. The latter became highway robbers and lived by plunder. All over France the roads were infested by parties of robbers, who made booty of everything they found.

They took from the farmer his lean cattle, his tumble-down cart, his poor tools, his broken plough, and his worn harness. If they thought he had money saved they held his feet to a fire to make him confess where it was hid. Those who did these things were not common robbers—they were quite often barons who had fought in the wars, and had taken to robbery after the fighting ceased. Many of them were rich. One of their ways of operating was thus: When they observed a town or a village which seemed to be worth robbing, they would gather their band of forty or fifty and march upon it in the night, avoiding the high road, and getting into the place about daybreak. Then they would set fire to a house, and when the people sprang half awake out of their beds, they would kill the men and fill the air with unearthly cries, so that it seemed there was an army in the place. Then the towns-people would run away, and the robbers would gather in the booty.

In many parts of France the peasants did not dare to stay in their houses, but lived in holes in the ground which were connected by underground passages. Sometimes women and children stayed in these holes for weeks together, while the men crept out from time to time to see if the robbers had gone away. Of course the fields were not seeded, and this meant famine.

When the famine pressed too cruelly, the peasantry rose against the barons and became robbers in their turn. They armed themselves with scythes, and pitchforks, and clubs, and knives, and such poor weapons as they could get, and fell upon the feudal lords and killed them, sparing none. This is called in history the Jacquerie.

Thus there were at this time in France four or five kinds of bandits, who were all trying to live on the country by murder and robbery: the regular robbers, who were disbanded soldiers; the followers of the Dauphin; the followers of Charles of Navarre; the peasants; and here and there soldiers of fortune—English, German, and French—who were seeking plunder. These parties all robbed each other, and fought with each other, and robbed peaceable people, and burned houses, and tore up vines wherever they went.

But the city of Paris stood like a rock in the stormy sea. Every man had taken up arms; they had chosen as their leader Stephen Marcel, the provost of the merchants. He raised great barricades against attack and manned them with men that could fight. Through the gates long strings of peasants, who had lost everything, and trembling monks and nuns, who had been driven from their houses, came streaming into the city for shelter. Paris took them all in. Marcel called a meeting of delegates from other cities, and, largely through the counsels of the wise Archbishop of Laon, they framed a plan of defence and government, which they required the dauphin to sign. He agreed to it;

broke his agreement; agreed again; and again refused to agree. The people grew sick of him, and when Charles of Navarre appeared in the streets they cheered him. On one troubled night they would have taken the dauphin's life, if Marcel had not thrust on his head a red and blue hood such as the city soldiers wore.

Then, after a little while, the people of Paris changed their minds and would have none of Charles of Navarre. Marcel still believed in him and went out to meet him one night to give him the key of one of the city gates. To him out of the dark night came the voice of John Maillart, crying,

"Stephen, what do you here at this time of night?"

"I am here," said Stephen with a voice which shook, "to guard the city over which I am set."

"You lie!" cried John. "You are here to betray us." And he struck him dead with a blow of his axe.

After a time the English let King John go, on his promise that he would pay a ransom of three million crowns. But he could not raise the money, and, like a man of honor as he was, he returned to his prison in London—it was a very comfortable prison—where he lived sumptuously. There he died and was buried in St. Paul's Cathedral. At his funeral four thousand torches, each twelve feet high, and as many tapers lighted the corpse to the grave. It was the least the English could do after keeping him prisoner for so many years.

Chapter XXII

BERTRAND DUGUESCLIN

A.D. 1364-1380

The next king is called in history Charles the Wise; his proper title is Charles the Fifth. One of his arms was crippled, and he was weak, so that he could neither hold a lance nor sit a horse. It had been said of him that he could not live long, as he had been poisoned in his youth, and the French grumbled when he came to the throne. But you may perhaps think, when you hear his story, that he may have served France better than a fighting king would have done.

He kept much at home; used to sit in his study in his palace and think all the time. He rose early, listened to all who called, walked in his gardens, and meditated and planned, while his band played music and his courtiers chatted. He had enough to think about. His kingdom was overrun by three pests, each of which seemed worse than the others; these were the followers of the King of Navarre, the English, and the soldier-bandits. He saw that, before anything could be done, these three must be conquered; and he looked about for a man who could conquer them. The man for the job he found in Bertrand Duguesclin.

This was a soldier from the northwest corner of France, which was called Brittany. He was nearly fifty years old, with a short figure, flat nose, green eyes, broad shoulders, and long arms. He was a fighter born. When he was only a common man-at-arms, a sorceress named Tiphaine had foretold that he would become a valiant knight, whereupon he married her by way of reward for her bright

CHURCH AT ST. DENYS

augury. King Charles sent for him, and asked him if he could rid the kingdom of the Navarrese.

"I'll try," said Duguesclin, and he marched forth at the head of his Bretons and inflicted on the Navarrese such a terrible beating that they gave no more trouble in that reign.

Then said the king, "Suppose you try to rid me of the English next."

This was not so easy. The English had a large army and an able soldier—Sir John Chandos—at its head. Duguesclin gave him battle, but was defeated and made prisoner. After a time he was ransomed, set at the head of another army, and went at it again. This time he gathered into his army most of the soldier-bandits of whom King Charles was as anxious to get rid of as the English; thus, like a wise general, intending to use one set of enemies to destroy the other. But again fortune was against him—he was beaten and taken prisoner.

This time the English had learned to fear him so much that they did not want to let him go for any ransom. He taunted them, saying that they must be terribly afraid of him if they dared not set him free for money, as the custom of that day was. This wounded their pride, and they grudgingly agreed to accept a ransom; then, piqued in their honor, Sir John Chandos and the Black Prince offered to lend him half the money. He thanked them, but raised it elsewhere, and once more got the command of an army. Now luck turned. Sir John Chandos died, and soon afterward the Black Prince, who had disgraced himself by sacking the town of Limoges, and putting every man, woman, and child in it to death, went home and died also. There was no one left in the English army who could hold his own against Duguesclin, and he pushed the English back to the sea, regaining all the rich country between the Loire and the Gironde, which the English had held, and much more territory besides.

Many of the soldier-bandits had been killed in his battles with the English. Others Duguesclin persuaded to go into Spain under the pretence of joining a crusade against the Moors. Thus he nearly cleared France of the most abominable vermin that had ever infested the country, and for the first time in many years the poor peasants could till their farms in peace.

This was the work of Duguesclin. The king made him Constable of France and loaded him with riches. But he did not live to enjoy them. He was taken ill on a march and died at the age of sixty-six. When he felt death near, he raised himself on his couch and kissed his sword, saying to his nearest friend,

"To you I commit it. I have never betrayed the king's trust."

And, turning to the soldiers round him, he added,

"Forget not, whenever you may be fighting, that priests, women, and children are not your enemies."

They buried him at St. Denys, by the side of the kings of France.

Two months afterward his friend the king followed

him to the grave. By wise management he had not only made France peaceful, but had got together large sums of money, which he spent in building grand palaces, with fine libraries and splendid galleries. He was generous to the poor and lived in his palace as became a king. His sideboard was loaded with gold plate. He had married a good woman, Jeanne of Bourbon, who set an example of gentleness and modesty to the ladies of her court. It may give you some idea of the manners of that day if you read her rules of behavior, as put into verse by a poet of her court. He said to the ladies:

"Do not be slovenly in your dress, nor put your fingers in the dish at table, nor blow your nose with the table-cloth. Do not rush into a room, but before you open the

INTERIOR OF CHURCH AT ST. DENYS

door give a gentle cough. Walk slowly to church, and do not run or jump in the streets. Those of you who cannot read must learn the hymns at home, so as to keep pace with the priests. Do not steal. Do not tell lies."

CHAPTER XXIII

A MAD KING

A.D. 1380-1422

WHILE Charles the Fifth was dying, his brother, the Duke of Anjou, hid in a room near the bed-chamber, and as soon as the king's death was announced stole the jewels and plate. With his plunder he went off to Naples, whose queen, in dying, had made him her heir. Two other brothers, the dukes of Bourbon and Berry, did not care to take either jewels or risks; they remained quiet, so the guardianship of the son and heir of Charles the Fifth, who was then a boy of twelve, fell to his other uncle, the Duke of Burgundy.

By way of training the boy, who was gentle and timid, the duke took him to a battle-field in Flanders, where the French had just defeated the Flemings with a loss of eight thousand men, and made him walk his horse over the dead bodies which lay in heaps. I dare say the brutal lesson did not help to strengthen a mind which was never very strong. At sixteen Charles was married to a Bavarian princess named Isabeau, who was fourteen, and after the marriage there was a triumphal entry into Paris, at which the finest festival ever seen was held. The common people were dressed in green, the gentlemen in rose color, the ladies in scarlet with gold belts; fountains ran with wine, milk, and rose-water. As the queen entered the St. Denys gate, two girls, dressed as angels, were lowered down by ropes, and asked her, with feigned surprise, if she hadn't come from Paradise? Then followed a dance which lasted three days and three nights. If this sort of thing could only have lasted, little Isabeau might indeed have fancied herself in Paradise.

But it did not last. At a masked ball the young king and four of his gentlemen disguised themselves as savages in cloth tights smeared with pitch, on which a thick layer of tow was stuck. The four gentlemen were tied together. Some careless guest held a lighted candle to the dress of one of them, and the tow caught fire. In an in-

ISABEAU OF BAVARIA

stant all four were ablaze. One of them saved his life by leaping into a water-butt. The other three were burned to death after agonies untold. The king was saved; his young aunt seized him, wrapped her skirt round him, and held him tight till the fire was put out. But the shock was terrible.

Then he fell ill of a fever and was very slow to recover.

When he got a little better he took the lead of a body of men to hunt a villain who had tried to murder his constable. It was the middle of summer; the sun's rays were scorching. He was riding through a sandy plain, where there was no shade. On his head he wore a scarlet velvet hood. He was dozing in the saddle, when a man ran up to him, seized his bridle, and shouted,

"King, go no further. You are betrayed."

The madman, for such he must have been, made his escape when the king's followers came up, but Charles, suddenly starting in his saddle, drew his sword and, crying "Forward! Death to the traitors!" fell upon his servants and pages and killed four of them before he could be disarmed. They took him back to Paris and found that he was hopelessly mad.

There were no doctors who could help him. He was sprinkled with holy water, made to confess, the communion was given him, but he got no better. He said his name was George, that he had no wife. Quacks came from distant parts and tried all kinds of medicines; one of them made him drink water in which pearls had been dissolved. But it did no good. Then the doctors stopped trying to cure him and endeavored to amuse him, which was the most sensible thing they could do. Playing-cards, such as are used to-day, were invented to divert him, and his queen, Isabeau, and the ladies of his court took turns in playing with him. Sometimes he would be well enough to talk quite rationally; but the lucid intervals did not last long, and he would soon relapse into sombre melancholy, when he would cry and moan that he was in such pain, and would nobody relieve him?

Meanwhile the Duke of Orleans, the king's brother, and the Duke of Burgundy, his uncle, strove for the mastery in France. Now one was up and the other was down; and whichever was down, and whichever was up, the people had to pay taxes which enraged them. The priests were on the side of the Duke of Burgundy, and refused to open the churches when the Orleans party were in control.

On the 22d of November, 1407, the Duke of Burgundy, whose name was Fearless John, and the Duke Louis of Orleans supped together, kissed each other, hung on each other's neck, and swore eternal friendship. Such love and affection had never been seen before. On the following evening, as Louis was going home at about eight, with only a few attendants, he was waylaid, in the Rue du Temple, by seven or eight men, masked and with red hoods on, who fell upon him with axes and swords and maces. He was heard to cry, "What's this? What's this?" To which his murderers answered, "Die! Die!"

DUKE OF BURGUNDY

After a moment the chief of them ordered,

"Out with your torches; he is dead enough."

And one of them striking him a heavy blow on the head with a mace to make sure, they all ran away, leaving the body in the street.

John the Fearless was not ashamed of his bloody deed. On the next day he said,

"What has been done has been done by my orders."

And he made haste to Burgundy, whence he returned to Paris with an army and compelled the poor mad king to give him a pardon. The priests preached sermons declaring that the murder was just, because the Duke of Orleans was God's enemy.

Then actual war broke out between the two factions.

The old Orleans party took the name of Armagnacs, from their leader, the Count of Armagnac; they threatened the city of Paris, which, in its old way, organized an army of its own for its own protection, with a butcher, a surgeon, and an executioner at its head. Neither the butcher nor the surgeon, nor even the executioner, however, could prevent the Armagnacs from getting possession of the place. They held it for a long time, and when the Duke of Burgundy sent a monk in to spy out the defences, the Armagnacs put him in a niche in a wall and walled him in. Then the Duke of Burgundy was declared a rebel, and his French estates were confiscated.

Three years afterward the keys of the city were stolen by a friend of the duke's; the gates were opened one dark night, a Burgundian army poured in, and the Count of Armagnac and all his followers were massacred. The count's body lay three days in the streets, and was kicked about by the Burgundians. So now Burgundy was up and Armagnac down.

This did not last long. Fearless John made an appointment to meet the dauphin on a bridge. When the duke appeared, a servant of the dauphin's bade him advance, as his master was waiting for him; he stepped into a side-gallery on the bridge and was instantly killed. So now Burgundy was down, and down to stay for the present.

During all the time these two factions had been fighting, the King of England, whose name was Henry the Fifth, had been conquering France bit by bit. The French met him in battle at a place called Agincourt, but once more they were so badly led that their knights and heavy men-at-arms, with the heavy armor which they wore and which their horses wore, were placed in a newly ploughed and marshy field. When the order came to move, they could not move. They were mired. The horses had sunk in the soft earth up to their knees, and partly from this reason the French were completely vanquished. After the battle the savage King of England cut the throats of his prisoners, refusing to admit them to ransom.

He was then master of so much of France that he thought he might just as well claim the whole; and indeed, so far as the French peasants and common people were concerned, it was quite possible that he might be an improvement on the mad king and the factions. He married the mad king's daughter Katharine, and in December, 1420, entered Paris, with the young Duke of Burgundy in deep mourning on one side and the mad king on the other. He became in name and in fact King of France, and Paris was so broken-hearted by the long struggles it had gone through that it had not a word to say by way of protest. The priests turned out in procession to meet the foreigner, offered him their relics to kiss, and performed high mass for him at Notre Dame.

He was not very cheerful himself. He had a presentiment that he would not long reign over two kingdoms. Eighteen months after his entry into Paris he died of a fever, and two months afterward the mad king also died. The French were much touched at his death. Living, they had thought little of the poor king, because of his infirmity; but when he was dead they wept over his grave.

JOAN OF ARC

Chapter XXIV

JOAN OF ARC

A.D. 1429–1431

After mad Charles died there were two claimants for the throne of France: his son Charles, who had been known as the Dauphin; and a baby, who was the son of Henry the Fifth of England and Katharine of France, the mad king's daughter. Charles was a puny youth with thin legs, who was so awkward that people laughed at him, and so poor that he could not pay for a pair of boots. The French, however, stood by him, while the English took the side of the baby. Charles's friends held the city of Orleans, and there the English besieged them. The siege lasted seven months without much gain on either side, though the besiegers from their towers threw stones weighing two hundred pounds into the place, and the French inside fired at the towers cannon-balls which sometimes hit their mark. If nothing unusual had happened this game of ball might have lasted a long time, but a new face was put on affairs by a most surprising event.

In the village of Domremy on the river Meuse, in Lorraine, there lived a farmer by the name of Arc, or Arcques, who had a daughter of nineteen, named Joan. She tended sheep in lonely pastures, and at evening-time loved to pray before a statue of the Virgin in the dimly lit village church. Both in the church and in the pastures she moped and brooded over the wrongs of her country, and she often fancied, as people do when they are low-spirited or when they have fever, that angels came down to her, and that she could hear their voices. You must remember that in those parts of France people were very ignorant and very superstitious. One day she fancied that an angel told her to go and help the king drive the English out of France, and she had so worked herself up by praying and fasting and brooding that she felt that she must do as the angel ordered. Though she was only a girl, and could neither read nor write, she believed that she would not have been called if there had not been a chance that she would be of use.

So she left her home, and with an uncle who was a wheelwright trudged over poor country roads, through woods and over hills, to a friend of the king's, to whom she told her story. He said she was a witch and had her forthwith sprinkled with holy water. But as she said the same things after she had been sprinkled as before, he began to be afraid of her. He gave her a horse and a sword and two squires to lead her to where the king was. She asked the voices what clothes she should wear, and they said "Man's clothes, of course." So she put them on, boots and spurs and all, and rode off.

The king received her in a hall which was lit by forty torches and filled with barons, and knights, and bishops, and priests. They questioned her, and cross-questioned her, and set traps to catch her; but she answered all their questions in a low, sweet voice, telling her story in so simple and truthful a way that she quite confounded them. Some were induced to think that she was a sorceress, and that the best thing to do with her was to burn her; but by this time her story had got wind, and the common people took her side so hotly that there would have been trouble if any one had tried to burn her then.

As for the king, he took her part. Her sweet face and gentle ways pleased him very much indeed. He gave her a suit of white armor, set her on a prancing white horse, ordered a page to carry her battle-flag, on which there was a picture of God, and armed her with a battle-axe, which she hung at her saddle-bow. Thus accoutred, she set out for Orleans; and there she put such new heart into the besieged French that they fell upon the English, and in ten days drove them away howling. Joan led the garrison, and though she was too tender-hearted to hurt any one, her battle-flag was always in the front of the fight. Twice she was wounded. Once, an archer shot an arrow into her neck, and the point came out behind. And once, one of those great stones which the English hurled with their machines struck her on the head and knocked her senseless. But when the arrow was pulled out, and the bruise on her head was dressed, she mounted her white horse and rode to the front in her old bold way.

When the English marched away she was known everywhere as the Maid of Orleans, and the common people began to worship and adore her. She even persuaded that poor-spirited creature the King, to go to Rheims and get crowned.

The English declared that it would never do to be beaten, and by a peasant girl. England was governed at the time by a priest—Cardinal Beaufort, Bishop of Winchester. He soon wrote to the armies in France that, cost what it might, the Maid of Orleans must be captured. It was easier to say this than to do it. Joan kept on riding at the head of the French, in her shining armor, on her white horse, and wherever she went the English made haste to get out of her way. They made an alliance with the Duke of Burgundy, and he sent an army to help them, but Joan beat the Burgundians as she had beaten the English. Among the priests and the nobles there were still some who said she was a witch, and in a sly way sprinkled her with holy water whenever her back was turned. But the French people trusted her, witch or no witch.

One early day, as she was besieging the town of Compiègne, her men-at-arms took fright and ran away, leaving her alone. Whereupon a Burgundian archer threw her from her horse and made her his prisoner. A roar of joy rose from the troops over the capture of this young girl. The man who took her sold her to John of Luxembourg; he sold her to the Duke of Burgundy; he sold her to the English.

"Now," said Cardinal Beaufort, Bishop of Winchester, with an oath and an ugly flash in his eye, "I don't think Joan of Arc will give me any more trouble."

They put the poor girl in irons and dragged her to Rouen, which was in possession of the English, to stand her trial for sorcery. As you know, the only sorcery she had been guilty of was putting fresh heart into the downspirited people of France. But a court was summoned, with the Bishop of Beauvais at its head, a vicar of the Inquisition at his side, and a score of priests to sit as judges—all of them sworn to do the dirty work of Cardinal Beaufort, Bishop of Winchester.

JOAN OF ARC IN BATTLE

Before this court, for sixteen days, Joan had to appear, and to answer all kinds of cruel and absurd questions. She was sick and broken down. Every night the poor girl was taken to her cell in the dungeon, where she was made to sleep with double chains around her limbs. Her feet were fastened to a chain at the foot of her bed, and, to keep her straight, her body was tied to an iron beam. Here torturers visited her and warned her that she would probably be put to the torture on the day following. She was not, but she suffered the agonies of torture in expectation. She had no friends, no advisers; the mean King of France never stirred hand nor spoke word to save her.

The trial had begun on the 21st of February, 1431. On May 31, at eight in the morning, she was taken out of her prison and placed in a cart with a confessor by her side. Eight hundred English soldiers, with swords drawn and lances in rest, escorted the cart. Ten thousand people lined the streets through which it passed. The cart stopped at the fish-market, in which three platforms had been built. One was for Cardinal Beaufort. Another was for the judges and the prisoner. On the third was a tall stake; its base was hidden by a pile of firewood. When Joan had taken her place a priest preached a sermon on her wickedness, and the Bishop of Beauvais urged her to repent. A silence fell; it was thought the doomed girl might say something. She was on her knees. As death drew near she was, like other girls, very much afraid, and cried and sobbed. She would have clasped her poor hands, but they were bound. She feebly murmured, "Good people, pray for me!"

No one who was present—neither the brutal judges nor the savage cardinal himself—could keep back his tears; as for the people, they broke out in sobs and groans.

But a soldier called to the priest who stood by Joan,

"What's this, priest? do you mean us to dine here?"

And two men-at-arms seized the Maid, dragged her to the stake, and roughly bade the executioner do his duty. She bowed her head, her lips were seen to move as in prayer, the flames rose, she gave one shriek—"Jesus!"—and all was over.

If you go to Rouen you may see, under the long shadow of the old cathedral tower, a statue of Joan of Arc, erected on the square where she was burned. And so long as the town of Domremy remained in the possession of the French it was a law of the French army that no regiment should march through it without presenting arms and having its band play a requiem.

The English—who were a very different people then

THE CATHEDRAL AT ROUEN

from the English of to-day—fancied that the death of Joan of Arc would remove their most dangerous enemy. But it did not help them much. The baby king never reigned in [illegible] death [illegible] in France [illegible] they [illegible]

[illegible] in name [illegible] in fact for [illegible] a creature that [illegible] can remem- [illegible] a beautiful and [illegible] always to have [illegible] gradually from [illegible] who became [illegible] Katharine, who had been [illegible] England, married a [illegible] after Henry's death; and [illegible] she lost her mad [illegible] English Henry, was [illegible] grandmother stood at [illegible] tears; but the [illegible] let him see her [illegible] without a friend to give her a cup of water [illegible] died.

LOUIS XI

Chapter XXV

LOUIS THE ELEVENTH

A.D. 1461–1483

About the middle of the fifteenth century the most splendid court in Europe was that of the Duke of Burgundy. He was a greater man than the King of France himself. He not only ruled over Burgundy, but his power was felt all through Holland, Flanders, Alsace, and Lorraine, and the country which lies between modern France and Germany, from the mouth of the Rhine to the rich slopes in which the blue Rhone begins its flow. Some places had sovereigns of their own. Liege was ruled by bishops, who were terrible fighters; and the lord of a large territory was a fierce baron, whose name was William de la Marck, but who was generally called the Wild Boar of the Ardennes. But they all bowed to the Duke of Burgundy.

He held his court at Brussels, and there he gathered around him the most learned scholars and the most gallant soldiers of the day; to attract them he created an order of the Golden Fleece, which was more thought of than any them on to a fight; while they were fighting the king took their towns. He was not fond of fighting himself. He was once induced to go to war, chiefly through the advice of a Cardinal Balue; but he was beaten, and he revenged himself against the cardinal by locking him up in an iron cage and keeping him there for eleven years.

It was during that war that he had the narrowest escape of his life. He went to see the Duke of Burgundy, the son of the old duke who had been at his coronation. They hated each other, and both knew it. Louis, fearful of being murdered, begged to be lodged in the castle of Peronne. When he went in the door was locked on him, and there he was a prisoner in the hands of his worst enemy. He was terribly frightened. When the duke visited him and asked him if he would help capture the town of Liege, which had revolted, and which Louis had solemnly vowed to succor in its revolt, the treacherous king replied,

"With a great deal of pleasure!"

They went, the duke and the king together, to Liege, which was counting confidently on the help which the king had promised. The place was soon taken. Then said the duke, "What would you do with Liege if it were yours?"

Said the king, smiling, "My father had a tree near his palace in which ravens had built nests, and at night their croaking disturbed him. He had the nests destroyed, but the ravens built them again and again. Then he had the tree rooted up, and he slept better afterward."

The duke took the hint. Every building in Liege was burned but the churches. The people were drowned and burned, or shot, or driven into the woods to perish of cold and hunger. And I suppose the duke slept better afterward.

But Louis was not the man to forget his little adventure in the castle of Peronne. He arranged a meeting between the King of England and himself. You may fancy how the kings trusted each other when you learn that at this meeting the two were separated by a lattice-work through which they talked, but which was too close to let a man's arm through. Here, through the lattice, a treaty was made by which for a large sum of money the King of England agreed to prevent the Duke of Burgundy from invading France. Shortly after that the duke made war on Réné, the Duke of Lorraine, one of his vassals. Louis helped Réné with money. A battle was fought. After the battle the Duke of Burgundy could not be found. It was not till two days afterward that his body was discovered, naked and frozen, partly hidden by the snow, and gnawed by dogs and wolves. Perhaps he understood before he died what he had made the poor people of Liege suffer. At any rate, King Louis understood how he had come by his end.

One by one Louis managed to get all his enemies among the feudal lords out of the way. To the Constable St. Pol, one of the greatest of them, Louis wrote that grave questions were pending at Paris in which his head would be of the greatest service. St. Pol came, and his head did serve, for Louis cut it off. The Duke of Nemours was shut up in an iron cage and was only taken out to be tortured and beheaded. Louis called on the Count of Armagnac and had him killed in his wife's presence. Another duke he sent to a prison for life. He was so suspicious of every one that one day he took the Duke of Nemours out of his iron cage and, having put him to the torture, asked him the question,

"Whom can I trust among the nobles of my court?"

The agonized man caught his breath and gasped,

"No one, sire; not one."

He lived a wretched life, as you may suppose. Toward the last he shut himself up in a castle at Plessis les Tours, which he made exceedingly strong, and garrisoned with Scotchmen. When he ventured out of the sight of the sentinels he trembled all over. When he took exercise he was accompanied by his barber, Oliver Daim, and his executioner, Tristan l'Ermite, who carried a hangman's rope in his pocket and often hanged people to the branches of trees without a trial when their behavior or their speech roused the king's suspicions. All three made jokes while the hanging was going on—coarse, poor jokes, such as you might expect from vile, brutal natures. When the Parisians saw the king with his two friends they ran away; women caught up their children and hid them.

He was always short of money—he spent so much in bribing feudal lords and kings, and in hiring spies to find out what was going on and what people were saying of him. He would never pay his servants their wages; when he was in good humor they coaxed him to give them a bishopric or an abbey or a rich wife; when no such chance offered they stole, and when the king found it out he made them divide. He spent little on himself. To the day of his death he wore, when he went out, an old coarse gray gown and broken hat like those in which he figured at his coronation. He said he could not afford to buy new clothes. But when he received envoys from foreign countries he wore a rich robe of crimson satin trimmed with fur.

He was very pious and never did anything without praying. In his youth he carried in the band of his hat a leaden image of a favorite saint; in his old age he wore saints all round his hat, and when prayers to one of them were not answered he tried the others in turn. He was greatly given to praying to the Virgin Mary, whom he appointed Countess of Boulogne, a place he much liked.

He had no friends. His wife was dead. His son he hated. When his daughter and her husband visited him, Oliver Daim and Tristan l'Ermite followed them about on tiptoe, suspecting them of a design to kill the king. His only pleasure through life, besides lying and cheating, was hunting. A year or two before his death he had a stroke of paralysis, which prevented him from mounting his horse. He then had little dogs trained to hunt mice, and the lame old man spent many an hour hopping round his room with these dogs, chasing mice which scampered from corner to corner, vainly looking for a hole to creep into.

He was terribly afraid of dying. And as he grew worse after his second stroke of paralysis, he sent to all parts of Europe for astrologers and physicians and had prayers said for him by the bishops and the most pious men in France, but he could not help seeing that his body was dying by inches. On August the 23d, 1483, he had a third stroke, and he died five days afterward. He had begged his attendants to warn him of the end, but to do it gently. When they saw that there was nothing more to be feared from him, they shouted the truth in his ear.

When you come to read larger histories of France than this, you will find that Louis the Eleventh is much thought of because he broke down the power of the feudal lords and made France larger than it had ever been before. This was a good work, and he deserves all the credit of it. But he was false, treacherous, deceitful, and cruel, and, as I think that falsehood, treachery, deceit, and cruelty are as disgraceful in a king as in a common man, I do not see how you can give him your respect or affection.

Chapter XXVI

THE GREAT LADY

A.D. 1483–1498

Louis the Eleventh left three children: Anne of Beaujeu, his eldest, who was twenty-two, and who was afterward known as the Great Lady; Joan, who was nineteen, and was married to Louis, Duke of Orleans; and Charles, who was thirteen. By Louis's will Charles was to succeed him as king, and his sister Anne was to be regent.

This arrangement suited all parties except the Duke of Orleans, who thought he should have been regent instead of Anne. He stirred up the people of Brittany—as though it mattered to them who was Regent of France—and they took the field against Anne. But she had not been called the Great Lady for nothing. She gathered an army under a gallant soldier named La Tremouille, swooped down upon the Bretons and their allies at a place near Rennes, and utterly discomfited them. She took her brother-in-law, the Duke of Orleans, prisoner, and put him in prison, locking him up at night for greater safety in an iron cage.

In that prison he pined and languished. His wife Joan, who was loving and true, though she was ugly and deformed, never ceased to beg his release from her sister Anne and her brother Charles, but in vain. He was at times so neglected that this faithful wife had to sell her jewels to get him food and clothes in his jail. Anne, the Great Lady, was unrelenting; she would not answer Joan's letters nor allow her to enter her presence. But Charles had soft moments, and in one of these, Joan begging him on her knees with many tears to let her husband go, he took horse, drew rein at the prison door, set Louis free, and fell upon his neck, kissing and hugging him as the custom of that day was.

I think you can figure to yourself the dark cloud which settled on the Great Lady's face when she heard of this freak of her brother's. She said nothing, but she thought to herself that it was time to get Charles married, so that he should have some one to look after him.

He was nineteen years old. Years before he had been betrothed to Marguerite of Austria, who was now a little girl eleven years old and at school. But the Great Lady had a much better match for him in her eye. The duchy of Brittany, one of the richest of the old feudal duchies, had fallen to a girl—Anne of Brittany, who was sixteen years old. She was pretty in face, but short, and lame in one foot, and though she tried to hide her lameness by wearing a high heel on the lame foot, it was easily noticed. But she had plenty of spirit, was bright and self-willed, and, being Lady of Brittany, she had suitors in swarms, from old widowers, with large families and pimply noses, to young gallants, with long swords and short purses. Among these she chose Maximilian of Austria, who was a giant, a good scholar, and a valiant soldier. She was betrothed to him, as Charles had been to Marguerite, and in those days, as you know, a betrothal was almost the same thing as a marriage.

The Great Lady perceived that a marriage between Charles and Anne would in fact be a union between France and Brittany, and she sent an envoy to Anne to find out her mind.

Anne replied that she was betrothed to Maximilian and rather liked what she had heard of him—she had never seen him ; she rather thought that she would like to be a giant's wife.

Thereupon the Great Lady invaded Brittany. You may think this a curious way of making love, but it was the way of the time, and Anne understood it. For, Charles being with the French army and Anne with the Breton army, a meeting was arranged between them; and the end of that meeting was that they were engaged on the spot and were married shortly afterward, the pope having agreed to annul the betrothals. Anne must have thought more of her people than of herself, for Charles was not a beauty. He was short and clumsy, with a big head, fishy eyes, fat lips which slobbered, a hooked nose, and a nervous twitching of eyelids and cheeks. To add to all, he could not read or write.

Such as he was, he now resolved to make the world hear of him, and, without reason, provocation, or pretext, in

CHARLES VIII. CROSSING THE ALPS

October, 1494, he crossed the Alps at the head of an army and invaded Italy, marching from Savoy to Naples. The Italians were so astonished that no one thought of resistance. On New Year's Eve, just as night fell, the French, lighting their torches as they went, marched up the main street of Rome, establishing guard stations, setting up gibbets to hang knaves on, and planting tents in the squares; while King Charles, in full armor, with his lance in rest, rode at the head of his body-guard, with trumpets sounding and drums beating all around him. The pope, who must have thought that Charles was out of his mind, sent word that he was very glad to see him, and would he please to call at the Vatican and pay his respects?

From Rome Charles went to Naples, and, it chancing to occur to him that sooner or later the Italians might object to being invaded in this way, he divided his army into two parts, leaving one at Naples, where it speedily melted away from hunger and disease, and taking with himself the other, which, after a smart battle near Milan, managed to cross the Alps again, and get home.

After this Charles considered himself a great conqueror, like Cæsar or Alexander the Great, and the French said that they were quite of the opinion that he was. Fêtes were given in his honor, at which the shows were more splendid, the dresses more gorgeous, the dancing more graceful, and the merry-making more vociferous than anything that had been seen before in France. To amuse the queen plays were got up under the direction of an officer who was called the King of the Fools, and who arranged spectacles which must have been like Christmas pantomimes you see at the theatres at this day. King and queen, courtiers and soldiers, did nothing all day but dance, sing, and frolic in these revels. France was fairly quiet. The old robber bands had been crushed out. Farmers ploughed their fields in safety. People were not in much danger if they neither stole nor killed. The gay nation was really gay. For the Great Lady, while king and queen frolicked, gave the people a good and just government.

All was thus going well when the king, walking through an unfinished corridor in a palace he was building at Amboise, struck his head against a beam. He did not at first notice that he had hurt himself, but went on talking and watching a game of tennis. Presently he staggered and

CHATEAU D'AMBOISE

fell. A mattress was brought; he was laid on it. They dared not move him; and on that mattress, in that dark and dirty corridor, with shavings and chips all around him, he died three hours afterward.

This was in April, 1498. Just four months afterward the great sailor Columbus first set foot on the continent of America. He had landed on several of the islands of the West Indies six years before. But it was not till August 2, 1498, that he discovered the mainland.

Chapter XXVII

LOUIS THE TWELFTH

A.D. 1498–1515

Charles the Eighth left no children; he was succeeded on the throne by that Louis of Orleans whom the Great Lady had kept so long in jail, and who was the husband of ugly Joan. He is known as Louis the Twelfth. You will be sorry to hear that his first act was to turn against the wife who had been so loyal to him in the days of his trouble.

In order to make it certain that Brittany would remain part of France, he got the pope to divorce him from his faithful Joan; then he married Charles's widow, Anne. It broke Joan's heart. She said meekly to her husband, "I hope, sire, that you will be happier with another than you have been with me." And then she shut herself up in a convent, and devoted the rest of her life to good works.

Like Charles, Louis made war on Italy, though there was no reason for the war, and neither side could gain anything by it, while it was sure to cause infinite distress and misery to the Italians, and was likely to end—as it did—in the French being driven home in defeat and disgrace. The French were, I think wrong-headed, and crazy for conquest and adventure, while the Italians were always fighting among themselves.

There was a duke of Milan whose name was Ludovico Sforza, but who was generally called the Blackamoor, because of his swarthy skin. He invited the French into Italy in order to overthrow the King of Naples. When he had got them in he turned against them and would not let them out. Him the King of France, with the help of valiant captains of whom I will presently tell you, hotly pursued and at last caught, though he had tried to hide among the Swiss guards, wearing his hair in a coif, putting on a crimson satin doublet and scarlet stockings, and holding a halberd in his fist. The Blackamoor was locked in a dungeon thirty feet under ground in the grim old castle of Loches; the walls of the dungeon were eight feet thick; through one barred window a thin ray of light crept in, and by leaning his ear to this window the prisoner could hear the shouts and the laughter of the courtiers as they jousted outside. In that castle, after many years' confinement, the Blackamoor died.

One of the most valiant of the French generals was a nephew of King Louis—a boy of twenty-three, whose name was Gaston of Foix. He was a born soldier, handsome, gallant, and one who never knew fear or pity. On Easter Sunday morning, in the year 1512, as he walked on the bank of a stream, he met a party of Spaniards who had crossed into Italy to help the Italians.

"Gentlemen," said he, "I am going to cross that stream to-day, and I will not recross it alive unless I win the day."

He went back to his tent and put on his finest clothes and his most splendid armor. But he had vowed to his fair lady—a curious person she must have been—that he would bathe his arm to the elbow in the blood of his enemies, and he cut off his right sleeve at the elbow. He did win the day, but on his way to his tent he was beset and stabbed to death. In his beautiful face there were fifteen sword-thrusts.

A still more glorious hero of these days was the Chevalier Bayard, "fearless and blameless." He started for the wars when he was only fourteen; he bestrode a little roan pony and wore a suit of satin and velvet, in the pocket of which was a purse containing six dollars. At the siege of Milan he pursued the enemy so hotly that he was taken prisoner and brought before the Blackamoor Duke of whom I have told you. Said Blackamoor, "Whom have we here?"

And when the boy explained how he had been taken, the duke, pleased with his manly speech and his open face, asked him what he would like?

"My horse and my arms," answered Bayard, "so I can get back to my master the King of France."

"Sir Captain," said Blackamoor to one of his men, "let his horse and his arms be found."

And he sent him back to his master, observing, "If all the men-at-arms in France were like him, I should have a bad chance."

At the siege of Brescia, Bayard was grievously wounded; he turned to his men and said,

CHEVALIER BAYARD DEFENDING A BRIDGE

"March on, comrades. As for me, I cannot pull farther, for I am a dead man."

They took him to a house where a woman lived with two daughters. Her husband had fled when the soldiers drew near, and her daughters had hidden under the hay in the garret. When the woman saw how badly Bayard was wounded, she bade the archers who bore him carry him into her best room, so she could nurse him.

"All that is in this house is yours by right of war," said she; "may it be your pleasure to spare my honor and my life, and those of my two young daughters."

"Madame," said the young soldier, "I know not whether I am to live or die. But so long as I live, your daughters and you shall be safe. If any come to this house to trouble you, say that I—the Chevalier Bayard—lie here wounded."

In five or six weeks he was well enough to get on his horse, and then the woman who had nursed him expected that he would demand ransom, as the custom of that day was. So, falling on her knees before him, with many tears and thanks for his gentle behavior, she offered him twenty-five hundred gold ducats in a steel box. But he only laughed and bade her fetch her daughters. The girls came in, pale and trembling, for those were rough times. The eldest said,

"My lord, we two poor girls, whom you have done the honor to guard, are come to take leave of you, to thank you, and, having nothing else in their power, to say that they will be forever bound to pray for you."

To which he answered,

"It is for me to thank you. Fighting-men are not laden with pretty things to present to ladies. But your lady mother has given me two thousand five hundred ducats: here is one thousand for each of you, and five hundred which I entreat your mother to give to the poor. Only I beg you all to pray God for me."

And with that he poured the gold into their aprons.

When his wound closed he returned to the army and

CHEVALIER BAYARD

fought wherever the enemy was met. He was the bravest soldier the king had, and he was generous and merciful. When he found that the people of a village had been driven into a cave, and two soldiers of his army had piled hay, straw, and wood at the mouth of the cave and stifled them, he caught the rascals, one of whom had but one ear while the other had none at all, and hanged them at the entrance.

He met his death like a soldier. He was shot while

crossing the Alps. When he felt the wound, he knew that it was mortal. He bade his men set him against a tree, with his face to the enemy. He confessed to a priest; then, to one who pitied him, he said, "I need no pity. I die the death of a man of honor."

And so indeed he did.

But all his honor and all his valor could not help the French to conquer Italy. After the bad Pope Alexander the Sixth there came a fighting pope, Julius the Second, who, when he was eighty years old, went out in his papal robes and pointed the cannon with his own hands. And then there came a very wise pope, Leo the Tenth, who made alliances with the princes all round him against the French, and in the end Louis had to creep back to France no better off than when he began. He made a bargain with Ferdinand of Spain, but was cheated, and when he complained that he had been deceived the Spaniard answered,

"The King of France is complaining that I have deceived him twice; he lies; I have deceived him more than ten times."

Louis had a little daughter whose name was Claude. He betrothed her to Charles of Austria, who was the son of a crazy daughter of this Ferdinand, named Juana. The betrothal took place at Blois. Crazy Juana, with her husband Philip, arrived at Blois at night, and climbed up the steep road to the castle by the light of torches of yellow wax fixed against the walls. Philip went first, between files of archers, to a room in which Louis was sitting by the chimney. Then came crazy Juana, whom Louis kissed and sent to his wife's apartments. The queen received her warmly, and Juana kissed her, and also as many of her ladies of honor as she could. Then the Spaniard was put to bed in her own room, where she was visited by six pages, bearing lights, and half a dozen ladies, bearing gold boxes full of sweetmeats, which were poured on the bed. At the door stood an apothecary to physic the strange lady in case she needed physicking, as perhaps she might after so

PORTAL OF THE CHATEAU DES BLOIS

much candy. And after all, the betrothal came to nothing. Claude married her cousin Francis.

It was soon after this that Queen Anne died. Louis was deeply distressed; she had been a good wife and a wise adviser. But it was decided that in order to insure the French alliance with England, he must marry the sister of the King of England. She was a pretty young girl of sixteen, who was already betrothed to one man and in love

MONUMENT TO CHEVALIER BAYARD

with another. Louis was a tall, thin man of fifty, who lived on boiled beef, took no pleasure in anything but hawking, was often ill, slouched in his gait, and went to bed when the sun went down. Still, the marriage took place. Louis only lived four months afterward.

Barring his foolish war with Italy, Louis the Twelfth was a good king, as kings went. He made a number of excellent laws, maintained order, and promoted trade and industry. It is said that in his reign there were fifty prosperous traders for one who could have been found in the reign of Louis the Eleventh. Travel was pretty safe, and public inns—which had come into use a few years before his time—were fairly good. Robbers were hunted down and severely punished. The people did not complain of being too heavily taxed.

The credit of most of the good deeds of his reign belongs to a wise priest who was his chief counsellor—Cardinal Amboise. He was one of the ablest men of his day, and one of the best and purest priests who had ever held power in France.

FRANCIS I., FROM A COIN

Chapter XXVIII

FRANCIS THE FIRST

A.D. 1515–1547

Francis the First, who succeeded Louis the Twelfth, was his cousin and had married his daughter. He was a handsome, dashing young man of twenty-one when he came to the French throne. As he grew older his face became gross and sensual. Louis the Twelfth, who knew him well, had warned his courtiers that when that big boy came to the throne he would spoil everything.

His first business was with Italy. The Italians were fighting among themselves. Milan was fighting with Venice, Genoa was fighting with Naples, Florence was fighting with Pisa, the pope and Spain were fighting with them all; and besides this, in many of the towns the people were fighting against their rulers, and the rulers were hiring Swiss and Germans to fight against their subjects. Such horrible confusion prevailed that from various places came invitations to Francis to take a hand in the fight on one side or another.

It was just the work he liked. And when he swooped

down on northern Italy with an army of sixty thousand men and won a great battle at Marignano, scattering the Swiss mercenaries, and sending them home ragged, wounded, with flags torn and bleeding feet, he felt very proud indeed. The French, too, were proud of him at first; but when they found that he increased the taxes and spent their money like water on his own pleasures they were not quite as proud as before. They found that he thought a great deal more of himself than of them. He spent his time in hunting and jousting and banqueting in castles on the Loire; when a Frenchman wanted to see him on business, he could not tell where to find him.

To gain the favor of the King of England Francis invited him to France, and the two monarchs met at a place since known as the Field of the Cloth of Gold. Each tried to outdo the other in splendor. Cardinal Wolsey, who was the minister of the King of England and looked like a king himself, appeared with a train a mile long, of mail-clad men-at-arms and gayly dressed courtiers on prancing steeds and snow-white mules, all covered with silver harness; the Constable Bourbon, who carried the sword of France before Francis, looked even more like a king, and bore himself so haughtily that Henry observed to Francis, "If I had a subject like that, his head would not be long on his shoulders." In order to cut a fine figure some of the French nobles made themselves poor for life.

The two kings slowly rode to the place of meeting, and when they met flung their arms round each other's neck, and embraced from their saddles.

Next day, to show his confidence, Francis called on English Henry before he was up and put his shirt on for him. Then the two kings went out to a tournament. At either end of the grounds were artificial trees made of cloth of gold, with leaves of green silk; along the sides were pavilions, tapestried with the most precious silks, satins, and embroidered cloths. Then followed tourneys, in which Francis showed more grace than the Englishman; archery contests, in which the English had the best of it; and wrestling-matches, in one of which Francis threw Henry more heavily than he liked. The two kings exchanged chains and tried to exchange coats, but Henry was so fat that Francis's coat would not button around him. This and the wrestling-match rather displeased the Englishman, and the kings parted without liking each other any the better for the meeting.

To console himself Francis invaded Italy again, and this time, having a great soldier, the Emperor Charles the Fifth, against him, the King of France came to grief. The time he should have given to preparing for battle he had spent on building a luxurious palace at Como, and the money which should have gone to his troops he had wasted on his pleasures. The battle was fought at Pavia, and was so hot that somebody who looked on said that he could see nothing but heads and arms flying in the air. Francis was completely beaten and taken prisoner. His army was destroyed. Some died of hunger, some of sickness, some sold their horses and clothes for food and got back to France so worn out by hunger, thirst, and cold that when they were taken in and warmed and fed, they died or went mad from the reaction. From that time to the days of Napoleon Bonaparte, the French never troubled Italy again.

When Francis was taken, he wrote to his mother that all was lost but honor. You may, perhaps, be inclined to think that by that time Francis had but little honor to lose.

He was taken a prisoner to Spain, and was only released on condition that he should marry the emperor's sister—his own wife, whom he had treated shamefully, having died—and should surrender certain territories to the emperor. He married the lady. But before he left his prison he made a secret declaration before a notary that he did not intend to carry out the rest of his bargain. He said he was a prisoner and not free to make a treaty. From which you may conclude that wherever he lost his honor, it *was* most certainly lost.

He reigned twenty years longer, and during that period he carried on four more wars with the Emperor Charles, in which neither side won much advantage. Between the wars, the two monarchs pretended to love each other like brothers. Once, Charles asked leave of Francis to cross France to go to Ghent, where a rebellion had broken out. When the king's fool heard of it, he made out a list of fools with the emperor's name at the head. The king, see-

FRANCIS I

ing the list, asked the fool, "How if I should let the emperor go through?"

"Then," replied the fool, "I should strike out the emperor's name and put yours in its place."

Francis let the emperor through, for all that.

These wars, and the vast sums which the king wasted on his pleasures, brought back the old troubles to the French people. The peasants could not till their fields properly; every penny workingmen made was eaten by tax-gatherers; the crops were short, and the poor people lived on bread made of acorns and soup made of weeds. The women grew thin and pale, and the voice of children crying from hunger was heard all over the country. Vast numbers of women and children died of cold and famine.

But the king had always money for new palaces, fine bronzes, pictures, and musical instruments; for jewels of gold, diamonds, and pearls; for velvets and silk from Genoa; for beasts and birds, camels, ostriches, and lions from Africa; for a clever card-player from Spain; for a horse for the royal cook, so that he could always be on hand for the king's dinner; for the beautiful ladies of the court, with whom Francis spent his time and on whom he lavished presents. He did not care much for his hungry people, but he cared a great deal for show. He wrote pretty verses himself, and he helped others who wrote, as well as those who built fine buildings or carved fine statues. It is the fashion to call his era the period of the Renaissance, which means that art and letters were then born again; and perhaps he had something to do with the birth. But it was much more largely due to a waking of the public mind from a sleep which had lasted a thousand years, and that waking was seen more plainly in religion than in anything else.

For a long time good Christians had been dissatisfied with the Church. They hated to see the popes mixing in politics and contending with kings; and they were not pleased with the tax which the popes levied on Christian

THE BURNING OF HERETICS

countries in the shape of Peter's pence, or with the raising of money by the sale of pardons for sins past or to come. In every country brave and intelligent priests had risen to protest, and to say that these things were wrong. But no two of them agreed what should be done, and the Church was able to break down each separately, either by burning him as a heretic, or by keeping him in prison, or in some other way.

Thus, John Huss, of Prague, protested, was caught, tried, and burned at Constance. Girolamo Savonarola, of Florence, was seized and was hanged and burned. John Wyckliffe, of England, was arrested and tried; the priests were afraid to execute him because when they proposed to do so an angry light came into the eye of the sturdy English people. John Calvin was driven out of France. But bold Martin Luther, in Germany, set the pope at defiance; and when the emperor called on him to take back what he had said, he defied him too. And the emperor, looking at the crowds who stood at Luther's back, and who, as they listened to his brave words, had a way of fingering their sword-hilts, thought to himself that this was a good man to let alone. That is how the Reformation, as it is called, took root in Germany.

In France people were very much mixed. Most of the bright men of the day were on the side of the Reformation; the best and brightest woman—the king's sister, Marguerite—was heart and soul with Luther. The king shilly-shallied after his fashion. He was a churchman on Monday and a Protestant on Wednesday; sometimes he changed his faith, like his shirt, every day. You never knew where to find him. But, on the whole, when a new and lovely lady came to court and smiled on him, he thought of nothing but her, and then the Church had its own way with the reformers.

Thus Peter Leclerc, an old and wise priest who agreed with Luther, was burned alive with thirteen of his friends in the market-place of Meaux. Thus Louis Berquin, who had written a book in favor of the Reformation, was sentenced to have a hole burned in his tongue, and to be confined between four walls, without pen, ink, or paper, for the rest of his life; a few days afterward the priests changed their mind, and he was burned alive. Thus John Leclerc, for tearing down the notice of the price at which the priests would sell indulgences to commit sin, was horribly punished: his right hand was cut off, his nose was

TORTURES OF THE INQUISITION

torn out, pinches of flesh were wrenched from his arms with hot pincers, a circlet of red-hot iron was bound round his head, and then his bleeding body was thrown upon the fagots and burned. And thus, in the year 1545, into the beautiful country of Vaud, where most of the people were Protestants, two columns of troops were marched, who sacked three towns and twenty-two villages, massacred three thousand people, sent seven hundred to the galleys, sold the children and young girls for slaves, and put up a sign on leaving that no one under pain of death should give shelter or money or food to any Vaudian or other heretic.

This was the beginning of the long struggle between the Church and the Reformation in France. For nearly a hundred years from the reign of Francis the First this history will be little else than a story of religious quarrels. It is a sad story. You might fancy that the good and wise Queen of Navarre saw what was coming when she wrote, on hearing of the persecution of the reformers after the death of Francis,

> "No father have I, no mother,
> Sister or brother,
> On God alone I now rely,
> Who ruleth over earth and sky.
> O world, I say good-by to you,
> To relatives, and friendly ties,
> To honors, and to wealth adieu,
> I hold them all for enemies."

Chapter XXIX

DIANA OF POITIERS

A.D. 1547–1559

The crown of Francis the First fell at his death to his son, Henry the Second, a young man of twenty-eight, robust, strong, and pleasant-mannered; but the real king during his twelve years' reign was a woman.

This was Diana of Poitiers, who was forty years old when Henry was crowned. Henry had married a lovely girl—Catherine of Medicis; but he cared nothing for her, and let Diana rule him in everything. The queen grieved in secret at being neglected—so much that one of her friends, named Tavannes, offered to go and cut Diana's nose off. But in her youth Catherine was gentle—she was not so gentle afterward—and was afraid of an open rupture with her husband's favorite; so Diana kept her nose.

There were at that time two great soldiers in the French army—the Constable Montmorency and the Duke of Guise. Of the latter and his family you will hear much more hereafter. The old chronic war breaking out between France and the Emperor Charles, these two led the French armies, and led them successfully, until the constable was beaten at Saint-Quentin and made prisoner. Then Guise came to the front alone. He made a sudden dash at Calais, which the English had held for two hundred years, and took it, in spite of the distich which the English had engraved on one of its gates:

"When lead and iron swim like wood,
A siege of Calais may be good."

When the emperor besieged the French at Metz—the

very place where the Germans besieged Marshal Bazaine twenty-two years ago—Guise made so stout a defence that he drove his army off, broken and shattered. So now the French people began to think a great deal of the Duke of Guise.

All this while the king was disporting himself with his lady friend at Paris. He did once take the command of his troops, but he did not keep it long. He liked pleasure better than fighting. He and his courtiers played at being wandering knights, spent their life in riding through the woods, and made believe they were very much surprised when dinner-time came to find a splendid meal laid out for them in a rustic arbor which had been built for the purpose, with superb paintings on the walls and priceless rugs on the floors. Of course, I need not tell you that these sports cost a great deal of money, but Diana knew how to raise it. She sold all the offices, from judgeships to places in the royal kitchen, and when the money came in too slowly she created new offices in order to sell them. As for the bishoprics and abbeys, she kept a list of them and sold them before they were vacant. With the money thus raised she established the wickedest court in Europe—a court in which men and women boasted of being vile, and base, and wicked, and in which a great noble founded a body-guard called the "Brave and Bad," to which no one could be admitted unless he had committed some crime.

King Henry enjoyed the gay life he led. On June 30th, 1559, he gave a tournament, and to be polite his courtiers allowed him to roll them in the dust. But there came a rough and brutal Scotchman named Montgomery, who did not understand a joke; he charged the king in downright earnest, and struck his visor so squarely with his lance that the lance broke, and a splinter went into the king's eye. He was taken from his horse, and his wound probed; it was found that the splinter had gone into his brain. He died ten days afterward in terrible suffering.

The Reformation made progress during the reign, though the king and the Guises were opposed to it and had a number of Protestants burned. King Henry himself was a trifler, and did not care much whether the Protestants were persecuted or let alone. But when one of his best soldiers, Francis d'Anbelot, declared that he was on the side of the Reformation, the king threw a plate at his head and locked him up in jail. For all this, the best people in France, one by one, drifted over to the Protestant side. Two thousand Protestant churches were founded in France during the reign of Henry the Second.

Chapter XXX

THE GUISES

A.D. 1559–1560

The rule was when a King died, that his widow should put on the blackest mourning and sit in a dark room for forty days. But when Henry the Second died, his widow, Catherine of Medicis, had too much work on hand to waste forty days in crying over a man who in the first bloom of her youth and beauty had preferred to her a woman of forty. She sternly ordered Diana of Poitiers to return every jewel Henry had given her; then she bade her be gone forever.

Her son Francis the Second, who had succeeded to the throne, she had married to a lovely girl, of whom you have heard, Mary Queen of Scots. He was sixteen, she fifteen; the queen-mother had an idea of a nursery in which these two children were to play all day long, with herself as head nurse, managing the government for them. But she reckoned without the Guises—the fighting Duke of Guise and the smooth, cunning Cardinal of Guise. They said that so long as the king was a child it was their proper business to govern France, and above all things to crush the heretics—by which term they meant the Protestants, who in France began to be called Huguenots. The leaders of the Huguenots were the Prince of Condé, who was a dandy, and a great favorite with the ladies, and was jokingly called the pretty little man, though he was brave as steel and could fight to the death; and the King of Navarre, who was a stupid person. Sometimes the Grand Constable Montmorency said that he was a Huguenot; but most times he said he was a Catholic, though he hated

AN EXECUTION AT AMBOISE

the Guises, and they hated him from the bottom of their hearts. There was no one in France who was as cunning as the two Guises. There had been a law passed in King Henry's reign forbidding Protestant church services under pain of death; this law the Guises resolved to carry out to the letter. First they got possession of the boy-king, his girl-wife—Mary Queen of Scots—aiding them with all her might, and the queen-mother not seeing her way to oppose them; then they had Montmorency dismissed, took everything into their hands, and began to burn Protestants at a lively rate. As they were short of money, Cardinal Guise stuck up a placard on the walls of the palace of Fontainebleau, where the boy-king was, in these words,

"All persons coming here with bills, and demanding money, will be hanged."

This, of course, enraged the king's creditors, and they plotted against the Guises, who were beginning to be hated. They were so much afraid that the people would fall upon them and make an end of them that they moved the boy-king to the strong castle of Amboise, and induced Catherine to appoint the Duke of Guise lieutenant-general of the kingdom, with power of life and death without trial. Catherine submitted with a wry face, because she could not help herself. Then the Guises turned on the plotters and executed them without mercy. Hundreds were hung, beheaded, or drowned in the Loire. The executioners would fasten six or eight persons to a long pole, sink the pole to the river bottom, and keep it there till all were drowned. What seems most shocking was that these executions took place after dinner in front of the castle of Amboise, and that the duke and the cardinal took the boy-king, his girl-wife, and the ladies-in-waiting to the battlements to see the executions and listen to the shrieks of the dying. You will not be surprised to hear that a good and wise old man, the Chancellor Olivier, turned to Cardinal Guise and exclaimed,

DUKE OF GUISE

"Ah! Cardinal, you are getting us all damned!"

These cruel deeds and the impudence of the Guises at last gave Catherine the opportunity she had been waiting for. She said the executions shocked her, and she suspended the law condemning Protestants to death. She ordered that the Huguenots be allowed to pray after their own fashion, provided they did not plot against the king. The Guises took their revenge by accusing the Prince of Condé, the pretty little man, of high treason. He had a mock trial, was found guilty, and was sentenced to death. But before he could be executed, as he was sitting one day playing cards with his jailers, a servant stole into the room and whispered in his ear,

"Our gentleman has croaked."

It was true enough. On the 5th of December, 1560, an abscess had burst in the ear of the King of France, and the poor boy had died, leaving his kingdom to be fought for by his brother, his mother, the Guises, and the Protestant leaders. Wise men saw that rivers of blood would flow before France would once more have peace.

Chapter XXXI

CATHERINE OF MEDICIS

A.D. 1560–1574

Francis the Second was succeeded by his brother Charles, who became known as Charles the Ninth. He was then ten years old. Throughout his reign and the succeeding reign, the most powerful person in the kingdom was Catherine of Medicis, the king's mother. You remember her as the patient young wife of Henry the Second, who would not allow Tavannes to cut off the nose of Diana of Poitiers; and as the bustling queen-mother, who had no time to sit in the dark when she became a widow, because she had work to do which required light. When her husband died, she felt that her time had come.

She was then forty-three years old, quite stout, with an olive complexion. She ate and drank a great deal, but kept herself well by riding or walking several hours a day. When Francis died she took Charles to sleep in her room, and for many years she never let him out of her sight. She received his visitors, opened his letters, never let his seal of state pass out of her hands, decided all public questions for him, and saw to it that he was always amused. The Catholic Duke of Guise had proposed to her to go into partnership with him to manage the kingdom; she pretended to be much struck by the idea, yet gave him no decided answer, but on the same day she invited his deadly foe, the Huguenot King of Navarre, to visit her secretly at midnight. You will understand her, if you bear in mind that she cared nothing for either religion. Her idea was to play the Protestants against the Catholics

CATHERINE DE' MEDICI

and to take sides with neither, but to keep power in her own hands.

It was a hard task. The French were all wild on the subject of religion—the Huguenots insisting on their right to worship God in their own way; the Catholics, who were the most numerous, insisting that there should be but one religion in the kingdom. Wherever the two met they fought, and the stronger of the two slaughtered the weaker. Battles raged almost every day.

The curate of St. Medard, at Paris, tried to drown the voice of a Huguenot preacher in a chapel near his church by ringing his bells clamorously; a Huguenot who went to remonstrate was killed; then the Huguenots burst into St. Medard, battered the priests, broke the crucifixes, smashed the statues, and drove out the Catholics howling.

The Duke of Guise, at the head of two hundred troopers, fell upon a Huguenot congregation at Vassy in Champagne, killed sixty, and wounded two hundred unarmed Protestants. At the news of the massacre Huguenots burst into fury everywhere, and you will not be surprised at it. When the duke passed men were heard to cry that they would willingly die if they could stick their daggers into his doublet. His life would not have been worth a sou if Constable Montmorency had not protected him.

The Huguenots, feeling that they must kill or be killed, took up arms, under the lead of the "pretty little man," who had not been executed after all, and old Admiral Coligni, who was a valiant captain and a gentleman of purest honor; they seized Orleans, Rouen, and other cities. The Catholics under the Duke of Guise besieged them. Rouen fell, but Orleans held out as in the old days of Joan of Arc. Guise wrote to Queen Catherine that the town must be destroyed, and every living being in it killed, "even the cats." As it happened, neither the people nor even the cats met this fate; but Guise, riding through his lines one dark night, was shot with a poisoned bullet, and there was an end of him.

All this time Catherine went on coquetting with both factions. She told every one she was on the side of Guise, and had him with her constantly; but at night she wrote sweet letters to the Huguenots, bidding them be of good cheer and to rely on her for help when the right time came. She always wanted to be on the winning side. When Guise was killed she believed the Huguenots would win, and in the king's name she issued an edict called the

Edict of Amboise, which gave the Protestants leave to worship in their own way.

This gave the country six years' peace. Then the war broke out again, and Catholics and Huguenots met in battle at Jarnac. A kick of a horse broke the pretty little man's leg, and one of the officers of the Duke of Anjou, who led the Catholics, and of whom you will hear more in the next chapter, shot him dead. His body was thrown on the back of an ass, with his head hanging down on one side and his feet on the other, and the soldiers threw mud on it as it passed. All these battles were cruel and bloody; not many prisoners were taken; when people fight for religion they have no mercy.

CHARLES IX

ADMIRAL COLIGNI

When Charles was fourteen he was proclaimed king, and his mother Catherine pretended to give up her authority. She even started for Italy, where she was born. But her son was lost without her. He could not even write a letter unless she was at his elbow. He sent for her to come back. She came, and ruled France with a higher and a more iron hand than ever. The cunning woman now believed that the Catholics were going to win, and made up her mind to put out of the way the Huguenot leader—the white-headed and gallant Admiral Coligni—not that she had any fault to find with him, nor that she objected to Protestantism, but because she thought that he stood in her way, and that if he were dead the Huguenots would lose heart and cease from troubling.

She conspired with the Duke of Guise, the son of the man who was shot at Orleans, and the two hired an assas-

THE THREE COLIGNIS

sin, who fired at the admiral as he was going home from the Louvre. The ball cut off two of his fingers, but did not kill him. Charles was, or pretended to be, so angry that his mother had to let him into the plot; she persuaded him that his life was not safe so long as Coligni existed. It was hard to convince Charles, but the poor, dull, muddled brain yielded at last, and he said,

"By God's death! since you think proper to kill the admiral, I consent, but all the Huguenots in Paris must die too. Give the orders at once."

A guard had been set around the admiral's house, and at the head of it was an abominable cut-throat in the pay of the Duke of Guise, whose name was Behm. Late that night—for the conspirators did not dare waste time, lest the king should change his mind—the cut-throat broke into the admiral's room, with a body of archers. The crippled veteran sprang out of bed, put on a dressing-gown, and leaned against the wall. Said Behm,

"Art thou the admiral?"

"Young man," replied Coligni, "thou comest against an aged and a wounded man. Thou'll not shorten my life much."

The assassin thrust a boar spear into the admiral's stomach, then struck him with it on the head. The archers stabbed him as he lay.

From the darkness of the courtyard, where archers' torches flashed a straggling light, the voice of the Duke of Guise rose,

"Behm, hast done?"

"It is all over, my lord," was the answer, and the body of the old admiral was thrown out of the window and splashed the pavement with his blood. Guise approached it, turned it over with his foot, wiped the blood off the white hairs with his boot, gazed on the face by the light of a torch, and said exultingly,

"Faith, it is he, sure enough."

Then he rode off. Next morning at daybreak the church-bells at Paris began to ring the tocsin, and in every quarter Guise's friends appeared in arms. They had been told that it was the king's will that all Huguenots should be massacred, and they were thirsty for blood. The rabble of Paris eagerly joined in the devilish work, and, as the Catholics were four or five times as numerous as the Protestants, there was no resistance. How many poor Huguenots were slaughtered in cold blood in Paris and in other towns—for the killing was contagious—it is difficult to say, but four thousand dead bodies floated down the Seine. This shocking event is called in history the Massacre of St. Bartholomew, because it occurred on St. Bartholomew's day.

MASSACRE OF ST. BARTHOLOMEW

Wicked Catherine, who plotted the massacre, did not reap the reward she expected. Religious war broke out again with more fury than ever. The great seaport of La Rochelle revolted against the king and turned out his officers. He besieged, but could not take it, and after losing some of his best captains he had to raise the siege and sign the Edict of La Rochelle, which gave the Huguenots freedom to worship in their own way. Neither the duke nor the queen had made much by the floods of blood they had spilled.

13

As for King Charles, he never forgave himself. His looks became sombre and downcast, and his head always drooped. He refused to drink wine or to eat anything but the plainest food. In order to tire himself, so as to get some sleep, he used to ride on horseback for twelve hours at a time. I am not surprised myself to read that he had visions, in which he saw dead men, lying stabbed on the floor by his side, and women, with blood flowing down their bosoms from gaping wounds, flying madly from the sight of him, with streaming hair and screaming children in their arms. He entreated his doctor, the great Ambroise Paré, who was himself a Huguenot, to find him some cure for these horrid visions; he begged for rest, rest, rest, but the wise old physician shook his head. He knew that the king's ailment was not to be cured by medicine.

He was not yet twenty-four years of age when he was attacked by an inflammation of the chest. He would not allow his mother near him, but to a faithful old nurse, who never left him, he moaned incessantly,

"Oh! nurse, nurse, what bloodshed and what murders! What evil counsel have I followed! O my God, forgive me my sins, and have mercy on me! I know not what hath come to me, so bewildered am I. What shall I do? I am lost, lost!"

In a day or two he died, in a fit of crying. Almost with his last words he rejoiced that his successor would not be a child, or one who could be misled by others.

Chapter XXXII

MORE WARS AND MURDERS

A.D. 1574–1589

Henry the Third, brother and successor of Charles the Ninth, was out of France when his brother died. He returned, and rather surprised the French by walking barefoot in a religious procession at Avignon, holding a crucifix and scourging himself with a whip. He was twenty-three years old. He had fought bravely enough in the religious wars, but he was a fop. He used to rouge his cheeks and dye his hair; he wore very expensive clothes of silver tissue, velvet, and satin, covered with lace and embroideries, and fringed with jewels and silver tags. Sometimes he masqueraded in woman's clothes. He laid down the most absurd rules of etiquette: no one could approach him nearer than a certain fixed number of feet; in the morning, when he awoke, a servant brought a glass of water and handed it to a courtier, who walked a few steps with it and then handed it to a prince of the blood, from whom alone the king was willing to receive it. It was not long before he showed that he was fonder of playing cup and ball, and other games, with idle favorites, than of attending to his duties of king. He had seen so much wickedness going on under his brother's reign that you will not be surprised to hear that he accused his younger brother of trying to kill him by scratching his neck with a poisoned ring.

This was not the man to make an end of the religious wars, which never ceased to rage and make life hideous for quiet people. Huguenots and Catholics would meet and fight until they were exhausted; then they would agree to a truce for a few months or years; when they re-

[illegible] the killing of a Huguenot by a Catholic [illegible] a Huguenot would rouse their blood, [illegible] begin again.

[illegible] formed a holy League to crush the Protestants [illegible] Henry of Guise, son of [illegible] Guise. In a battle Henry had been shot [illegible] had carried off part of one ear and [illegible] from which he was called the [illegible] The League put an army in the field [illegible] wherever they met them. In [illegible] an army in the field and set [illegible] Navarre, one of the most glorious [illegible] in France. Between the two, King Henry [illegible] now this way and now that; he was a poor [illegible] who had no mind of his own, and his mother, Catherine, [illegible] was over sixty, fat and gouty, was not able to help him much.

At Poitiers, when Henry of Navarre was near him, he agreed that the Huguenots should be let alone; at Paris, shortly afterward, when the Man with the Scar [illegible] over him, with a scowl on his scarred face, he took it all back and ordered the persecution to go on. But under brave Henry of Navarre the Huguenots learned to fight. They met the king's army, which was led by one of the king's chief favorites, at Coutras; the Catholics were terribly beaten, the favorite being left dead on the field. The Huguenots might then, with the help of some German Protestants who had come to their assistance, have made an end of the League; but Henry of Navarre, with all his noble qualities, had one great weakness: he never could resist a pretty face, and the beautiful Corisande of Grammont imploring him to visit her after his victory, he obeyed and lost his opportunity. While he was at the feet of pretty Corisande, Guise drove his army back and entered Paris.

When he passed through the gate, he covered his face with his cloak; but the people quickly recognized him and shouted,

HENRY III

"Hurrah for Guise! Hurrah for the pillar of the Church!"

He went straight to the palace of Queen-mother Catherine, who lifted her fat body from her couch and grew very pale when he entered. She said, with a forced smile, that she was glad to see him, but that she would rather have seen him at any other time. He bade the old woman conduct him to the king. She was carried to her sedan-chair, and he walked beside her, bareheaded, in a white damask doublet, with a black cloak, and boots of buffalo-hide. The people shouted with joy to see him, women flung flowers on his head from the windows, and one girl pushed through the crowd and kissed him. He entered the Louvre, with head erect and proud face, through a double row of frowning archers, who were surprised to see him, and at length met the king face to face.

Said Henry: "What brings you here? I ordered you not to come."

Said Guise: "I am here to offer your majesty my humble services."

And he stalked out with his chin in the air. Then every one, and Catherine better than any other, knew that it was war to the death between these two, and that Guise meant to make himself king.

A riot breaking out in Paris, the king could not put it down and had to humble himself and ask Guise to do so. Catherine called on him to thank him and asked him frankly,

"Is it your intention to take the crown from my son's head?"

"Madame," replied the duke, "the medicine may be bitter, but it will do good."

Next day King Henry, with a light cane in his hand, and a troop of tiny dogs of which he was strangely fond at his heels, walked to where a carriage was waiting and drove into the country, leaving Paris in the hands of his enemy. Guise put his own people in all the strong places and filled the city with his troops. His sister, the Duchess of Montpensier, went about with a pair of golden scissors at her belt; she had bought them, she said, to cut the king's hair off when he abdicated and became a monk.

The king went to Blois, where that curious collection of noblemen, priests, and representatives of the people which the French called the States-General, and which we should call a congress, was about to assemble. There, as ill-luck would have it, Guise followed him. For once—it was the

MURDER OF GUISE

only time in his life—Henry made up his mind and stuck to his resolution. He sent for Crillon, who commanded the regiment of guards, and asked him,

"Think you the Duke of Guise deserves death?"

"I do, sire."

"Very well," answered the king; "I choose you to give it to him."

"I am ready," said the guardsman, "to challenge him."

"That," said the king, "is not what I want. He must be struck down unexpectedly."

"Sire," said Crillon, "I am a soldier, not an assassin."

Others were not so scrupulous. The morning of the 23d of December, 1588, was dark, cold, and dismal; it was raining heavily. A royal council was to meet at seven, and the duke was to attend. Henry had filled the rooms round the council chamber with Gascon soldiers, who knew what they had been sent for and were ready for the work. He was pale and trembled all over. He went into his bedroom when Guise came in. The duke shivered a little from cold and asked a page to bring him some of the sugared plums he used to eat in the morning. Just then a messenger told him the king desired to see him. As he raised the tapestry which closed the king's chamber, five Gascons sprang upon him, stabbing him in the throat, chest, and side, with cries of "Die, traitor!" The duke had strength enough to drag them across the room, then fell dead before the bed, choked with his own blood.

A door opened, and the quaking king thrust his pale face into the room, stammering, "Is it done?" Seeing the dead body of the Man with the Scar before him, he plucked up courage enough to approach it and muttered,

"How tall he is! He looks even taller than he did when he was alive!"

On the day following the Cardinal of Guise was taken into a gallery where four soldiers stood with drawn swords and bidden to prepare for death. He made no reply, but knelt down with his face against the wall, and as he prayed a soldier drove his sword through his body.

Henry made haste to tell his mother, now bedridden with her gout, what he had done. The grim old woman heard him out.

"I hope," said she, "that the cutting is right. Now for the sewing."

That did not concern her long. Thirteen days afterward she was dead herself.

All the Catholics of France flew into a frenzy when they heard of the murder of the Duke of Guise. Madame de Montpensier, the sister of the dead man, led a procession through the streets of Paris, barefoot, in a loose robe, with her hair streaming over her shoulders, and screaming like a madwoman. Hundreds of ladies followed her lead. Crowds filled the streets, some singing dirges, some roaring

ASSASSINATION OF HENRY III

curses, all raging at the assassin. Men waved swords and pikes; women gave their jewels to pay for troops. If King Henry the Third had appeared at that time in his own chief city his reign would not have lasted even for the short period which it was to endure.

There was but one thing for him to do—and that was to throw himself upon the mercy of Henry of Navarre, the Huguenot leader. They met, by appointment, at Plessis les Tours—the king in shabby clothes and moving with a gait which was more slouching than ever; Henry of Navarre gorgeous in olive-green velvet doublet, scarlet cloak, and white plume, smiling loftily, and stepping like a king. It did not take them long to make a treaty by which the Huguenots were to be free from persecution; and then the two Henrys, with forty-two thousand men at their heels, marched on Paris, where the brother of the murdered Duke of Guise, Mayenne, was ruling as if he had been king.

Henry of France lodged at a house at St. Cloud, from which he could see Paris and watch the fighting. At eight in the morning of August 1st, 1589, a servant told him that a monk wished to see him. He was a mean-looking Dominican, by name Jacques Clement, cadaverous, wild-eyed, and probably crazed by the religious wars of the period. The king accosted him pleasantly, saying, "Well, friend, what news from Paris?"

The monk handed him a letter and, while the king bent his head to read it, drew a long sharp knife from his sleeve and drove it into Henry's stomach so furiously that it stuck in the wound. The king pulled it out and cried,

"The monk! He has killed me!"

Guards came running in and spitted the murderer with their swords as he stood against the wall with his arms outstretched. But it was too late to do anything for the king. He died next morning, having called upon his friends to support his successor, King Henry of Navarre.

MEDAL OF HENRY IV. AND MARY OF MEDICIS

Chapter XXXIII

HENRY THE FOURTH

A.D. 1589–1610

When the news of the murder of Henry the Third reached Paris, Madame de Montpensier, who never forgot nor forgave, mounted her carriage and drove furiously through the streets, like a madwoman, screaming,

"Good news, friends, good news! Henry the Third is dead and done for!"

But neither she nor her friends the Leaguers were better disposed toward the Protestant Henry, who was saluted by his officers and the people round them as Henry the Fourth, than they had been toward Henry the Third. They swore that they would never, never, submit to be ruled by a heretic king. And the Duke of Mayenne, who was now the head of the Guise family and of the League, sallied forth, with much blowing of trumpets and flourishing of banners, to make an end of the Huguenots, which they said they were sure to do in two or three days, or at most a week. They were not so sure of that when Henry met them at Arques, and beat them soundly; and they were still more doubtful after he had met them at Ivry, at ten o'clock one morning, and sent them flying in every direction before the noon-bell rang. It was at this last battle that Henry bade his soldiers, if they were confused in the fight, to look for his white plume and make for that, because there the fight would be hottest.

The Leaguers still held Paris, however, and there Henry besieged them. They had a large force of their own, and the King of Spain had sent an army to help them. Henry encircled the city with strong works, and pretty soon the provisions of the garrison began to fail. You remember that when Edward the Third of England besieged Calais, and the garrison turned out of the city the old men, the women and children, to make their provisions last the longer, cruel Edward let them die of hunger between his lines and the walls. Henry not only let the old men and women and children pass through his lines, but occasionally, when a convoy of bread or beef tried to get into the city, he pretended not to notice it, and it passed through. After the siege had lasted off and on for nearly four years, and the Leaguers were all quarrelling among themselves, the French quarrelling with the Spaniards, and Mayenne quarrelling with the citizens, a few of the more reasonable people concluded that it was time to end the agony, and sent word to Henry that they would let him in.

The morning of March 22d, 1593, was dark and rainy. Henry started from St. Denis, with two divisions of his army, a little after midnight, and ploughed through the mud till five in the morning, when they reached the Gate of St. Denis and the New Gate, both of which were opened as they approached. The provost of the tradesmen handed Henry the keys, and his troops marched through street after street without meeting any resistance; they camped in the squares while he went to the Louvre. He would not allow a man to be harmed; he even permitted the Spaniards to get away with bag and baggage. Other towns followed the example of Paris, and so Henry the Fourth got his kingdom at last.

But Henry was too wise a man to believe that, in those days of bigotry, a Protestant king could rule peaceably over a people four-fifths of whom were Catholics. He saw that his becoming king would not end the religious war—that as soon as people had got over their exhaustion they would fall to fighting again. And it broke his heart to think that he should be the cause of endless warfare in his country.

CHATEAU OF HENRY IV

You can hardly fancy the frightful condition to which this strife between Catholic and Protestant had reduced France. Everybody went armed. Every one was suspected, and many a one was killed for fear he might mean to kill some one else. In the country, when a stranger was seen coming along the road, householders got on the roofs of their houses to inspect him, and if they did not like his looks they shot him without asking questions. When a man paid a visit he left his gun and sword in the porch outside the door; if he did not he ran some risk of being stabbed by a host who wanted to be on the safe side. Families were divided—father against son, brothers against brothers. And this had gone on for fifty years.

Henry consulted the wisest men—Catholic and Protestant—and they agreed that, for the sake of his people, he ought to belong to the Church which most of his subjects preferred. It was a bitter struggle; at first he scorned the idea of appearing to change his religion for the sake of becoming king; he spent months in doubt; but at last he decided to follow the advice of his counsellors. He drew an edict granting full freedom of worship to the Huguenots (it was known as the Edict of Nantes, and was not put in force till after the events I am now relating), then, on Sunday, July 25th, 1593, he went in great state to the Cathedral of St. Denis, where the Archbishop of Bourges, in flowing robe, with a mitre on his head and a crook in his hand, nine bishops, and a swarm of priests, stood at the grand entrance to receive him.

Said the archbishop: "Who comes here?"

Said Henry: "The King of France."

"What does the King of France want?" asked the archbishop.

"To be received into the bosom of the Church."

"The King of France may enter."

So the king went in, was duly baptized, and became a Catholic, so far as baptism and blessings could make him one.

I cannot describe to you the joy of the French people—Protestant and Catholic. They understood that this meant peace. A few Huguenots murmured, but when, afterward, they read the Edict of Nantes, which for nearly a hundred years was the charter of religious liberty in France, they made no more objection. The pope stormed and railed and declared that he would never admit Henry into the Church; but as Henry was in it already, with or without his leave, his wails did not impress people very much. The King of Spain, who was a besotted bigot, sent an army into France to punish Henry for doing that which Spain had always wanted him to do; but he merely spent a great sum of money and wasted many lives without accomplishing anything.

After a time the Duke of Mayenne begged Henry's pardon and became a dutiful subject; the son of the Duke of Guise was glad to take an office under him; even spiteful Madame de Montpensier gave him her hand to kiss, with a becoming blush. He was so manly and generous and genial, he had such winning ways, that no one could remain his enemy long.

He was, however, in terrible straits for money. These wars cost vast sums; the people were all poor and could not pay taxes. He was so poor himself that, when he had subdued all his enemies and was king without dispute, his shirts were all torn, his doublets out at elbows, his cupboard so bare that he had to go round among his friends to beg a dinner or a supper. He spent many sleepless nights planning how to raise money to carry on the government.

All his life he had loved and had been loved by beautiful women. He married twice, each time unhappily. His first wife, the daughter of Catherine of Medicis, was an odious creature, who led so shameful a life that the king would not live with her and at last divorced her; his second was another Medicis, of whom you will hear in the next chapter, and who was not by any means a nice person. You heard in the last chapter of pretty Corisande of Grammont, at whose feet Henry hastened to lay the first news of his victory at Coutras. After her, a lovely girl, with curly hair and soft blue eyes, whose name was Gabrielle d'Estrees, was for many years Henry's closest friend. She had a clear head as well as a tender heart; he always sought her advice in the trying times through which he passed, and she generally advised him well. Sometimes, as ladies will, she forgot herself, and Henry had to teach her that, much as he loved her, he was the master. Once she quarrelled with one of Henry's best friends and wanted to drive him from the court. When Henry heard of it he went to her with that ugly light in his eyes which his enemies had often seen in battle.

"Madame," said he, "let me hear no more of this. I would have you to know your place. I would rather part with ten lady-friends like you than one man-friend like Rosny."

She died suddenly, poor thing, and was supposed to have been poisoned. After her Henry chose Henriette d'Entragues and Mademoiselle de Montmorenci to be his favorites. His heart was so loving that he was lost if he had no woman to pet and tell his secrets to. But no one ever took in his heart the place which had been Gabrielle's.

You will not be surprised to hear that, in that age of wars and treacheries and murders, ruffians were found to try to assassinate this good king. He had scarcely got settled at Paris when a lad of nineteen, named John Chastel, attended one of his receptions and stabbed him in the face with a knife, without seriously injuring him. He confessed that the Jesuits, who had brought him up, had taught him that it was allowable to kill kings who were not approved by the pope. Chastel was put to death with horrible torments, and the Jesuits were expelled from Paris. Of course you know that at the present day the Jesuits do not teach any brutal nonsense of that kind.

A number of other attempts were made on Henry's life, but he scorned to take precautions and laughed at the idea of his dying by murder. It was not till his wife, Mary of Medicis, insisted on being crowned in great state that a curious presentiment came over him. He said to his counsellor Sully,

"I shall die in this city and shall never go out of it.

HENRY IV. OF FRANCE

They will kill me; my enemies have no remedy but my death."

And for a long time he steadfastly refused to attend the coronation, greatly to the queen's chagrin. He told her,

"I have been told that I was to be killed at the first grand ceremony I undertook, and that I would die in a carriage."

The queen still persisted and teased him so constantly that he, who could refuse nothing to a woman, finally consented to go.

His carriage was being driven along the street of La Ferronnerie, when a cart got in the way and forced the driver to slack up, and to draw close to the shop of an ironmonger. In the doorway stood a man who, as the carriage slackened its speed, sprang upon the step and struck the king twice with a knife, the last thrust entering his body between the fifth and sixth ribs and making a deep hole. Henry uttered a low cry; one of the gentlemen, who had not noticed the assassin, asked,

"What is it, sire?"

The king answered in a faint voice, "It is nothing," and spoke no more. They carried him to the Louvre and laid him on his bed; he remained speechless and insensible for two days and then died.

François Ravaillac, the murderer, was a madman who had gone crazy on the subject of religion. He was torn in pieces by wild horses for his crime. But even that horrible death did not expiate his murder of the wisest, and bravest, and gentlest, and noblest king France ever had.

CARDINAL RICHELIEU

Chapter XXXIV

CARDINAL RICHELIEU

A.D. 1610–1643

Two or three minutes after King Henry the Fourth expired the royal chancellor entered the room of Mary of Medicis. She read his face and, springing to her feet, cried, "Is the king dead?"

"Madame," answered the chancellor, "the king can never die. Here is the king."

And he laid his hand on the head of her son Louis, who was a boy nine years old. He was known as Louis the Thirteenth.

When Mary of Medicis married Henry she was twenty-seven years old—tall, fat, with staring eyes and a forbidding air. Henry never loved her and never trusted her. When he died she was thirty-seven—vain, obstinate, vindictive, and suspicious. She did not care for her son, whose education she neglected, and whom she allowed to spend his time in playing tennis and billiards, setting bird-traps, and painting little pictures on scraps of paper. When he was fifteen she married him to Anne of Austria, a Spanish princess, who was also fifteen, pretty and graceful, with blue eyes and a quantity of light hair. The two children seemed to take a fancy to each other, though the little queen could hardly move in her heavy green satin dress embroidered with gold, and was glad to get it off and play at romps with her boy-husband.

Mary of Medicis, the queen-mother, kept the business of government in her own hands, and to advise her she took into her employment the ablest statesman you have read of in this history—Richelieu.

You may be surprised to hear that he was a bishop when he was twenty, but in those days bishoprics were property which could be handed down from father to son or from brother to brother, like a field or a watch. He was so poor when he was created a bishop that he had to buy a second-hand bed to sleep on, and made himself a muff out of a fur belonging to his uncle. But if he was poor in money he was rich in brains, as you will see.

The queen-mother had brought from Italy a woman she liked, Leonora Galigai, and her husband Concini, and had loaded them with riches, titles, and honors. She had created Concini, who was a very common person, a marquis; and, as you may suppose, the French grew jealous of him. He was a foolish talker, and some of his boastful speeches were reported to the king and angered him. One day the Italian kept his hat on in the king's presence—this was the straw which broke the camel's back. No one who kept his hat on before the king was fit to live.

On the 24th of April, 1617, the captain of the King's Guard bade a few trusty men put pistols in their pockets when they went on guard. When the Italian marquis made his appearance the captain stepped up to him and said,

"I have the king's orders to arrest you."

"What! arrest me?" cried the marquis, clapping his hand to his sword.

At that four or five guardsmen fired their pistols at him, and he fell dead.

Everybody said that this would be bad for Richelieu, who had been a close friend of the dead man; but, strange to say, it turned out that he was a still closer friend of the man who succeeded Concini in his offices—De Luynes. At this time it took a pretty sharp observer to keep track of Richelieu's friendships and his enmities.

The queen-mother was furious at her favorite's death, and went to the country, taking Richelieu with her. For quite a long time mother and son were foes and never met; but at last Richelieu reconciled them, and to reward him the king got the pope to make him a cardinal and took him into his own service. From that time he ruled France, and ruled it wisely and well.

It would weary you to read the story of the cunning tricks by which he managed to outwit the enemies of France, and set them all fighting one against the other, so that at the end of the fighting France was more powerful than any of them. Though he was a cardinal of the Church, more than once in Germany he took the side of the Protestants against the Catholics, the better to weaken both. And at home, while he captured the great Protestant town of La Rochelle from the Huguenots, after a siege in which hundreds of men, women, and children died of hunger, he was quite fair in dealing with the Huguenot party, allowing no man to be persecuted because of his religion. In this way he made France a peaceful country, in which every one could attend to his own business, and pray in the church he liked best, without troubling himself about what his neighbor believed, or how or where he prayed. Richelieu had no money troubles. With the help of his wise minister, Sully, Henry the Fourth had left a large sum of money in the treasury when he died. Richelieu increased it, though the people made no complaint of being over-taxed.

But, as you may suppose, he could not do all these things without making enemies. One of them was the young queen, Anne, who turned out a flirt, and was always coquetting with the Duke of Buckingham, the Duke of Orleans, who was her husband's brother, or some one else. The cardinal watched her closely; she found it out and vowed vengeance. From that time plot succeeded plot, and it required all the cardinal's wit and skill to defeat them.

The Duke of Orleans planned to murder the cardinal in his own palace. The deed was to be done in the night. Shortly before midnight a party of the duke's men-at-arms knocked loudly at the cardinal's door. It was opened, and, of all unexpected persons, the cardinal himself stepped out, serene and calm.

"Ha !" said he, with a wave of his laced wristband, "the duke deigns to pay me a visit. I will go meet him."

And stepping into a carriage, he drove off like the wind, leaving the assassins staring at each other.

When the duke awoke next morning, you may fancy his surprise when he saw the cardinal standing by his bedside, handing him his shirt.

"Your royal highness's men," said he with a smile, "did not find the beast in his lair."

One of the conspirators in this plot — Chalais — was caught and condemned to death. To prolong his life, his friends gave the executioner a large sum of money to go away; but another executioner was procured, who did not know his business, and who chopped thirty-one times at the poor fellow's neck before he succeeded in cutting his head off.

The cardinal knew that Queen Anne was in the plot, but for the present he was content with a mild punishment. He introduced to her a new envoy from the pope, of the name of Mazarin; you will hear more of him by and by. "Madame," said Richelieu, with a bow and a smile, "you will doubtless approve of him, he is so like the late Duke of Buckingham."

The old queen-mother quarrelled with the cardinal because he would not consult her about the business of state. She did not do her plotting in secret, as her daughter-in-law did, but went round everywhere howling that Richelieu was a knave and a liar and a crocodile, and that he ought to have his head taken off before supper. The cardinal pretended to be very much distressed at having lost the favor of his good, kind friend Madame Mary of Medicis, but he went on governing the country all the same; and the king, who did not know much, still knew enough, at that time, to choose rightly between his mother and the cardinal. Queen Mary went off boiling with spite and muttering that God would repay, though he did not pay every week.

Richelieu was satisfied that Queen Anne was secretly writing letters to her brothers in Spain, though Spain and France were at war at the time; his spies had convinced him of that, but he could not get hold of the letters. Suddenly, without any warning, he arrested her confidential valet, La Porte, and shut him up in the Bastile. It chanced that Anne had among her maids of honor a beautiful girl named Marie d'Hautefort, who was so charming that when she was only fourteen the king himself had fallen in love with her, and had pursued her with calf-love until she had pluckily told him he did not please her at all. This Marie, who was as brave as she was pretty, now went to the Bastile in the dress of a servant, and found that La Porte was in one of the lowest dungeons of the prison, and that two stories above him a young nobleman of her acquaintance, named De Jars, was also locked up. She got admission to De Jars, and gave him a paper on which was written,

"The queen is in danger. Do not betray her."

De Jars broke a hole in the floor of his cell and passed the paper to the prisoner below him, and he, being a friend of De Jars, broke a hole in his floor likewise and lowered the note down to La Porte.

Whereby it came that when La Porte was examined, he declared on his honor that he had never carried any letters from the queen to the envoys of Spain, had never received any from them, and could swear that no letters had ever passed between them and the queen. If it had been necessary, he would have sworn that the queen had never written any letters to anybody and that she didn't know how to write. The cardinal, taking a pinch of snuff and settling his scarlet velvet gown around him, remarked with a sigh, "I wish I could get as faithful a servant as that."

Another friend of the queen's, who probably knew all about the letters to Spain, was the Duchess of Chevreuse. The cardinal locked her up in a castle. One day, as she was driving through the grounds, she managed in the carriage to slip off her clothes, and put on the doublet, hose, boots, and wig of a man; then, with a sword by her side, she leaped from the carriage, ran to a place where a horse stood saddled and bridled, and rode to Bayonne. A gentleman who met her said as she passed,

"If you were not dressed as a cavalier, I should say you were the Duchess of Chevreuse."

"I have the honor," said the pretended cavalier, laughing, "to be related to that lady"; and putting spurs to her horse, she did not draw bridle till she stood on Spanish soil.

These narrow escapes so frightened Queen Anne that she sent for Richelieu and confessed. The poor little woman, trembling all over, and sobbing and crying, knelt at the feet of the great cardinal, who, in his scarlet robe, with his lace collar, his diamond star, and his lofty smile, looked like a king. He knew how weak this woman was. He patted her on the back as a father might.

"Madame," said he, "let the past be forgotten. But conspire no more with Spain against your country."

She swore by her crucifix that she would not, and then she went on conspiring just as before. The cardinal knew that she would, and he bought her servants, and read every letter she wrote, and knew of every plot she made as soon as it was formed.

Meantime her husband was inconstant as a weathercock.

Sometimes he declared that he would not be king if he had not the cardinal to advise him. Then again he would wring his hands and whine, "Will nobody rid me of this terrible priest?"

Richelieu felt that he was not safe unless he had a faithful friend near the king's person. For that work he chose a handsome, dashing young fellow named Cinq-Mars. The two young men became fast friends. Cinq-Mars taught Louis how to catch magpies and how to train dogs; they carved wooden toys together, and sometimes they went into the royal kitchen and made candy, under the direction of the royal cook. The king grew as fond of the young man as a boy is of his sweetheart; he made him a member of his privy council. This was too much for the cardinal. He required the king to revoke the appointment. Then Cinq-Mars, like the others, began to plot against the man who had made him.

If he had been wise, he would have taken warning by the end of Mary of Medicis. That terrible old woman had gone too far at last, and the knave and crocodile had turned upon her and sent her into exile in Germany. Neither England nor Holland nor Spain dared receive her. By the cardinal's advice her son Louis broke with her and refused to send her money. There were times when she had not a meal a day, nor money to buy firewood to keep her warm. She chopped up her table and chairs to make a fire. When the end came, she told her confessor that she forgave her enemies; but when he advised her to send a ring to Richelieu in token of forgiveness, she answered, "That is too much," and turned her face to the wall and died.

The other queen, Anne, had learned her lesson at last, and would have nothing to do with Cinq-Mars and his plots; but the Duke of Orleans and other revengeful courtiers begged to be counted in. In the old way, they made a treacherous treaty with Spain, and, likewise in the old way, the cardinal found it out and got a copy of the treaty, which he sent to the king. Cinq-Mars soon received word that he had been found out. He hastened to the king, but Louis would not see him. "His soul," said the king, holding up a frying-pan in which he was making candy, "is as black as the bottom of this pan."

So he was arrested, tried, and convicted of high treason, as also was his friend De Thou. He was sentenced to be put to the torture, but just as he was taking off his doublet an order came from the cardinal to leave out this part of the sentence. He stepped with firm tread to the courtyard of the castle of Pierre Encise, and refused to have his eyes bandaged. Seeing the block, he marched silently to it, threw off his cloak, knelt down, and bent his neck to the headsman, who, with a single blow of his axe, put an end to his life. He was just twenty-two years of age, and the darling of the fair ladies of the court.

"Now," said the cardinal to the king, "I think your majesty will have peace."

Louis sighed and made no answer. Both he and the cardinal had had warnings that a life of turmoil is seldom long. Richelieu was very ill; at times his pains seemed more than he could bear. He took great care of himself. When he travelled he went by water, if he could, in a splendid barge, which was escorted by a fleet of small boats full of priests, physicians, men-at-arms, servants, and wine, rich food, and delicacies; on each shore a squadron of cavalry escorted the barge. When he could not travel by water he was carried in a litter, which was borne by twelve gentlemen of his guard, who marched bareheaded. It was covered with damask, and was so large that, besides the cardinal, it contained a bed, a couch, a table, a mirror, and a chair for his secretary. When it came to a walled lane which was too narrow to let it pass, the walls were broken down; and where it had to be taken into a house, it did not enter by the door, but a hole was broken in the wall, and the litter was hauled up an inclined plane with ropes.

When the cardinal reached Paris, after the trial of Cinq-Mars, he was very ill indeed. He sent for the king and took his leave of him.

"Sire," said the dying man, "I bid you adieu forever in this world. I leave you a kingdom more powerful than ever. To retain it you have only to choose your councillors wisely."

The king left the death-bed and strolled through the cardinal's picture-gallery, making remarks about the pictures. A doctor arriving, the cardinal asked him,

"How long have I to live? Tell me the plain truth."

"Monsignor," answered the physician, "in twenty-four hours you will be dead or cured."

He died next day at noon. Word was sent to the king, who quietly observed,

"He was a great politician."

Four months afterward Louis lay dying himself. "I am soon going," he said, "to lay my bones in St. Denis. It will be a hard journey, for the roads are bad." He grew peevish. His bedroom was full of courtiers who came to ask after his health. They annoyed him, as you might imagine. He said,

"These gentry come to see how I shall die. If I should get better, I will make them repent their curiosity."

His wife Anne, who was true and tender to him at the last, never left him. When the doctor said, "I can feel no more pulse," she clasped her arms round him, and thus, at the age of forty-two, on May 14th, 1643, he breathed his last, with his head on her breast.

He had been King of France for thirty-three years. But, if it had not been his good fortune to have a minister like Richelieu, you would have had no more reason to remember him than you have to recall the names of the feeble and worthless kings whose story I have told you. Under Richelieu, France became the greatest power in Europe, and this was due to his wisdom, his boldness, and his prudence. But he had no idea of liberty; it never occurred

LAST MEETING OF THE STATES-GENERAL

to him that no nation can be really great unless it be also free.

From the beginning of history the French had taken a small share in governing themselves through the States-General, in which the nobles, the clergy, and the people were represented; and besides this, each province had a parliament, which chiefly occupied itself with lawsuits. These were not very formidable bodies when they were opposed to the king; but, such as they were, they kept alive the idea of freedom. Cardinal Richelieu crushed them out of existence. He took all power into his own hands, and scoffed at the idea of sharing it with any one. I make no doubt that in so acting he paved the way for the explosion which came a hundred and fifty years after his time. If he had left the French some show of liberty, perhaps they might not have been so rabid to grasp the reality, and to avenge themselves on those who had so long kept them out of their own.

When you think of him, you must give him credit for having used his power to encourage French letters, science, and art. Before him France lagged behind other nations. Italy had long before produced books which you may read with pleasure to-day; Spain had given birth to Cervantes and Lope de Vega; Shakespeare's plays were being performed in London when Richelieu was a little boy. While France was devoted to religious wars, nothing else was thought of. When peace came, through the Edict of Nantes, poets, philosophers, and men of science arose. Richelieu encouraged them all.

He founded the French Academy, which is in full vigor to-day, and has counted among its members the greatest writers in France. He established the Garden of Plants, which contains to-day, as it has always contained, the largest collection of beasts, birds, reptiles, and plants in the world. He rebuilt the Sorbonne, the great school where the science of the human mind was studied. He founded the Royal Printing-office. He encouraged the Society of the Hôtel Rambouillet, which counted among its members all who were witty and wise in France. Under him Corneille, Ronsard, and Malherbe began to create French poetry, and Pascal and Descartes taught the French how to write prose. Before the time of Richelieu, the deepest thinkers of the day, such as Erasmus and Bacon, wrote in Latin.

THE HOLY CHAPEL AT PARIS

Montaigne, Calvin, Rabelais, Amyot, and other Huguenots set the example of writing in French. Richelieu encouraged the practice, and it was under him that the French language first became what it is—a language which you will love the more the better you understand it.

When you weigh the cardinal in the balance, you must offset his treason to liberty with his great services to the cause of human knowledge.

Chapter XXXV

CARDINAL MAZARIN

A.D. 1643–1651

At the death of Louis the Thirteenth, his widow, Anne of Austria, became regent, and chose for her chief counsellor the Italian Cardinal Mazarin, rather to the chagrin of the proud French nobles, the Duke of Orleans and the Prince of Condé. She took her little son, who was a fair-haired, handsome boy of four, to the Parliament of Paris, and the child, standing on a stool, bowed his little head, and gave the members of the parliament his little hand to kiss.

At first all went smoothly, but before long disputes arose between Mazarin and the parliament on the subject of taxes. France was carrying on expensive wars in Germany and Spain, and the cardinal had to provide money, which he could only do by laying fresh taxes; the people refused to pay the taxes, and in some places broke out in revolt. The rioters were called frondeurs, or slingers, from the frondes, or slings, which Paris boys used in their street squabbles. They had the parliament on their side, with old, bald-headed, long-bearded Matthieu Molé, who was as bold as a lion, at its head, and among its leaders an intrepid member named Broussel. When the regent sent orders to the parliament to do this and do that, Broussel declared flatly that he would not obey them.

That afternoon, as he was quietly dining with his son and daughter in his house, in a narrow street near the Seine, the lieutenant of the guard and a body of soldiers broke in, seized him, and carried him off. An old woman who kept Broussel's house rushed to the window, crying,

PARLIAMENT IN SESSION

"Help! Help! Rescue the father of the people! Help!"

Every man threw down his tools and ran toward the Palais Royal. By the time they got there they were such a crowd that the Swiss troops let them break their ranks, and the palace was surrounded by a surging mass of people shouting,

"Give us Broussel! We must have Broussel!"

Anne, at whose side stood Mazarin, declared with set teeth and scornful eyes that she would never give him up —never, never!

"Then, madame," said Marshal Meilleraye, "by to-morrow there will not be a stone left of all the buildings in Paris."

That night twelve hundred barricades arose in the streets of Paris, one of them within a hundred yards of the Palais Royal. Still Anne held out. It was not till Matthieu Molé took her by the hand, showed her her little son playing in the courtyard, and said, "That child is losing his crown," that she burst into tears and flounced into her room. Then Mazarin issued an order for the release of Broussel. Paris went wild when he appeared in the streets; he was hoisted on men's shoulders, and carried round through crowds, which threw up their hats and shouted "Broussel! Broussel! welcome back!"

This was the first victory of the people over the throne; you will hear of more such before you finish this book.

For the time the storm was over. But the square-caps, as the members of the parliament were called, did not love the cardinal any the more for their victory, and the proud nobles, the Prince of Condé and the Duke of Orleans, hated him worse than ever. The Prince of Condé wrote him a letter, in which he addressed him as "most worshipful flunky," and the people hooted him when he appeared in the streets. After a time Anne and he grew tired of this treatment, and secretly slipped out of Paris by night with the boy-king.

They fled to St. Germain, where the palace was very grand, but as there were no sashes in the windows, they were boarded up; there was no firewood, there were no bedsteads, so that even the ladies had to sleep on mattresses on the floor, and the rats were so numerous that they had to send back to Paris for cats. The Prince of Condé, who was at St. Germain, threatened to besiege Paris. In order not to be behindhand with him the frondeurs took the Bastile.

Then followed a number of skirmishes, which had no result except to cost the lives of people who cared little either for the cardinal or for the Fronde and to stop all business in Paris. This led to sober thought, and after a time the people, who wanted no more wars, invited the queen to come back. She came, and Mazarin got back to power, though the boys of Paris still shouted, when they saw him in the street,

"Down with Mazarin! Down with Mazarin, the Italian cardinal!"

Seven figures, stuffed with straw, and in cardinal's robes, were hung to lamp-posts, and two oil paintings, nailed on one of the bridges, showed the Italian with a rope round his neck, and a list of his crimes written out underneath.

The vindictive Italian struck at his enemies by imprisoning the Prince of Condé and the Duke of Longueville. At this the quarrel burst out as fiercely as ever; the parliament passed a vote that Mazarin should be sent into exile, and he, feigning to submit, left Paris and went to Brussels. The people imagined that the queen had gone with him and had taken the king with her. They broke into the Palais Royal, and a mob of ragamuffins forced their way into the splendid bedchamber where the boy-king slept, under gorgeous curtains and with tall mirrors on every side. There they saw him soundly sleeping on his pillow, and they went out on tiptoe. Then the people went home and slept soundly too, feeling that the cardinal was gone, and that the king was not.

The sleep was followed by a sharp awakening. Mazarin came back. The parliament offered a reward of a hundred thousand crowns for his capture, dead or alive. He captured his would-be captors and put them in jail. He came leisurely on to Paris; the queen and her son went to meet him and escort him to his palace; the parliament gave up the struggle against him; he took charge of the government as before, and held it till he died of gout, on March 9th, 1661, at the age of fifty-nine. He had been eighteen years in power, and had made so much money that his income was larger than the king's.

BARRICADES AT PORTE ST. ANTOINE IN THE CIVIL WAR OF THE FRONDE

esses around him, he could simper and smile and flirt. You would not think to-day that his company was very choice. The ladies wore their hair combed back from their foreheads, and powdered; their heads were hidden under hats like diadems, and their hoops swung to and fro when they walked. They were so bold that they looked like boys in disguise, and sometimes they talked like very rude boys. The men wore pigtails, powder, and patches; from their wristbands and the knees of their breeches hung long lace frills. If the ladies looked like boys, the gentlemen looked like girls at a masquerade.

The best people in France crouched at the king's feet. A smile from him made them happy; a frown plunged them into despair. They worshipped him, toadied to him, basked in the light of his eyes. The greatest men in the kingdom, thinkers who were famous, poets whose verses were in every one's mouth, soldiers who had won battles, nobles whose ancestors had been at the Crusades, fought with each other for the honor of holding the king's candle when valets took off his clothes at bed-time. When he was in bed, the haughtiest dames and the fairest girls in France sat at his bedside reading to him. All were splendidly dressed and beautifully mannered. Everybody spent money like water. Carriages had come into use in Paris with Henry the Fourth. That valiant soldier, who rode into battle with a smile, never dared ride in one, for fear of being upset. But under Louis the Fourteenth rich people kept gorgeous carriages, and drove prancing horses with golden harness through the streets, which, as there were no sidewalks, was not pleasant for people who were on foot.

In the year 1660, when Louis was twenty-two, he married Maria Theresa of Spain. She was rather good-looking, though short; her teeth were bad—there were no dentists in those days—her hair was fair, her eyes blue, and her complexion perfect. The Spanish fashions of that day were queer. Maria Theresa wore at her betrothal a white dress with heavy gold ornaments and a huge white cap, while her ladies in waiting wore low dresses which showed their skinny necks; they had quantities of false hair, and enormous hoops which wobbled as they walked.

The poor queen did not have a happy life. Louis treated her coldly and neglected her for other ladies; her jealousy affected her mind, so that she became half-witted. She lived, however, twenty-three years as Queen of France, and when she died she begged her husband with her last breath to marry Madame de Maintenon. This was a lady of fifty, who had been married in her youth to a cripple, and had outlived him. She possessed uncommon judgment and tact, and had completely mastered the king by devoting herself to his service and never annoying him by jealousy. Louis married her, as his wife had bidden him; but the marriage was kept a secret, and Madame de Maintenon never took the title of queen. She did not make much by her grand marriage. For thirty years she was the slave and nurse of a crabbed, selfish tyrant, who was always either flirting with young girls, or sitting silent and morose in his arm-chair, or whining for medicines for some new ailment. When Louis died, she went to live at a country place, and was as soon forgotten as if she had never been mistress of France.

Louis had not been long on the throne before he began to yearn for glory. He dreamed of blood and battles and triumphal marches and plains strewed with the dead. It probably never occurred to him that war would waste the lives and the substance of his people. Indeed, I fancy he never thought of his people at all. He wanted to figure in history as a conqueror, like Alexander the Great, or Cæsar. For nearly fifty years, with some short intervals, he followed his bent, and made war in turn on the English, the Dutch, the Germans, and the Spaniards. He declared war on England in 1666, just as his mother was dying. The peace of Utrecht, which ended the wars, was signed in 1713. By all these wars France gained but a few scraps of territory, which added nothing to her greatness. She would not have gained these but for the genius of her great generals—Turenne, the great Condé, Vauban, Luxembourg, and others. What she lost I have now to tell you.

When Louis became king, he found that the money matters of the kingdom were in the hands of a thief named Fouquet, who, like Mazarin, made an immense fortune, and gave parties at which every guest found a purse of gold on his dressing-table for use in the card-room. Louis got rid of him, and set over his treasury a wise minister named Colbert. It was Colbert's business to find money to carry on the king's wars.

This he did; but it broke his heart, and brought his gray hairs to a miserable grave. He lived to see one tenth of the whole people get their bread by begging. Persons who could not afford to eat meat themselves were forced to buy meat to feed soldiers who were quartered on them. That noble priest, Archbishop Fénelon, told the king to his face that he had made France one great hospital. Every able-bodied man was forced into the army, and there was no one to till the fields or to work in factories or wait in shops. Riots round the bakers' stores were every-day affairs. The farmers' cattle had been seized and sold for taxes. In one place, while a farmer was burying his dead wife, a tax-collector broke into his house, wounded him, beat his maid-servant with a stick, and killed his daughter. The peasants were driven to eat the grass of the fields and the bark of trees.

All this while Louis was not only carrying on monstrously expensive wars, but was building a palace at Versailles which you can see to this day—it cost over a hundred and fifty millions of livres—a palace at Marli, a castle at St. Germain, any number of splendid residences in Paris for himself and his friends, public buildings for glory, four or five triumphal arches, and was completing the Louvre. He did not even stint himself in his private expenses. On a little junket of a few days which he took to Versailles

MADAME DE MAINTENON

he spent about sixty thousand dollars of our money, one half of which went in gambling. One of the king's lady friends lost a million livres one night at cards, another spent twenty thousand dollars on Christmas presents. I need not tell you that when the king and the court set such an example of reckless waste and brutal indifference to the sufferings of the people, society was sure to become wicked and rotten. In this case the rottenness showed itself in a peculiar way. A curious epidemic of poisoning broke out.

The story goes that the first poisoners came from Italy. I do not know how this may be. But it is certain that Henrietta of England, wife of the Duke of Orleans, drank a glass of succory water, and immediately turned pale with agony. They would not let her have the physician she wanted. A canon of the Church called to confess her; he advised her to submit to the will of God. Some courtiers came, and made light of her pains. Her husband was surprised, but did not stay with her. The only one who remained by her side was the great preacher Bossuet, who was with her when she expired, the day after she had drunk the glass of water. It was given out at the court that she had died of cholera.

Then other persons of high rank died under surprising circumstances, and in every case after a short illness. Sudden deaths became so common that the government created a special court, called the Burning Chapel, to look into them. This court caused the arrest of a woman whose name was Marie de Brinvilliers, and who was a marquise and surprisingly beautiful. Her story was horrible. After her marriage she fell in love with a man who was said to have learned from an Italian the way to make a famous poison, then called aqua tofana, which was in reality a solution of arsenic. He told the secret to Marie.

She tried it on her chambermaid, and on sick people in the hospitals, and, finding it answer, she poisoned her father, her two brothers, and her child. She then took to poisoning from pure love of the thing, and put to death a number of people whom she did not know and whom she had no reason to hate. She was caught by a policeman who disguised himself as a priest, and wormed out of her many secrets when she went to confess. She retracted her confessions before the Burning Chapel. But when she was laid on an iron bed in the torture-chamber, and the ropes round the pulleys began to pull her beautiful arms and legs out of their sockets, she screamed, and confessed everything. She had put to death an astonishing number of people, and Paris rejoiced when she was led limping from the torture-chamber to the stake and was burned alive.

Another female poisoner, you may be surprised to hear, was Olympia di Mancini, niece of Cardinal Mazarin. She was summoned to appear before the Burning Chapel, but refused, and fled to Spain. Her reputation had gone before her, and neither the king nor the Court of Spain was glad to see her. After a time they relented. She became intimate with the queen, and one day her majesty took a glass of milk from her hand. The queen only lived a few hours. The Spanish police tried to catch the murderess, but she fled.

You will not perhaps be sorry to hear that this wicked woman wandered through Europe for twenty-seven years, hunted out of place after place when people learned who she was. She had not a friend in the world, and in her old age she had not a penny.

Chapter XXXVII

MORE PERSECUTION OF THE HUGUENOTS

A.D. 1680-1715

About the time when Louis the Fourteenth was being assured by his courtiers that he was a greater warrior than Cæsar, a greater statesman than Charlemagne, and a greater monarch than had ever before lived, it occurred to him that it would be a fine thing to crush out the Huguenots, and to have but one religion in his kingdom.

At first, his idea was to break down the Protestants by degrees. He told his officers that Protestantism was a malady caused by hot blood, which should be treated with gentleness rather than with severity. Thus, he let the Huguenots pray in their own churches and in their own way; but he forbade their becoming lawyers or doctors or members of the parliament. In those days, there were no barracks for soldiers; the men were quartered on citizens, who had to lodge and feed them. Louis ordered that soldiers should be quartered on Huguenots rather than on Catholics. As the soldiers were often ruffians, who maltreated the household that housed them, stole all they could lay their hands on, and in case of remonstrance beat those they robbed, it was a cruel hardship to have them as lodgers. The troopers sometimes made things pleasant for the family which boarded them by beating drums day and night, the drummers relieving each other at intervals, so that nobody could sleep.

By annoying the Huguenots in this and other ways, by seizing their ministers and thrusting them into jail, and torturing some into submission, the king induced many Huguenots to recant their religion and become Catholics.

Madame de Maintenon, who had become very pious and thought a Huguenot had no right to live, felt sure that Louis was going to bring back all his subjects into the Church. She was well seconded by a minister of the king named Louvois. But still there remained a few thousand Huguenots whom neither persecution could subdue nor danger shake, and who stood firm by their religion through all. To overcome these, Louis the Fourteenth revoked the Edict of Nantes—which Henry the Fourth had issued to be forever a guarantee of religious freedom in France. The revocation was made known on the 17th of October, 1685; the edict had given peace to France for eighty-seven years. When it was repealed, Protestants had no rights whatever. They were forbidden to pray. Their churches and chapels were torn down. Their ministers were locked up in filthy dungeons. Their children were baptized by force by the Catholic priests. And finally they were forbidden to leave the kingdom. Madame de Maintenon, who was the king's adviser in all this business, said that she intended to make the Huguenots ridiculous. It was, I think, France that was made ridiculous in the end.

In Languedoc the women were fiery; they are so to this day. They refused to change their faith. The king sent word to have all of them who were not of noble birth whipped on the bare back and branded. In the Cevennes, a cruel priest filled his house with Huguenot prisoners. The peasants rose one night, tore him shrieking out of his house, and stabbed him to death with fifty-two stabs. Each peasant explained his stab. "That's for my father, broken on the wheel!" "That's for my brother, sent to the galleys!" "That's for my mother, dead of grief!" And so on.

In spite of the order forbidding Protestants to leave the country, some four or five hundred thousand did so, including some of the most skilful and industrious artisans in France. They came to this country, or went to England, Belgium, Holland, or Germany, and took their skill and their knowledge with them, so that some of the most prosperous industries in France died out. Those who remained kept their faith a secret. For a hundred years after the Revocation of the Edict of Nantes, Huguenots had no rights in France. Their marriages were no marriages; their children were not lawful children; when they died, they had no right to decent burial. But the Huguenots lived through it all, and are flourishing and giving great men to France to-day, when the memory of Madame de Maintenon and Louvois and Louis the Great taints the air like a carcass that has lain in the noonday sun.

You will not be surprised to hear that the last years of this tyrant were gloomy and miserable. He had lost his sons, his eldest son's wife, his grandson, and nearly all those whom he had loved; he was alone. "I," said old Madame de Maintenon, "am compelled to endure his whims, his silence, his ill-temper; he never says a kind word to me." His confessor had been a good and gentle priest named Father la Chaise; when you go to Paris you will see the fine cemetery which bears his name. He was succeeded by a rough Jesuit named Le Tellier, who worried the king to death about his soul, and kept him in deadly fear of dying. The old man—he was seventy-seven—had not an hour of peace.

An ulcer appeared on his leg, and mortification set in. The odor of the sore was so offensive that all his family left him, and, after great suffering, he died at last on September 1st, 1715, with no one near him but servants, priests, and doctors; not one single person whom he had loved, or who had professed to love him.

You will find in larger books than this that the reign of Louis the Fourteenth is considered one of the most glorious in French history. This distinction is not due to any merit in the king, but to the fact that under his reign men of genius appeared in almost every branch of human knowledge. Some of the books of that period are out of print; but a great many others you can read with as much pleasure to-day as the French felt when they first appeared. I suppose that as long as the French language lasts people will love to read the comedies of Molière, the tragedies of Corneille and Racine, and the poems of Boileau; the sermons of Fénelon, Bossuet, and Bourdaloue; the wit and wisdom of Pascal, La Rochefoucauld, and La Bruyère; the fables of La Fontaine; the letters of Madame de Sévigné. There was no good music as yet in France, nor were there great paintings; but you can see to this day how well the architects of the time of Louis the Fourteenth knew their business. We have no better soldiers to-day than Turenne, no bolder sailors than Duquesne, and no more skilful fort-builder than Vauban. It was natural that the age which saw all these great men flourish together should be considered a golden age.

I am afraid that, when you think of Louis the Fourteenth, you may remember him less by these illustrious Frenchmen than by the recollection of his cruel wars, of his dreadful persecutions of the Huguenots, and his brutal tyranny. It was under him that the infamous prison of the Bastile became a dungeon where the king, or one of his courtiers who had the king's ear, could imprison a man for life without trial and without telling his friends where he was. When the doors of the Bastile were opened, after the death of Louis the Fourteenth, a poor Italian was found who had been locked up there for thirty-five years, and had never been told what he had been arrested for. He knew no one, had no money, and begged for the privilege of going back to jail and ending his days there.

A prisoner who did die in the Bastile, and about whom there has been much discussion, was the Man in the Iron Mask. This man had been for many years a prisoner on the island of St. Marguerite when he was brought to the Bastile in 1698 by Saint Mars, at the time the latter was appointed governor of that prison. He was brought in a closed carriage which was surrounded by mounted guards, who had orders to shoot him if he spoke. He wore a velvet mask set on an iron frame, and was forbidden to remove it under pain of instant death. In the Bastile he saw no one but the governor, who carried loaded pistols at his belt. The prisoner had been told that if he tried to remove the mask or to speak, the orders were to blow his brains out. He lived that silent life for several years. When he died, he was buried secretly at night in St. Paul's burial-ground, and every particle of his clothing except the mask, which he still wore after death, was burned.

THE BASTILE

Now, the question is, Who was the Man in the Iron Mask? You will find in large histories attempts to explain who he was. One of the most plausible of these is that he was a twin-brother of Louis the Fourteenth, who was thus secluded from the world to prevent his setting up a claim to the throne. I hardly think that you can believe this, nor do I see how you can agree with other writers, who have tried to identify the Man in the Iron Mask with another personage. The only thing that you can be sure of is that there was such a man, and that he suffered this cruel imprisonment for life for no offence that is known. All the rest is mystery.

Chapter XXXVIII

THE REGENT ORLEANS

A.D. 1715–1723

When Louis the Fourteenth died, the heir to the throne was his great-grandson Louis, who was a boy five years old. His great-grandfather had appointed a council of regency; but Philippe, Duke of Orleans, said he would be sole regent, and the parliament, which was glad of a chance of showing its spite to the dead king, replied: So he should. He gave money to the soldiers; they got out their firelocks and their pikes, and everybody then agreed that Orleans should be sole regent.

He was a stupid person, who was always led by the nose by somebody. When he was a young man, his uncle, Louis the Fourteenth, ordered him to marry Mademoiselle de Blois, against his mother's wishes; he obeyed, and the next time he went to court, his mother called him to her side and boxed his ears before the whole assemblage. He walked out without a word.

His first business was to bury his uncle, and this he did in a shabby way. There was no grand procession; only a few carriages followed the body of him who, according to the courtiers, had been the greatest general and the greatest statesman and the greatest monarch in history. By the side of the road to St. Denis, where the kings of France were buried, tents had been set up, and roysterers drank in them, guzzled in them, and sang coarse songs as the corpse rolled by.

The regent began hopefully, however. He reduced the army, set free a number of prisoners in the Bastile, and checked the persecution of the Protestants. But he was too easy-going and lazy to stick to any line of conduct, and the Bastile soon began to fill up again, and the Protestants to feel the iron hand of the Church. Philippe's idea was to have a good time, and his idea of a good time —and the idea of his courtiers too—was to get drunk, to associate with low, vicious people, and to boast of doing things which good people never do, or are ashamed of doing. He bragged of his wickedness, and the court bragged of its wickedness, and both of them had good ground for the brag. You may fancy what good society was like in France when such people were at the head of it.

The Regent Orleans lived under the thumbs of pretty, dissipated women; he was also governed by two men in turn.

The first of these was, when the regent made his acquaintance, an abbé and a tutor. His name was Dubois. He was a little, thin man, with a face like a weasel; so base and corrupt and mean and false that I know of no viler creature in history. He won the regent's heart by doing for him dirty work which no gentleman would have touched. He was, however, bright and witty and good company; he made a pretty fair politician, when chance threw politics in his way. This man the regent took to his bosom and made one of his chief advisers. As he called himself an abbé, he was supposed to belong to the Church; he applied to the pope to make him an archbishop, and the pope, who was at first staggered by the impudence of the request—it being as well known at Rome as in Paris that Dubois was a blackguard—at last consented, probably remembering that there had been archbishops before who were not angels.

Then the weasel-faced rogue asked to be made a cardinal. People laughed to split their sides at this, but Dubois never gave up anything on which he had set his heart. He begged, he cajoled, he threatened; he crawled like a serpent, roared like a lion, scratched like a cat. He told lies morning, noon, and night, and when he told the meanest lies he prayed the loudest. He cringed, and bribed the pope's nephews and friends; he reminded the pope that he let no day pass without sending to Rome either jewels or books or presents of some kind. The head of the Church was so hard pressed that at last he lay down and died, in order, as they said at the time, to get rid of Dubois. But a new pope was chosen. He was poor. Dubois sent him cartloads of silver money taken from the treasury of France. It is said that he forwarded sums which were equal to two million dollars of our money to Rome. He finally begged the Protestant King of England to intercede for him; and George the First, who regarded the thing as a monstrous good joke, wrote to the pope that in his opinion the weasel-faced knave ought to be a cardinal. The pope was only too anxious to please the Protestant king, and Dubois got a cardinal's hat and was happy.

The great lords of France refused to sit at the council-board with him; but the regent made him prime-minister, and Cardinal Dubois became ruler of the kingdom. Not for long, however.

He was made a cardinal in July, 1721. In August, 1723, he undertook to review a regiment, though he had never learned to ride. His horse jolted him up and down so roughly that an internal abscess, caused by his bad habits, burst, gangrene set in, and he died. At the last, he refused to take the sacrament, because there was no one of higher rank than a priest to anoint him with the holy oil. He said that no one of inferior degree to a cardinal should smooth his path to heaven.

The regent's other leader was a Scotch gambler, named John Law. He was a fascinating fellow, young, handsome, witty, dashing, graceful, a king of hearts, and a brilliant man of business. France was in desperate straits for money; the regent had neither credit nor coin. Law persuaded him that if he could start speculation among the people the government would be able to float paper money, and to pay off enough of its debts to be easy in its circumstances. The regent agreed to anything which would furnish him means to give his little suppers and to present diamonds to his fair lady friends. So Law had a chance to try his plan.

CARICATURE OF JOHN LAW

The first part of it succeeded very well indeed. All France went mad on speculation. All over the French colonies, and in all sorts of odd places throughout the world, towns were built—among others the city of New Orleans on the Mississippi; it was named after the regent—and every town was owned by a company, which issued shares of stock. Companies were started to carry on every business you can think of, and some businesses you never heard of. All of them issued shares; everybody was wild to buy them; the shares went up day after day, and everybody seemed to be making a fortune. Great lords, bishops, generals, lawyers, merchants, court ladies and ladies'-maids, gentlemen and valets, all crowded into the little Rue Quincampoix, where the shares were manufactured, and scrambled for them. On some days the throng was so dense that people were crushed to death near Law's office.

This went on for six months. Then it began to be noticed that there was not so much gold and silver in people's pockets as usual; the only money which passed from hand to hand was paper. Then prices began to rise. A pair of stockings cost in paper ten dollars of our money; a yard of cloth, twenty dollars. Then everybody wanted real money for their goods, paper money dropped in value to nothing, the speculators were ruined, and the government was worse off than it had been when John Law began his financial tricks and juggleries. The people mobbed him and smashed his carriage. He had to fly from Paris. But he was a crank, not a rogue; he went away almost without a dollar, and spent his last years in poverty in Venice, persisting to the end that his system was all right, if he had been allowed time to work it out. He had had all the money in France in his hands; he did not take a franc for himself.

It was in the regent's time that the plague—that awful disease of the East—paid its last visit to France. It was brought to Marseilles by a ship from Asia Minor. It was more terrible than any disease of our day. It struck down chiefly strong men and women in the flower of their age; those whom it did strike generally died within twenty-four hours. Everybody who could fled from Marseilles—the rich men, the officials, the members of the parliament, the lawyers, the merchants, and even the doctors. Happily there was in that city an intrepid priest—Bishop Belzunce. He stayed.

All around him his attendant priests, his servants, his choir-boys, died; he stayed, and spent day after day walking on foot among the dying and the dead, holding a cup of water to the parched lips of the stricken, soothing them, giving them the last consolations of the Church, and directing the burial of the corpses. After a time other priests joined him, and gave their lives for the afflicted. Out of twenty-six Jesuits, eighteen died of the plague; out of fifty-five Capuchins, forty-three died of the same disease. Priests of other orders were just as heroic. When you think of the wrong-doings of priests in the chapters you have read, remember the Marseilles plague, and give due credit to the Church.

I do not hear that the regent went to Marseilles when the plague was raging, or that he allowed the dreadful news from that city to interfere with his merry suppers. He diverted his mind with pleasanter pastimes than visiting the sick.

On the 2d of December, 1723, he was sitting with the lovely Duchess of Falaris, who was as bright as she was pretty. The regent leaned his head on her round white shoulder, and said,

"Duchess, tell me one of those fairy stories you invent so well."

She stroked his head with her jewelled hand, and began,

"Once upon a time, there was a king and a queen—"

She got no further. The regent's head had fallen into her lap. She sprang up and rang for help; doctors and servants rushed into the room. But it was too late. Philippe of Orleans was dead—dead of a stroke of apoplexy, brought on by the wicked life he had led.

Chapter XXXIX

LOUIS THE FIFTEENTH

A.D. 1723-1774

When the regent died, the great-grandson of Louis the Fourteenth was thirteen and was already King of France, under the name of Louis the Fifteenth. That was in the year 1723. He lived till 1774, two years before our Declaration of Independence; so that his actual reign lasted fifty-one years, one of the longest in French history. During about thirty-five of these years he carried on wars against Germany, England, Austria, Italy, and Spain; and though he was not beaten in all the battles, the end of the wars was that France lost all her colonies in North America, nearly all her provinces in India, several of her islands in the West Indies, nearly all her navy, scores of millions of treasure, and about a million men who were killed in the battles, or who died from wounds or disease afterward. You will perhaps think that France ought to have learned the lesson that war does not pay. But she had not.

I should tire you if I told you the story of these wars. One war was like another; each battle was a copy of the last; sometimes one side won, sometimes the other; but in every case a great number of poor fellows, who had nothing to do with the objects of the wars, were killed or crippled, and the people who stayed at home had to stint their children in food and clothing to provide money to feed and pay the soldiers. There was one battle fought near the town of Fontenoy, in Belgium, between the English, Dutch, and Austrians on the one side, and the French on the other. The story goes that a regiment of English guards, led by the king's son, met a regiment of French guards, led by a great French noble; and that an English officer, taking off his hat, called out,

"Gentlemen of the French guard, fire first!"

To which a French officer, also taking off his hat, replied,

"Fire yourselves, gentlemen of England! We never fire first."

Upon which the Englishmen fired a volley, and laid the front rank of the Frenchmen low.

You can believe this story if you think it probable. I think myself that an officer who let his men be killed, when he had a chance of saving them, didn't understand his business; and I suspect the officers of the French guard understood theirs.

Notwithstanding his endless wars, Louis the Fifteenth was not as wild for blood and glory as his great-grandfather. He preferred ladies' society to the society of camps. When he was fifteen, his friends looked round for a princess to marry him to. Madame de Prie, who took the delicate matter in hand, made out a list of ninety-nine who would answer; the list included fifty-five Lutherans, thirteen Calvinists, and three Greeks. Out of the lot the choice fell on Mary Leczinska, a Polish girl who was stupid and homely and seven years older than Louis. Her father had once been King of Poland, and was living on a small pension which the French allowed him, at Wissembourg, the place where one of the great battles in the Franco-German war took place. He was so overjoyed when he heard that his daughter had been chosen over the other ninety-eight, that he ran into her room, crying,

"Fall we on our knees, dear daughter, and thank God!"

I hardly think that Mary would have thanked God heartily if she could have foreseen her married lot. For her husband led even a worse life than the regent. He was always ruled by some woman or other, and he generally preferred the worst woman he could find. After many changes, he fell into the hands of a cunning schemer named Jane Poisson, who, after two years' chase, managed to catch him at a masked ball. She was pretty and smart; the king made her Marquise of Pompadour. For twenty-four years her will was law. She had an income of half a million dollars of our money, three castles, four palaces in the cities, and several estates; she made and unmade magistrates, judges, and generals; nothing was done without her direction. Even the king trembled when her voice rose in anger.

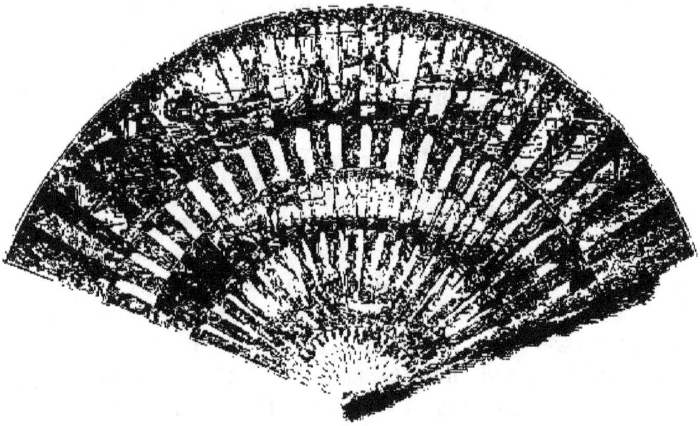

FAN OF LOUIS XV. PERIOD

When he grew tired of her he sent her away, and put in her place a girl who had been a milliner. Her he created Countess Dubarry, and she ruled him to the end. She was not as proud as Madame of Pompadour, and spent much of the money which the king gave her in works of charity. But the people of Paris could not forgive her for what she had been, and when the dreadful days of the guillotine came round, they found her out — she was an old, gray-haired woman then—and they cut off her head.

I am happy to say that Louis the Fifteenth was the last French king who led a dreadfully bad life. Of him you cannot think too ill. They said of him in his old age that his wickedness would have shocked even the Regent Orleans.

For a large portion of his reign, Louis's chief councillor was a wise and good priest named Cardinal Fleury, who, I imagine, must have been sorely distressed at the life his king was leading. He was seventy-three years of age when he became prime-minister, and I suppose he had enough to do to look after the money matters of the kingdom, and to settle the constant trouble with the people and the parliaments. In one way and another the king spent on his own pleasures and on his friends something like thirty million dollars of our money every year, and it was hard to get this sum out of an overtaxed people like the French, though these did number at that time some twenty million souls.

With the exception of a short period, when there was no war raging and the harvests were very good, the people were in dreadful poverty throughout this reign. They knew it was in part the king's fault, and when they met him driving in his splendid carriage, with the prancing horses and the golden harness, and the whiskered guards cantering round it, and some ravishing marquise by his side, they did not shout "Long live the king!" as Louis would have liked, but groaned in a hollow voice,

"Want! Famine! Bread!"

I have mentioned to you the parliaments which were held in several provinces, and which met, at set times, at Paris, Toulouse, Aix, Rouen, Rennes, and other towns. For a long time the chief business of these parliaments was to hear lawsuits; but ever since the time of Louis the Thirteenth they had tried, greatly against the wish of the kings, to take a hand in public affairs. The Parliament of Paris now drew up a paper in which they said that it was all wrong to lock up people in the Bastile without giving them a trial, to shave and imprison women who did not attend church, and to refuse to give the sacrament to dying persons who had notions of their own about the way to manage churches.

This brought a storm about the king's ears. Two cardinals and twenty-seven bishops hastened to Versailles to protest against the impudence of the parliament. Madame of Pompadour said she had never heard anything like it in her life. The king wrote a pettish letter to the parliament, begging to be let alone with his fair lady friends. Parliament refused to open the letter, but sent a written protest to Cardinal Fleury. The cardinal refused to receive it. Then fifty members of the parliament, all in their long scarlet robes, went to Marli, in fourteen carriages, and demanded to see the king. He would not see them. They drove home, and told how they had been shown the door. That night the cardinal arrested one hundred and thirty-nine members of the parliament, including the presidents, and locked them up in prison in distant parts of France. The pot, you see, was beginning to boil.

The Parliament of Rouen ordered an inquiry into the cause of the high price of bread. It was forbidden to ask questions, and when it insisted, it was dispersed by soldiers. The Parliament of Dijon sent a remonstrance to the king, reminding him that he ought to govern according to law; the members who drew up the remonstrance were put in jail. Just before the Parliament of Paris was dispersed by the king, it had dissolved the Jesuit society and closed the Jesuit houses. The Jesuits complained that they were persecuted. I suppose they had forgotten the way in which they had handled the Huguenots.

Troubles began to thicken round the king. Poor, plain, stupid, patient Mary, his wife, died; his son and his son's wife died also; the heir to the throne was a boy of eleven, who afterward became Louis the Sixteenth. The king had had a warning which reminded him of Henry the Fourth. One day, as he was walking down the grand staircase of the marble court at Versailles, a man ran against him and drove a penknife into his side. Louis clapped his hand to the wound, and drew it away, covered with blood. The man was seized.

It turned out that he was a crank named Damiens, who had no reason for seeking the king's death. The wound proved trifling. But Damiens was convicted of an attempt to kill the king, and, according to the old barbarous law, was sentenced to be torn to pieces by wild horses.

VOLTAIRE

When the day came for his execution—which was to take place in one of the great squares of Paris—the windows of every house in the square were rented to sight-seers. The highest nobles and the finest ladies of the court went to see the show. Enormous prices were paid for seats at windows. After the sentence was read, four wild horses were hitched to the ankles and wrists of the prisoner, and each was started, with shouts and lashes and goads, in a different direction. The horses were balky, and could not understand what was required of them. After they had made many starts and had spent over two hours in furious galloping, with men at their sides whipping them, they tore off the wretched man's arms and one of his legs. The other leg still remained attached to the body; the executioner had to cut the tendons before it could be separated. All this while Damiens lived and filled the air with his shrieks, while the nobles clapped their hands when the horses made a great rush, and the fair ladies fanned themselves and giggled to each other about their dresses and their flirtations.

Sorrow had made the king a mournful man. He had a good daughter who became a nun, and who besought her father to repent and amend his life. On the other hand, Madame Dubarry and the court were all for keeping up their deviltries, and would not hear of the king's reforming. Between the two the king was drawn now this way and now that; but the nun generally got the worst of the tussle. Louis was quite willing to pray and play at piety, but he couldn't give up his wicked pleasures. It was not till he fell ill of the small-pox that he shut his door in Madame Dubarry's face. On the 10th of May, 1774, a few weeks before the first congress of the American colonies met at Philadelphia, he died in great pain, with his features distorted by his terrible malady.

As many great Frenchmen flourished under Louis the Fifteenth as under Louis the Fourteenth; but their greatness showed itself in a different way. They cared less for writing poetry or even fine prose than for philosophy, science, and high politics. Voltaire, Rousseau, Montesquieu, Diderot, D'Alembert, and Buffon laid down the principles of free government with a force and clearness which have never been surpassed; they showed the iniquity of royal tyranny, and the absurdity of a privileged nobility, just at the time when the iniquity and the absurdity were most flourishing. Everybody—especially the court and the nobility—devoured their books, and quoted them to each other with praise. It never seemed to occur to them that some day the people might want to put these fine princi-

JEAN JACQUES ROUSSEAU

ples into practice. They were blind as bats to the meaning of the lesson they learned so well.

You may remember the reign of Louis the Fifteenth as the period when the French empire in North America ceased to exist. At the time he came to the throne France owned all Canada—which included the territory from Nova Scotia and New Brunswick to the great lakes—Ohio, Indiana, Illinois, and Michigan, both banks of the Mississippi to its mouth, and the country lying back of the west bank from the southern end of Louisiana to Northern Missouri. At the end of Louis's reign the French flag did not float over a foot of this territory. The whole of it had passed into the hands of the English, except Louisiana, which had been ceded to Spain.

LOUIS XVI. FROM A COIN

Chapter XL

LOUIS THE SIXTEENTH

A.D. 1774–1789

Louis the Sixteenth was twenty when he succeeded his grandfather as King of France, in 1774. He was an awkward, shy lad, slow of speech and timid in manner, fond of books, and delighted when he could shut himself up with a friend who was a locksmith, and forge and file locks and keys. His intentions were good, though his mind was narrow. He purposed to lead a decent life, and to do his duty by his people. His wife, Marie Antoinette of Austria, was a giddy girl, who adored dancing and fancy balls. She laughed at etiquette, and made an intimate of her dressmaker. She loved setting new fashions. Under her lead, the ladies of the court would sometimes wear simple white muslin gowns like their waiting-maids ; and then again they would crown themselves with lofty mountains of gauze, flowers, and feathers, so that their heads appeared to be in the middle of their bodies. Marie Antoinette had blue eyes, a fine figure, small hands and feet, a graceful carriage, and a most brilliant complexion. I am glad to be able to add that she was not the wicked woman which she was accused of being when the French turned against her, though people thought it an unfortunate omen when fifty-three persons were crushed to death at her coronation.

In order that you may realize the causes of the Revolution, of which I shall have to tell you the story in this and the succeeding chapters, you must know something of the condition of France during the reign of Louis the Sixteenth.

In the first place, you must understand that, outside of the cities, the people were either nobles, churchmen, or peasants. The two former classes were everything, the last class nothing. Most of the taxes which were collected by the kings to support their armies and their courts were paid by the peasants; the nobles and clergy paid little or nothing. Within their domains the nobles, and the clergy —who were often feudal nobles themselves—were masters of the peasants. The peasant was bound to send his wheat to be ground at the nobleman's mill, to have his grapes pressed at the nobleman's press, to have his loaves of bread baked in the nobleman's oven. The nobles kept deer and hares and rabbits and game birds which fed on the peasant's crops; he was forbidden to kill the game, and in some places he was forbidden to mow the grass for fear of breaking the partridge-eggs, while in others he was not allowed to manure his fields for fear of injuring the flavor of the game.

Each peasant was bound to put in so many days' work every year on the roads, and he was not paid for his work. He had to pay rent to the noble for the land he cultivated, though it was his own; when he sent his stuff to market, the noble collected a tax on it. The peasant could not sell his land without paying a fine to the noble. When he got into trouble, he had to take his lawsuit to a court of which the noble was the judge. When he crossed a bridge, he paid toll to the noble. When he had grown his crop and sold it, the Church came down upon him for its tithe.

The nobles and the clergy were generally fairly well educated for that age. The peasants knew nothing. Their mayors could not read or write; their tax-collectors could not add up a column of figures. Between the times of Henry the Fourth and Louis the Sixteenth, the land-tax, which was called the taille, had increased tenfold. It was levied on parishes as a whole; if one land-owner would not or could not pay, the others had to make up the deficiency. I need not tell you that the nobles and the priests came to despise people who were so ignorant and so spiritless as to submit to such wrongs. They regarded the peasants as brutes.

A noble was free to thrash a peasant with his heavy hunting-whip, and the peasant was so cowed that he never struck back. The noble took from the peasant his wife or his daughter, if he fancied either. The poor, dark-faced grubber of the earth, in his ragged clothes and his wooden shoes, had to stand it. When the crops failed and the peasants starved, a noble governor of Dijon told them that the grass was coming up finely; they had better go and browse. A noble could order one of his peasants to spend the night in beating the ponds with a stick, to prevent the frogs from croaking and disturbing his noble sleep.

In the cities, there was another class of Frenchmen, who were called burgesses. These were above day-laborers, and yet below churchmen and noblemen—they were merchants; shopkeepers; makers of cloth, tools, bricks, and iron ware; lawyers, doctors, druggists, bankers, and the like. They were not as ignorant as the peasants, and many of them were rich. But they could not associate with the nobles, and were an inferior class—not to be beaten with hunting-whips, but to be made to keep their distance—and who, when they visited a noble, stood in the hall and were jeered at by lackeys. They were not often suffered to interfere, or to have any opinion on public affairs.

When Louis the Sixteenth settled down to the government of the country, he began to root out some of the more grievous wrongs which had been handed down from former kings. He put a stop to torture. He forbade further interference with the Huguenots. He abolished the law which forbade a peasant-girl from marrying without

LYONS

the consent of the noble on whose land she lived. He improved the prisons. One of the commonest offences of that day was smuggling, which is the natural fruit of bad tariffs. There is a story, which I believe to be true, of a man named Monnerat, who was falsely accused of smuggling. He was arrested, thrust into an underground dungeon, and kept there for six weeks on bread and water; then he was removed to another prison, where he lay twenty months without trial. When he got out, he easily proved that he had been taken for some one else, but he got no redress from those who had so cruelly wronged him.

But the more the king tried to reform wrongs, the more angry the people grew at their having existed. They were awaking to their rights, and began to talk very loudly indeed. They first tried what could be done through their parliaments. These bodies spoke out fearlessly, and even threatened. Louis had a succession of ministers—Maurepas, Turgot, Necker, Calonne, and Brienne; Turgot was the best of them. Each in his turn tried to pacify the parliaments or to put them down. Neither thing could be done.

In Brittany a parliament met at Rennes. The king ordered it to disperse; it refused. The king sent a regiment to enforce his orders. Fifteen members of the parliament fought duels with fifteen officers, and a committee of twelve members went to Versailles to protest. When the twelve were locked up in the Bastile, eighteen more members went to demand them back; and these not returning, fifty more followed them to the king. Meantime the brave Breton people came trooping into Rennes from north and south and east and west, all with swords and pikes and guns in their hands.

At Grenoble, orders from the king commanded the parliament to disperse. The church-bells rang the tocsin, and the mountaineers of Dauphiné came hurrying into Grenoble. The king's troops fell back, and the mob, seizing the governor, swore they would hang him to his own chandelier if he did not convene the parliament in the city-hall that very day and hour.

The Parliament of Paris had a dispute with the king over money matters and taxes. The king had his plan for raising money. The parliament declared that the country was drifting into bankruptcy, and refused to agree to the king's plan. He declared that he would put it in force whether they liked it or not. M. d'Espremesnil shouted that this was despotism. Another member, De Montsa-

BRETON PEASANTS

bert, moved an inquiry into what had been done with the last money raised by taxes.

On the next night, while the parliament was in session, every member in his scarlet gown and with a very grave face, an officer of the guards entered, and said he held a warrant for the arrest of Espremesnil and Montsabert. Would the members present kindly point them out? A member started to his feet and cried,

"We are all Espremesnils and Montsaberts. Find them if you can."

The officer retired. Returning next day with a doorkeeper who knew every member by sight, he bade him point out the men he was in search of. The doorkeeper, looking Espremesnil and Montsabert straight in the eye, said he could not see them.

The king dissolved the parliament and forbade it to meet again. Louis had a scheme of his own. He called an assembly of the Notables.

This extraordinary body consisted of a hundred and forty-four members—seven princes of the blood, fourteen bishops and archbishops, thirty-six dukes and other noblemen, fifty councillors and magistrates, all appointed by the king, twelve deputies of districts, and twenty-five city officials. I need not tell you that this assembly did not settle the troubles of the nation.

There was one man in France who understood the situation. This was a great big man, with a red, blotched, pock-marked face, a head of hair like a lion's mane, and a voice like thunder; a man who, when he spoke, made other men tremble, he looked so like an angry giant. His name was Mirabeau. He had led a riotous youth, and had spent years in prisons to which he had been unjustly condemned. He was now boiling over with wrath, and spluttered in his rage,

"We must have a meeting of the States-General, and we must have it at once."

Straightway all France, with one voice, demanded the meeting of the States-General. This body had not met since the time of Mary of Medicis, one hundred and twenty-five years before. It consisted of representatives of the nobles, the clergy, and the third estate, by which term the people were meant. It would not now be considered a fairly representative body; it embraced delegates from two classes which had no right to separate representation, and it did not embrace any one who could fairly speak for the peasants and the workingmen. But, such as it was, it was the nearest approach to a real congress which France had ever had, or could hope to have at that time. You will see, as we go on, that it did good and thorough work. The day of its meeting was set for May 2d, 1789.

Before we begin its history, I must tell you something of two rather important events which occurred before it met.

LOUIS XVI

The American Revolution began with the battle of Lexington in April, 1775; the Declaration of Independence was issued on July 4th, 1776. On April 17th, 1778, a French squadron sailed from Toulon, in France, to aid the United States in obtaining their independence. A gallant young Frenchman, of whom you will hear more—General Lafayette—had already joined Washington's staff. For three years the French helped your forefathers with men, ships, and money, and at the surrender of Yorktown their services were one of the chief causes of the victory. The French took the side of the United States in order to feed their ancient grudge against England, and not from love for the revolted colonies. But perhaps it is not best to inquire too curiously into motives. It is enough for you to know that France was our friend when we sorely needed a friend, and that it will become you to be grateful to her accordingly.

The other event of which this history must say something is a story of a necklace.

On the 18th of August, 1785, Cardinal Rohan, a member of one of the noblest families in France, was arrested on his way to the church where he was going to celebrate mass, and was taken into the king's private room, where Louis sat very stern, with his wife Marie Antoinette sitting opposite him and sterner still.

"Cardinal," said the king, "you bought some diamonds of Boehmer?"

"Yes, sire."

"What did you do with them?"

"I understood they had been sent to the queen." And the cardinal began to tremble and to turn red and white.

"Who told you they were for the queen?"

"A lady," stammered the cardinal; "the Countess of La Mothe-Valois."

"Did it seem natural to you," asked the queen bitterly, "that I should give such a commission to Madame de Valois, whom I despise, to be executed by you, to whom I have not spoken for years?"

"I have here," said the cardinal, with much confusion, "a letter from your majesty on the subject." And he handed the letter to the king. One glance at it was sufficient.

"The letter is not in the queen's handwriting, and the signature is a forgery."

The cardinal replied that he was so overcome that he could not stand; might he retire into the next room?

That night he was taken to the Bastile. The story of

the diamond necklace was this: It was worth three quarters of a million dollars of our money. The Countess of Valois coveted it, and begged the cardinal to buy it for her. He did not care to spend so much money, but he bought it, telling the jeweller it was for the queen. Whether Madame de Valois deceived him, and persuaded him that she had an order to buy it for the queen, or whether he conspired with her to use the queen's credit to cheat the jeweller, was never rightly known. The cardinal was tried before the Parliament of Paris and was acquitted; Madame de Valois was convicted, and was sentenced to be whipped, branded, and imprisoned. Meanwhile the necklace disappeared—the stones were probably sold separately. The queen never forgave the cardinal; and, on the other hand, the people never forgave the queen for buying, as they supposed, seven-hundred-thousand-dollar necklaces when the poor were starving.

MIRABEAU

CHAPTER XLI

MIRABEAU

A.D. 1789–1791

IN the early months of 1789 the French people elected members of the States-General. The elections passed off quietly; but at Paris the shop of a man named Revillon was robbed, because he was said to have declared that fifteen cents a day was pay enough for a working-man; and at Aix, in Provence, a hot-headed noble ordered the troops to fire at the people, because they insisted on voting for Mirabeau. The nobles had refused to choose Mirabeau, though he was a marquis; so he hired a store, set up a sign, "Mirabeau, Dry-goods Dealer," and was chosen as a deputy of the third estate. It had been settled that the States-General should consist of twelve hundred members, three hundred to represent the nobles, three hundred to represent the clergy, and six hundred to represent the third estate, or, in plain words, the people.

On the 2d of May the king received them at Versailles. The morning was wet; the nobles and the clergy got out of their carriages and entered the palace, leaving the members of the third estate standing outside in the rain.

On the following Sunday the members attended mass together, the nobility in garments of cloth of gold, with silk cloaks, lace neckties, and plumed hats; the common clergy in surplices, mantles, and square caps; the bishops in purple robes; and the deputies of the people in their common every-day clothes, and looking shabby by the side of the others. The king and queen and court were there in splendid attire, flashing with diamonds; the streets leading to the church were hung with tapestry and purple velvet spangled with lilies, and lined with troops whose bands played martial airs.

When the States-General met for the despatch of business, it appeared that one great hall had been provided for the general meetings of all three classes, another hall for the separate use of the clergy, a third for the separate use of the nobility, but none for the separate use of the third estate.

"Oh, well," said Mirabeau, "we'll sit in the common hall."

As it turned out, this occupation of the common hall by the third estate made the nobles and clergy figure as outsiders.

The name of States-General appearing cumbersome, that of National Assembly was adopted on the suggestion of the Abbé Sieyès. The body was sometimes called the Constitutional Assembly; in this country it would have been called a constitutional convention. Then the members of the third estate, finding that the members from the Church and the nobility raised objections to uniting with them for the business they had to do, declared that they themselves were the Assembly, and the other orders might join them or not, as they pleased. On this the king took possession of the hall, and when the members approached it next day they found the doors locked and soldiers guarding them.

Next door to the Assembly Hall was a tennis-court—a dark, bare room without seats. In that room the members took refuge, and there they declared that, wherever they chose to meet, they would remain the National Assembly. They pledged themselves to each other never to separate till they had done the work the people had set them to do.

Three days afterward the king ordered them to meet him in the Assembly Hall. There he told them that he intended to govern the kingdom in his own way, and he bade them go home. Then he stalked out.

The nobility and part of the clergy followed, but not a member of the third estate budged or opened his mouth. A king's officer spoke up:

"You have heard the orders of the king. Go!"

Said Mirabeau: "We will not go. Tell your master that we are here by the will of the people, and we will not be driven away except by bayonets."

Pretty soon the nobility and the clergy got frightened. Some of them went to the Assembly, and of their own free will gave up their privileges and agreed to pay their taxes and submit to the laws like other people. Numbers of soldiers of the French Guards began to desert and to take the side of the Assembly. But the king had gathered round him several regiments of Germans and Swiss, who fought for pay and cared nothing for the rights of the people. A procession, marching through the streets of Paris, was fired upon by German soldiers, and several people killed or wounded. This was first blood.

The people of Paris sacked the gunsmiths' stores and armed themselves with muskets which they found in the vaults of the Invalides. With these they attacked the Bastile, on July 14th, 1789.

The Bastile was a fort which had been long used for a prison. Its walls were nine feet thick, and it had eight towers which overlooked Paris. Soldiers said that it could not be taken without heavy cannon, and the people had none. But there were only about one hundred soldiers in the work, and a mob of many thousand Parisians surrounded

BREAKING INTO THE INVALIDES

it, all panting with rage. They literally broke into it by force of numbers. The governor, a brave old soldier named Delaunay, had refused to surrender and had tried to blow the fort up. But at last, when the last drawbridge had been lowered, and the roaring, surging mob were pouring like a flood into the work, he hoisted the white flag. The invaders scattered all over the prison in search of prisoners; they found seven of them in prison cells; one had been there for thirty years, another since his childhood. They also found on the walls piteous stories that had been scratched by prisoners who had died there. The sight of these pitiful inscriptions and of the poor captives, gaunt and pale from their long imprisonment, so infuriated the people that they wrenched Governor Delaunay from the guards who had him in charge, chopped him in pieces with axes and knives, and set his head on the point of a pike.

That night, as the king was sleeping, after planning with his courtiers an attack on Paris at the head of his Germans and Swiss, an attendant shook him till he woke and told him the news.

"Why!" said Louis, yawning, "this is a rebellion."

"Sire," said the attendant, "it is a revolution."

Next day he hastened to the Assembly, prepared to yield everything. He entered the hall with no guard. "Gentlemen," said he, "you have been afraid of me. I put my trust in you."

But the people had got over being fooled with smooth words. A national guard was raised in Paris, and every member wore a blue-and-white cockade. The king put one on his own hat, so as to be in the fashion. The people cheered mightily when they saw it on his head; but that did not prevent their catching Foulon, one of his ministers—who, like a noble of whom I have told you, had said that the people might eat grass if they were hungry—tying a necklace of thistles round his neck and a bunch of grass round his waist, tearing him from the hall where he was going to be tried, dragging him down the stairs, now head down, now head up, hanging his half dead body to a lamp-post, and marching round Paris with his bloody head on the end of a pike. The French were dreadfully in earnest by this time; all the piled-up passion of centuries was boiling over at once.

In the country parts, where the peasants had borne such dreadful hardships from their feudal lords, the same things were done. Castles were stormed, gutted, and burned; in many cases the owners and their families were massacred, I am afraid, with dreadful cruelties. In larger books than this, you will read touching stories of the rescue of ladies of noble family by faithful servants from furious peasants, who would be satisfied with nothing short of the extinc-

STORMING THE BASTILE

tion of the class which had oppressed them so long and so mercilessly.

All this while the Assembly was trying to make new laws for France. It was found impossible to mend the old ones. A young man of whom you will hear more—his name was Robespierre—proposed to build from the ground up, and though he was a poor speaker, with a harsh voice and a bad manner, his head was so clear that the Assembly paid a great deal of attention to him. The king seemed to be paralyzed; he went about in a feeble way, asking advice of every one he met; the queen was far more of a man; she gathered foreign soldiers and young French noblemen round her, and made ready for the death-grapple that she saw coming.

She was not the only woman who was at work. Bread was frightfully scarce in Paris. Women could not feed their children. One day, when they found there was no bread at the bakers', a crowd of women collected together, and, arming themselves with bludgeons, broomsticks, cutlasses, hatchets, and pikes, marched to Versailles, under the lead of a vagabond named Maillard, to see the king. As they marched other women joined them, and so did some men. They were a sorry crowd, wild-eyed, bedraggled, dirty, coarse, foul-mouthed, many of them drunken, and most of them barefoot. What made them so terrible was that they were hungry. The king received a few of them and tried to pacify them with sweet words. He clasped one virago to his royal bosom. A regiment of life-guards endeavored to push them back without opening fire, but lost several of its men. At last General Lafayette, who had returned from this country and was the darling of the people, arrived at Versailles, got most of the women back to Paris, where bread had been provided for them, and dispersed the mob of men who had followed them. He could only do this, however, by undertaking that the king should go back from Versailles to Paris and stay there.

The king and queen started from Versailles at one in the afternoon. One hundred members of the Assembly followed them in carriages. In front of the king's carriage marched the remnant of the furious mob of women of the day before, waving pikes and singing horrible songs. Before them straggled men carrying two heads of life-guardsmen on the ends of pikes. Behind the king rode his guards, unarmed; and all along the road Lafayette had scattered soldiers to guard his majesty against a sudden attack.

DEATH OF GOVERNOR DELAUNAY, OF THE BASTILE

Considering how Louis had fought against returning to Paris, where the mob frightened him, I am a little surprised at his address to the mayor when he reached the City Hall.

"I return with confidence," he said, "into the midst of my people of Paris."

There was one man in whom the king really had confidence. That was Mirabeau. Both king and queen saw him frequently in secret at night, and took counsel with him. It has been said that he was in their pay. I think it likely that he took money from them, because he was always wasteful and needy; but I hope that what he did for them was prompted by sympathy and not bribery. The "tiger that has had the small-pox," as Mirabeau called himself, would naturally feel proud of protecting a king.

Whatever his motive was, it was soon going to disappear, for Mirabeau was dying. The nearer death came, the more powerful he grew. In the Assembly he had always been a tower of strength—he was now master. Under the fire of his eye and the thunder of his voice the boldest quailed. His doctors told him he must die if he did not abstain from wine and work. He drank heavily that very day, and spoke five times in the Assembly. On the 20th of April, 1791, he bade a friend open the window of his room.

"I am going," he said, "to die to-day. Sprinkle me with flowers, fill the air with music and perfume, so that I can sink quietly into everlasting sleep."

They gave him a soothing potion, his head dropped to one side, and he was gone.

When he was dead, every one declared that he was the only man who could have pulled France through the present agony. Everybody went to his funeral. All Paris put on mourning and wept. He was buried in the Pantheon as a national hero. But a few years afterward, when some one found his letters to the queen, showing his tender sympathy for the poor woman in her sorrow, the angry mob of Paris called him a traitor, tore open his tomb, and scattered his ashes to the winds.

CHAPTER XLII

THE KING'S FLIGHT, IMPRISONMENT, AND DEATH

A.D. 1791-1793

THE king returned to Paris, to find himself a prisoner. The Assembly believed that he was plotting with foreigners to put down the French people by force of arms—which was, in fact, the case—and kept watch of him accordingly. It had intercepted despatches of his and of the queen's, which showed that, while he was professing to love the people, he hated them in his heart, and was only waiting for an opportunity to set his foot on their neck once more. A few hot-headed members of the Assembly said as much in their speeches; their more prudent colleagues kept silent, but they thought all the more. I am not surprised that Louis came to believe that his life was not safe at Paris, and resolved to run away. But it was not in him to be honest or truthful. While he was making his plans for flight, he told every one that he would stay in Paris to the bitter end. He assured General Lafayette that he would remain where he was; he told his minister, who told the Assembly, that he had never dreamed of leaving France.

Nevertheless, in the night of June 20th, 1791, disguised in the gray coat and periwig of a valet, with the queen and his sister, his children and their governess, he left Paris in a travelling-carriage from the Porte St. Martin. He had for escort three life-guardsmen disguised as servants; and a stanch friend of the queen's, Monsieur de Bouillé, had stationed parties of troops on the road which he was to follow. When the next morning dawned, he was far on his way to Flanders.

At nine in the morning the Assembly met. Almost

everybody knew of the king's escape, and nobody seemed to mind it. The Assembly discussed the event quite calmly, and simply sent for the ministers of state, and directed them to take their orders from it instead of from the king. In their secret hearts the Assembly thought it was a good riddance. He was so false a creature that they foresaw they might have to deal with him roughly some day. As a matter of form they directed Lafayette, who commanded the National Guard, to have him pursued and brought back. But privately they all hoped that he had got so good a start of his pursuers that he would be able to cross the border before he could be overtaken. He was, in fact, at Chalons, on the Marne, when Lafayette's troopers started, and was pushing on as fast as fresh horses could draw him.

But it was not the fate of this man to be saved. At St. Menehould, a few miles from Chalons, Louis put his head out of the carriage and was recognized by Drouet, the son of the postmaster and a strong Republican. Drouet took horse, rode madly through the night to Varennes, on the little river Aire, and warned the National Guard that the king was coming, on his way to join the enemies of France. Bouillé, the queen's friend, had some hussars in the place; but they refused to fight against the people. When the king's carriage came lumbering up and crossed the river bridge, it found the road blockaded by a carriage which Drouet had upset on purpose; a crowd of men, with loaded muskets and torches flaring in the black night, barred the way.

Said the captain of the national guard of Varennes: "You are the king?"

Said Louis: "I am not. I assure you that you are mistaken."

But others came up who recognized Louis from his likeness on silver coins, and he had to confess that he was the king.

While the crowd were discussing what should be done with him, Lafayette's aide-de-camp, who had ridden faster than the leaders of the Assembly intended, appeared at Varennes with orders to bring back the royal family to Paris. The people of Varennes were sorry for the king and queen, whose grief was touching. A baker's wife would have hid them, if she could. But the National Guard was firm; Lafayette's guards were approaching; at eight in the morning the carriage, with six fresh horses, started on the return journey to Paris.

HOUSE OF THE JACOBIN CLUB

The weather was hot. The carriage was eight days on the way. When it entered a town or a village the people turned out in a body to see it pass. Some jeered, but more were sorry, seeing what was coming. When the king entered Paris, he saw the walls placarded with a notice posted by order of the Assembly:

"Whoever applauds the king shall be whipped; whoever insults him shall be hanged."

took refuge, and there they declared that, wherever they chose to meet, they would remain the National Assembly. They pledged themselves to each other never to separate till they had done the work the people had set them to do.

Three days afterward the king ordered them to meet him in the Assembly Hall. There he told them that he intended to govern the kingdom in his own way, and he bade them go home. Then he stalked out.

The nobility and part of the clergy followed, but not a member of the third estate budged or opened his mouth. A king's officer spoke up:

"You have heard the orders of the king. Go!"

Said Mirabeau: "We will not go. Tell your master that we are here by the will of the people, and we will not be driven away except by bayonets."

Pretty soon the nobility and the clergy got frightened. Some of them went to the Assembly, and of their own free will gave up their privileges and agreed to pay their taxes and submit to the laws like other people. Numbers of soldiers of the French Guards began to desert and to take the side of the Assembly. But the king had gathered round him several regiments of Germans and Swiss, who fought for pay and cared nothing for the rights of the people. A procession, marching through the streets of Paris, was fired upon by German soldiers, and several people killed or wounded. This was first blood.

The people of Paris sacked the gunsmiths' stores and armed themselves with muskets which they found in the vaults of the Invalides. With these they attacked the Bastile, on July 14th, 1789.

The Bastile was a fort which had been long used for a prison. Its walls were nine feet thick, and it had eight towers which overlooked Paris. Soldiers said that it could not be taken without heavy cannon, and the people had none. But there were only about one hundred soldiers in the work, and a mob of many thousand Parisians surrounded

BREAKING INTO THE INVALIDES

it, all panting with rage. They literally broke into it by force of numbers. The governor, a brave old soldier named Delaunay, had refused to surrender and had tried to blow the fort up. But at last, when the last drawbridge had been lowered, and the roaring, surging mob were pouring like a flood into the work, he hoisted the white flag. The invaders scattered all over the prison in search of prisoners; they found seven of them in prison cells; one had been there for thirty years, another since his childhood. They also found on the walls piteous stories that had been scratched by prisoners who had died there. The sight of these pitiful inscriptions and of the poor captives, gaunt and pale from their long imprisonment, so infuriated the people that they wrenched Governor Delaunay from the guards who had him in charge, chopped him in pieces with axes and knives, and set his head on the point of a pike.

That night, as the king was sleeping, after planning with his courtiers an attack on Paris at the head of his Germans and Swiss, an attendant shook him till he woke and told him the news.

"Why!" said Louis, yawning, "this is a rebellion."

"Sire," said the attendant, "it is a revolution."

Next day he hastened to the Assembly, prepared to yield everything. He entered the hall with no guard. "Gentlemen," said he, "you have been afraid of me. I put my trust in you."

But the people had got over being fooled with smooth words. A national guard was raised in Paris, and every member wore a blue-and-white cockade. The king put one on his own hat, so as to be in the fashion. The people cheered mightily when they saw it on his head; but that did not prevent their catching Foulon, one of his ministers—who, like a noble of whom I have told you, had said that the people might eat grass if they were hungry—tying a necklace of thistles round his neck and a bunch of grass round his waist, tearing him from the hall where he was going to be tried, dragging him down the stairs, now head down, now head up, hanging his half dead body to a lamp-post, and marching round Paris with his bloody head on the end of a pike. The French were dreadfully in earnest by this time; all the piled-up passion of centuries was boiling over at once.

In the country parts, where the peasants had borne such dreadful hardships from their feudal lords, the same things were done. Castles were stormed, gutted, and burned; in many cases the owners and their families were massacred, I am afraid, with dreadful cruelties. In larger books than this, you will read touching stories of the rescue of ladies of noble family by faithful servants from furious peasants, who would be satisfied with nothing short of the extinc-

STORMING THE BASTILE

tion of the class which had oppressed them so long and so mercilessly.

All this while the Assembly was trying to make new laws for France. It was found impossible to mend the old ones. A young man of whom you will hear more—his name was Robespierre—proposed to build from the ground up, and though he was a poor speaker, with a harsh voice and a bad manner, his head was so clear that the Assembly paid

Paris was in danger. Then the mob grew more frantic than ever, and many people—priests, friends of the king and queen, nobles and their servants—were thrust into jail. On Sunday, September 2d, a whisper went round that the jails were not safe. In every prison the jailer took away the prisoners' table-knives; most of them sent their families away.

You remember the procession of hungry, drunken, and bedraggled women at Versailles in 1789. That procession was led by a brutal vagabond named Maillard. This Maillard now collected three hundred ruffians like himself, fell upon carriages in which twenty-four priests were being moved from one prison to another, and murdered every one. Then he went from prison to prison and did the same thing everywhere. The jailer would be bidden to bring out his prisoners. In the horrible confusion which prevailed at that time, he would suppose that Maillard had authority for what he was doing and would obey. Then a form of mock trial would take place in the prison yard: Maillard would say—in a formula which had been agreed upon between him and his fellow-ruffians—"Take him to La Force" or "Set him at liberty." The prisoner would pass through the wicket, and, once outside, the gang, with sword and pike and hatchet, would make an end of him. In this way, on that 2d and 3d of September, about a thousand poor prisoners were done to death with savage cruelty by Maillard and his three hundred; and five or six thousand more were murdered away from the prisons.

Among those who perished was the beautiful Marie de Lamballe, the queen's friend and the sweetest woman at court. As she was going through the farce of a trial, a drummer-boy struck her down with a stick. She was quickly despatched with sword and knives; her body was cut in pieces, and each piece carried around Paris on the point of a pike.

Another cruel death was that of the Archbishop of Arles, an old, white-haired priest. They dragged him out into the yard.

"Are you the archbishop?" asked a ruffian, whose hands and face were smeared with blood.

"I am," said the priest intrepidly.

"Then take that," said the assassin, striking him on the head with his sword. Again and again he struck, till the old man fell; then a pike was driven into his breast with such force that the iron head came off and put an end to his agony.

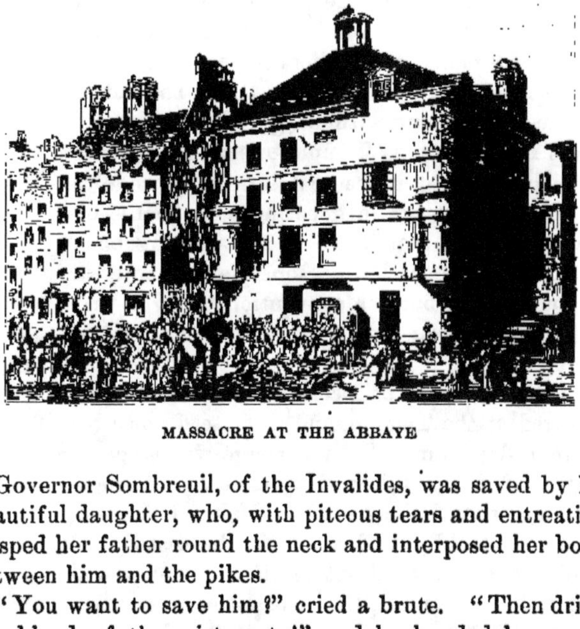

MASSACRE AT THE ABBAYE

Governor Sombreuil, of the Invalides, was saved by his beautiful daughter, who, with piteous tears and entreaties, clasped her father round the neck and interposed her body between him and the pikes.

"You want to save him?" cried a brute. "Then drink the blood of the aristocrats!" and he handed her a can which he had filled with blood.

She drank, and her father was released.

When the news of the massacre reached people's knowledge, a cry of horror arose. The Assembly ordered the murderers to be put on trial. The Commune, which had given money to Maillard and his gang, began to make excuses. The clubs were silent. The army boiled over with rage. Lafayette threw up his command. It looked as though the infamous wretches who had committed the murders of September had wrecked the revolution, though they were only a handful and had no one behind them. The fact was that such confusion reigned that no one knew whom to obey, and things had got to grow worse before they could get better.

The massacre took place on the 2d and 3d of September. On the 21st of the same month the Legislative Assembly, finding itself unable to restore order, made way for a new assembly, which was called the National Assembly. This new body abolished royalty in France. But it had yet to decide what was to be done with King Louis, who, with his family, was in the gloomy Temple prison, guarded by rough jailers, who thought it was patriotic to be rude to them. It spent many weeks in debating, and finally, on December 3d, it decided that it would try the king on a charge of treason to the nation. Robespierre wanted a sentence without a trial, but the convention thought that a king should have a trial like other persons accused of crime.

At eleven in the morning of December 11th the mayor of Paris appeared at the Temple, and in a stern voice ordered Louis to follow him. Their carriage was escorted by troopers, preceded and followed by cannon. At half-past two the king entered the Assembly Hall. The president looked at him coldly, and bade him be seated and answer the questions that were put to him. He answered them all; then he demanded the assistance of counsel. This was granted, but when the trial adjourned for the day he was not allowed to see his family. They went to bed in an agony of suspense, not knowing what had happened. The trial lasted fifteen days; and after that, for several days, the members of the convention debated. Vergniaud and the Girondins would have saved the king if they could have found a way to do so without failing in their idea of their duty to the people. Robespierre and the Jacobins were for his immediate execution, guilty or not guilty. Every one was curious to see how the Duke of Orleans, the king's cousin (who now called himself Philip Equality, in order to curry favor with the people), would vote on the question.

PARTING BETWEEN THE KING AND HIS FAMILY

The vote was taken on the 15th of January, 1793, and Louis was found guilty by 683 votes out of 749 members. Philip Equality was one of the 683. On the following day the vote was taken on the punishment which should be inflicted. The voting began at half-past seven in the morning and lasted all that day, all through the next night, and all the next day. When the vote was counted, President Vergniaud rose and in a solemn voice declared,

"Seven hundred and twenty-one votes have been cast. Two hundred and eighty votes are for imprisonment or exile; seventy-two for death with long reprieves; three hundred and sixty-one for death unconditionally. I therefore declare that the punishment of Louis Capet is death."

Philip Equality had sneaked up to the voting-desk, and, with the ashen hue of a coward on his cheek, voted death.

All through the thirty-six hours' session ladies had been present, eating ices and oranges and drinking liquors. The gallery was full of people who brought bottles of wine, and kept betting on the course of the voting, and clapping and stamping when the vote pleased them. Many slept, and snored while the life and death of him who had been master of France were trembling in the balance.

Louis was alone in his room when his lawyers entered to give him the bad news. Before they spoke he said, with a sad smile,

"There is a legend in our family that, before a death, a lady dressed all in white appears to the one who is to die—I saw the white lady last night."

The king was allowed to send for a priest and to see his family. His wife, his sister, and his son threw themselves into his arms, and for an hour and a half they spoke in broken whispers mingled with sobs. Their grief was so touching that the brutal guards drew off, so as not to overhear what they said.

At five in the morning of January 21st, all the troops in Paris were under arms, and in the dark morning fog drums were beating, bugles blowing, horses tramping, and heavy guns rumbling over the pavement. Louis rose early, shaved and dressed himself, heard mass, and took the communion. At half-past eight a tremendous clatter of hoofs and wheels resounded through the street on which the Temple stood, the door of the prison was flung open, and San-

EXECUTION OF LOUIS XVI

terre, the brewer, in gorgeous uniform and with a savage frown on his face, appeared in the king's room at the head of ten soldiers.

"You have come for me?" asked the king.

"Yes," was the curt answer.

A servant offered him his overcoat.

"I shall not need it," said Louis. "Give me my hat. Now, sir"—to Santerre—"lead on."

The carriage, which was surrounded by troops, took two hours to traverse the silent crowd in the streets, on the way to the place of execution. Louis conversed calmly with the priest and the brewer. When the carriage stopped he alighted, pushed back the guards who would have undressed him, threw off his coat, hat, and neckcloth, and opened his shirt; then, with a firm tread, he mounted the scaffold and began to speak to the vast crowd of people.

19

"I die innocent of the crimes which have been laid to my charge. I pardon those who have caused my death, and I pray to God—"

Just then Santerre signalled the drums to beat; they drowned his voice, and at the same time cries in the impatient crowd summoned executioner Sanson to do his duty. He and two assistants roughly seized Louis, threw him on the plank, shoved the plank under the groove, the blade of the guillotine fell, and the king's head rolled into a basket, while his blood spurted upon the boards and trickled upon the sawdust under the platform.

Paris was uncomfortable all that day. Shops were closed and shutters put on the windows. People were horror-stricken. Even Republicans were shocked, and the king had still some friends who were furious. The day before, as Lepelletier, the President of the Parliament of Paris, was sitting down to eat his dinner at a restaurant, a life-guardsman approached him and asked,

"Art thou Lepelletier, the villain who voted for the death of the king?"

"I am Lepelletier," said the president, "but I am not a villain."

"Take that for thy reward!" said the man, plunging his sword into Lepelletier's side.

Pieces of the dead king's clothes and handkerchiefs dipped in his blood sold at enormous prices and were treasured as relics. The members of the convention did not sleep soundly for many nights afterward. The wives of some of them swore they would never, never lay their heads on pillows beside theirs.

France was probably unsafe as long as Louis lived. He could not resist the temptation to conspire with her enemies in order to keep the kingly power. Let us thank Providence that in this country there are no dangers which require such desperate remedies.

Chapter XLIII

MARAT AND CHARLOTTE CORDAY

A.D. 1792–1793

Among the members of the convention who had sentenced Louis to death, some, such as the Girondists, whose leader was Vergniaud, did so from a sense of duty to their country; others, like most of the Jacobins, acted from pure hatred of kings because they were kings. Of these Robespierre was the leader—I shall tell you of him in the next chapter; but the most active and noisy of the king-killers was John Paul Marat.

This man had been a monster from his birth. He was only five feet high, with a prodigiously large head and a hideous face. He had wild, glaring eyes and a mouth gaping like the mouth of a toad. He affected to glory in uncleanness, and went about in a ragged coat, a broken hat, boots without stockings, a pair of old leather breeches, and a dirty shirt which was always open, showing his yellow chest. He lived in the midst of filth and squalor, not because he liked them, but because he wanted to show how poor and humble he was.

At the time the troubles in France began he came to Paris from his native home, and started a newspaper which he called the *Friend of the People.* In this paper, which was shockingly brutal and indecent, he wrote articles day after day telling the people of Paris that all would be well with them if they killed nobles and priests enough. At first he thought about six hundred of the best people would do, but afterward he raised his figure to two hundred and seventy thousand; and sometimes he seemed to think that everybody should be killed except himself and the subscribers to his paper.

Now, you know that a person of this kind would not give us any trouble at all. We should lock him up in a well-conducted insane asylum and keep him there. But, a hundred years ago, in France people were unsettled in their minds. They felt sore over the wrongs they had suffered and nervous about the trouble they were going through. There were numbers of people who were not sure whether there might not be some truth in Marat's bloody doctrines. When he kept preaching day after day that all would be well if throats were cut, people's reason was so shaken by the astonishing changes that were taking place around them that they didn't know but he might be right. So Marat came to be a most mischievous, as well as a most abominable, creature.

He made so much noise that he became a popular leader, and was appointed a member of the Paris Commune. It was he who put into Maillard's head the idea of massacring the prisoners, but his notion was different from Maillard's—he was for setting fire to the prisons and burning the prisoners alive. At one time Lafayette resolved to lock him up, but he escaped. Then the Assembly ordered his arrest, but Robespierre stood his friend, and he went free. Then he became president of the Jacobin Club, and it became very dangerous indeed to quarrel with him. He insisted on forcing his way into the Assembly and lecturing the members on their weakness in sparing lives. He was one of the loudest bawlers for the execution of the king. His speeches, like his articles, were all on one text, "Kill! kill! kill!"

He was so mad on the subject of killing that one day, when he forced himself into the Assembly and disgusted the members till one of them proposed his arrest, he drew a pistol and threatened to kill himself then and there. You may perhaps regret that he was not allowed to fulfil his threat.

Of course, as all the French had not lost their heads, and

CHARLOTTE CORDAY IN PRISON

indeed as most of them, at bottom, continued to distinguish between right and wrong, there were many who loathed and despised Marat, without being on the side of the king. Among these was a young lady whose name was Charlotte Corday.

She was a motherless girl who lived with an aunt in the pretty old town of Caen, in Normandy. Her people were poor, but Charlotte had been well-educated; she spent days sitting by a fountain in the sunny square of her aunt's house, poring over books, and trying to understand the stirring times in which she lived. She had no girl friend, and though in secret she loved a young soldier named Franquelin, they were not engaged; she had never told her love. She was tall, with brown hair; her face was pleasant, rather than beautiful; she was very straight and strong, as the Norman girls generally are. This girl now resolved to give her life to rid France of the monster Marat.

On a sunny morning in July, while the lizards were gliding along the top of the stone fences, and the big Norman cows were lying down in the fat grass after their breakfast, Charlotte came out of her home, handing a toy to a neighbor's child.

"Here, Robert," said she, "this is for you. Be a good boy and kiss me; you will never see me again."

At seven in the evening on July 13th, she left her lodging in Paris for the broken-down shanty in which Marat lived. She wore a plain white gown, with a silk scarf round her neck. On her head was a Norman cap, fastened with a broad green ribbon, and with a lace trimming which fluttered in the wind. Her hair hung loose down her neck. In her dress she hid a long, sharp knife with a black handle. She walked with steady step and asked for Marat.

He was in his bath, which was covered with a filthy cloth, spotted with ink. His head, shoulders, and right arm were all that could be seen of him; in front of him a board covered with papers lay across the bath. When he heard Charlotte's voice, saying that she came from Caen and wished to see Marat, he shouted,

"Let the citizeness in."

As she stood by the bath he questioned her about Caen. She answered him simply, giving him the names of the Girondins who were there—people whom she loved and whom he hated. As he wrote down their names he ground his teeth and growled, licking his cruel lips,

"They shall all go to the guillotine within a week."

At this she could no longer restrain herself. She drew the knife from her bosom and, with a strong, swift motion, drove the blade up to the hilt into Marat's heart, then drew it out and flung it on the floor. Marat gave one cry, "Help! help!" and died. His blood gushed in a flood and crimsoned the water in the bath. A servant-man, rushing in, knocked Charlotte down with a chair, and a woman who kept Marat's house jumped on her as she lay and almost stamped the life out of her.

THE COAST OF NORMANDY

Pretty soon the lodging was full of people, who glared at Charlotte. She—pale, silent, quite composed—stood motionless; when questions were put to her she said that she alone had killed Marat. She was hurried to prison; on entering its door, with her hands tightly bound by cords and her arms griped by soldiers, her strength gave way, and she fainted.

By the time she was put on her trial she had recovered her coolness. To the president she said,

"It was I who killed Marat."

"Why did you kill him?" asked the court.

"Because of his crimes."

"Who were your accomplices?"

"I had no accomplice."

It did not take the jury long to find her guilty, and Fouquier Tinville, who was public prosecutor, pressed for immediate sentence. She had scarcely got back to her room in the prison when the executioner appeared, with a long red chemise and a pair of scissors in his hand. With the scissors he cut off her long hair—she begged one lock for a young artist who had taken her portrait in prison. Then she drew on the red chemise of the condemned over her other clothes, her hands were bound behind her back, and she was thrust into a cart without springs, which jogged slowly through the streets on its way to the square where the guillotine stood. Just as the cart started a thunder-storm with rain burst over Paris. But it did not scatter the rabble which swarmed in the street, and which followed the cart with groans and hisses.

The women who had marched to Versailles a few years before were all there, and cursed Charlotte with their foul tongues.

She stepped upon the platform as lightly as her pinioned arms and her long chemise permitted. When the executioner tore away the handkerchief which covered her neck a blush overspread her face. In an instant strong hands flung her down upon the plank, the blade fell, and from her neck a jet of blood spurted. The executioner, who was even more brutal than such people usually are, seized the head by the hair, held it up before the people, and slapped the poor dead cheeks with his open hand.

That night the rabble of Paris said that the friend of the people had been avenged.

A hundred years have passed since then, and see how

public opinion has changed! To-day, Marat is accounted one of the worst scoundrels who ever figured in history; and Charlotte Corday, murderess as she was, has taken a place among the heroines who have ennobled humanity and given their lives to save others. Statues, paintings, and poems commemorate her deed, while France would like to forget that Marat ever lived.

HOTEL DE VILLE

ROBESPIERRE

Chapter XLIV

ROBESPIERRE

A.D. 1792–1794

In order to give you a consecutive story of Marat, I passed over events which happened before his death. I must now turn back to them.

There was confusion enough in Paris while the king lived; it grew worse after his death. Not only did the political clubs try to govern the country, but forty-eight new bodies, called sections, which were not by any means composed of the wisest or best men in Paris, undertook the same thing, and in the Assembly itself two parties arose which contended for the mastery. One of these was called the Girondists. Their leader Vergniaud I have already mentioned. He was a pure man, honestly seeking the freedom and happiness of France, and without a thought of himself or ill-will for any one. He was a sublime orator, who could stir men to fury or melt them to tears; but he was hardly strong enough for those rough times.

The other party was called the Jacobins. Their leader was Robespierre. He was a lawyer—a small, lean man, with a mean face, but a dandy in his dress. He wore fine clothes and what ladies nowadays would call a corsage bouquet. He was not like Vergniaud. He was cold, calculating, cruel, and was always thinking of himself and ready to strike down every one who stood in his way. He told every one that he was the most virtuous person in France, and, as virtuous people were pretty scarce at that time, he gained a good deal of credit in consequence.

Another leader of the Assembly was Danton. He was like Mirabeau in looks—a big man, with a shaggy head of hair and a roaring voice. He was violent and bloodthirsty, but clear-headed. His motto was: "Boldness! boldness! boldness!" Robespierre at first liked him, then grew jealous of him; you will see how the flowered dandy disposed of him in the end.

Meantime all Europe had formed a coalition against France to punish the French for the execution of their king. They had gathered a great army on the Rhine, and, with the help of the nobles who had left their country and were called Emigrants, proposed to march on Paris. They were held in check by French armies under Lafayette and Dumouriez. But after a time these generals became so disgusted with affairs at Paris that they threw up their commands. Lafayette entered Germany and was thrown into an Austrian prison. Dumouriez went to England. The Assembly ordered every able-bodied man to enroll himself in the army, and appointed a Committee of Public Safety to look after traitors at home. A revolutionary tribunal was also appointed to try persons suspected of disloyalty to the nation, and it was specially provided that it should not be bound by the rules of law. A bad plan, as you will see. It was easy for a Jacobin to say he suspected this or that person, and thus the prisons were kept pretty full, though the tribunal did its best to thin them out by finding almost everybody guilty.

The tribunal began by sending General Custine and a number of citizens of Rouen to the guillotine on a charge of disloyalty. Two new members were then added to the Committee of Safety, Billaud Varennes and Collot d'Herbois, than whom there were no wickeder or more bloodthirsty villains in France. They insisted that a reign of terror should be established to cow people.

All of these measures were opposed by the Girondists, who did not like the guillotine and had no love for blood. But they were fiercely insisted on by Robespierre and his followers. The Jacobins even went so far as to demand that the Girondists themselves, Queen Marie Antoinette, who was still in the Temple prison, and the Duke of Orleans, who called himself Philip Equality, should be brought to trial as enemies of the people.

The poor queen had languished in her jail ever since the king's execution, but for some time she had the comfort of the society of her daughter and her sister-in-law, Elizabeth. Her son, the young dauphin, had been taken from her. She was now removed to the Conciergerie prison, and placed in solitary confinement in a damp, ill-smelling room. A man who had been a robber mounted guard over her and was in her room day and night. Her clothes were worn out and in rags, her stockings were in holes, and she had no shoes. Both she and the dauphin had been intrusted by the Assembly to the guard of a wretch named Hebert, who had been ticket-taker at a theatre and had stolen the receipts.

She was brought to trial on October 14th, 1793, just ten months after the execution of her husband. She was only thirty-eight years old, but her hair was snow white, her beauty was gone, her color had faded, her cheeks were

MARIE ANTOINETTE

sunken. She had not been a loyal queen to France, but any man with a heart in his bosom would have pitied her now. It did not take long to find her guilty. She dressed herself all in white, cut off her hair with her own hands, gave her poor, thin wrists to the executioner to bind them behind her back, and went to her rest meekly and bravely.

I may as well tell you here of the fate of her son, the dauphin. He was locked up in the Temple prison with his father and mother, as you remember, on August 13th, 1792, when he was seven years old. On July 3d, 1793, he was dragged from his mother and shut up by himself in a room which was full of rats. He was a timid, nervous child, and trembled when a rat scurried past him. For two years he lived in that room, with no one to play with, no one to speak to. His bed was never made, his windows were never opened, his underclothes were hardly ever changed. He had no books to read and no light at night. Under this treatment both his body and his mind gave way. He sat the livelong day in a chair, and when his keeper, a cobbler named Simon, who shamefully neglected and abused him, came in and spoke to him, he would make no answer. At last he lost his mind altogether, and it was a happy release when he died, at ten years of age.

Having started in on their reign of terror, the Jacobins followed it up. Just a fortnight after the queen's death they arrested twenty-two Girondists, with Vergniaud at their head, and held them for trial on a charge of treason. They were the flower of France, the wisest and purest men of the Revolution. But they were accused by Robespierre of having conspired against the republic, and, of course, they were convicted. When they left their prison in the morning, they promised their fellow prisoners to let them know how they had fared. They kept their promise by singing the verse of the Marseillaise hymn—

"Allons, enfans de la patrie,
Le jour de gloire est arrivé."

(Come all ye sons of France,
The day of glory's come at last.)

That night they spent in cheerful conversation. When day dawned, Vergniaud took his watch, scratched his initials and the date on the case, and sent it to a young lady to whom he was tenderly attached, and whom he had intended

THE DAUPHIN IN THE TEMPLE

to marry. They were borne in five carts to the guillotine. As they stepped on the platform, all, with one accord, sang the Marseillaise. The chant grew feebler and feebler as singer after singer fell on the fatal plank. At last only Vergniaud was left. With his last breath he sang—

"The day of glory's come at last."

The Jacobins murdered women as willingly as men. They sent to the guillotine Madame Roland, one of the most beautiful and gifted women of the day, but a Girondist. She died bravely, saying,

"O Liberty! What crimes are committed in thy name!"

Then followed poor old Madame Dubarry, who struggled and fought with the executioner; Madame Elizabeth, sister of Louis the Sixteenth, who died bravely; and a host of other women, many of whom were young and beautiful, and whose only fault was that their husbands, or their brothers, or their fathers had been nobles or stood in the way of the Jacobins.

As for the men, the executioner wore himself out in putting them to death. Danton was put on his trial, was not allowed to produce witnesses, and was executed; so was Camille Desmoulins, one of the brightest members of the convention, who had been an intimate friend of Robespierre, and was the husband of one of the loveliest and sweetest women of that day; so was Lavoisier, the great chemist; so was Bailly, one of the best and purest Frenchmen who ever lived. The spies of the Committee of Public Safety hunted down every one who had been a noble or a priest, or who was opposed to bloody murder; they, their wives, their children, and even their servants, were sent to prison, and in three or four days many of them were guillotined. The guillotine was the great show of Paris; some days as many as fifty persons had their heads cut off; when the number fell as low as twenty, the rabble grumbled that they were cheated.

Men made jokes about the awful blade which severed so many necks; they called it the Little Tickler. Vile women used to take their knitting and watch the executioners from chairs which were kept for them, from day to day, round the platform on which the terrible instrument of death stood. They kept count of the victims by means of knots in their worsted. I think that many of the people of Paris at that time had gone mad.

What happened at the capital happened elsewhere.

A broken-down actor named Collot d'Herbois, who was a friend of Robespierre and was called the Tiger, was sent to Lyons. He arrested hundreds of priests, nobles, and other people, old and young men, women, and even young children; and, finding that he could not kill them fast enough with the guillotine, he made them stand in long rows and shot them down with artillery. After each discharge of the great guns soldiers went round to finish with their bayonets those who still breathed. When three women begged of him the lives of their husbands, he had them tied to posts near the execution ground, so that their husbands' blood should spurt on them. This brute was afterward exiled to Cayenne, and killed himself by drinking a bottle of brandy at a sitting.

At Nantes, the murder business was in the hands of a man named Carrier. He, like Collot d'Herbois, found the guillotine too slow; he used to put two or three hundred priests, nobles, and others, with women and children, into boats; when the boats reached deep water in the river

EXECUTIONS OF THE GIRONDISTS

Loire, plugs in their sides were pulled out, and the boats sank to the bottom with their living contents, the hatches being battened down. Sometimes Carrier would entertain his friends by giving them a show of men and women tied together in pairs so that they could not move their arms or legs, and thrown into the river; he and his friends thought it capital fun to watch their helpless struggles. He lived to be guillotined.

Another savage Jacobin was Couthon. He was Robespierre's bosom friend, and sent many a good man to the guillotine. His time came at last. When he ascended the platform he could not be laid on his face, as he was frightfully deformed; the executioner had to lay him on his side, so as to cut his head off. All these wretches, as you see, got their puuishment in this world.

I need not tell you that when these horrors were going on business was greatly disturbed. People did not pay taxes. The government could not borrow money; it issued paper-money called assignats, which very soon fell so much in value that a loaf of bread cost twelve dollars of our money. The butchers' and grocers' stores were robbed, and after a time they only opened their doors to those they knew; but still numbers of people starved. Everybody was afraid of his neighbor, for fear of being denounced as an enemy of the nation. The women were in great distress, for the churches were closed, and at the instigation of Robespierre the Christian religion had been abolished by law.

But this could not go on forever. The people of Paris sickened at last of the daily butcheries. Shop-keepers began to put up their shutters when the dreadful carts passed, and in the St. Antoine suburbs sturdy workmen frowned and scowled when Robespierre's wonderful virtue was spoken of. He had put his leading rivals out of the way. But new rivals were springing up all around him, and in the Assembly and among the people a feeling of loathing for never-ending bloodshed was growing. He stayed away from the Assembly for a month to see if it would subside. When he returned, in his blue coat and brass buttons, nankeen breeches and blooming nosegay, members affected not to see him. Those who did set eyes on him glared at him. No man took his hand. You see, there was hardly a member there who had not lost some loved one through this man. A murmur rose, and swelled and swelled and swelled, until at last it became a roar from right to left and gallery and floor,

"Arrest the traitor! Down with the tyrant! Down with him!"

He rose, staggered, turned red and white, tried to speak, but his tongue was too dry to make sounds. He could only froth at the mouth in his rage. A member shouted,

"It is Danton's blood that is choking you."

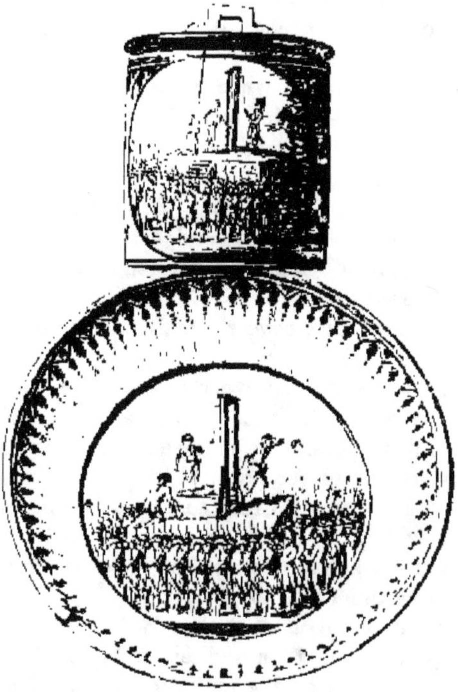

MEMORIAL CUP AND SAUCER OF THE GUILLOTINE

In such wild tumult as even that tumultuous Assembly had never known before, amid howls and groans and shouts and shaking of fists and tearing of hair, Robespierre was declared to be an outlaw, and was sent to be tried by the very court he had created to convict innocent men of being traitors. To prevent a rescue by his Jacobin friends, an intrepid soldier named Barras patrolled the streets. Brought to bay at last, with rage in his heart and curses on his tongue, Robespierre drew a pistol and shot himself in the face. But the wound was slight; he was put on a board, and carried to the rooms of the Committee of Safety, and laid on a table. He still wore his blue coat, nankeen breeches, and white stockings; he kept stauching the blood from his face with bits of paper, until a surgeon dressed the wound.

It was four in the afternoon when he was taken to the guillotine. Soldiers pointed him out with the points of their sabres; men hooted, women hissed and spat as he passed; the executioner made him stand up and roughly tore the bloody bandage from his jaw. He shrieked with the pain, while from the crowd round the guillotine a gray-haired woman, all in black, sprang forth and, stretching a skinny arm, cried shrilly,

"Descend to hell, villain, covered with the curses of every mother in France!"

This time when the knife fell every one breathed more freely. In a week from the time of his execution the guillotine went out of general business, and ten thousand people who were in prisons for political offences were set free. A weight was lifted off every soul, and the people, eager to show their disgust with the crew which had ruled them so long, took Marat's remains out of his grave in the Pantheon and threw them into the gutter.

During the twenty-two months that Robespierre had held the chief power, one thousand eight hundred and sixty-two persons had died by the guillotine in Paris; and this is besides those who had been put to death by his agents at Lyons, Nantes, Bordeaux, Marseilles, and in La Vendée. Ingenious writers have tried to explain that Robespierre's motives were good, and that he really believed that he was doing right. I think myself that he wanted to climb upon a throne by a bloody ladder, and that the happiness of his country never troubled him at all.

Chapter XLV

THE LAST OF THE ASSEMBLY

A.D. 1794–1796

After the fall of Robespierre, Paris had a rest. Fouquier Tinville, who had sent so many innocent people to their death, and his friend Carrier, followed him to execution, but the dreadful processions of carts to the guillotine were stopped.

This, however, was only a breathing-spell. There was no power anywhere strong enough to preserve order, and people had not yet settled down to quiet lives after the excitement of the Reign of Terror. The Assembly claimed to rule France, but the Jacobin Club also claimed to have a good deal to say about that, and the forty-eight sections of Paris were quite sure that they ruled that city. Among the three, fights were constantly breaking out.

Paris and most of the other French towns were in dire straits. Owing to the turmoil which had prevailed all over the country the fields had not been properly tilled, and grain was scarce. The Parisians were put on short rations—first, a pound of bread for each person per day, and next, only two ounces. The winter of 1794–95 was extremely cold; all the rivers froze over so solidly that in Belgium, where war was raging, a regiment of cavalry captured a fleet of war-ships which were frozen in the ice. When the Seine froze over no fuel could be got into Paris, and the poor people suffered terribly from cold.

While they were shivering and starving another class of people, who had kept out of the trouble of the past five years and who still had money, and who had made money by speculating in assignats or buying church lands or supplying the armies, were leading gay lives to console themselves for the anxieties they had undergone. They dressed splendidly and gave fine entertainments. The men wore their hair in rolls, huge cravats, short coats with long tails, vast waistcoats, and tight trousers; they all carried thick sticks —not for show. They were called "gilded youth," "incredibles," "muscadins." The ladies wore long gowns with high waists and no hoops; their hair was done up in fillets and bound with a single ribbon; on their feet they wore sandals fastened with ribbons which crossed each other over the ankle, and stockings with fingers for each toe, on which it was fashionable to wear rings. The men wore powder in their hair, the ladies not. The churches had opened again, and people could pray at the altars if they wanted to; the theatres remained closed.

HAT WORN IN 1795

All the men, and especially the young men, of this better class were opposed to the Jacobin Club; and when the Jacobins began in their old way to hector and bully the Assembly, and to trample the laws under foot as a parcel of savages might have done, the gilded youth resolved to see how hard they could hit with their thick sticks.

They did not arm themselves with guns or pikes or knives; but whenever the Jacobins pranced through the streets, calling for the life of this good man or that good man, and ranting and roaring, the gilded youth began hitting them on the head with their thick sticks. The Jacobins were so much surprised at finding that the gentlemen, as they sneeringly called them, could fight, that they thought there must be some mistake. They went back to their club, called out their biggest bullies, and sal-

A REPUBLICAN ADDRESSING THE PEOPLE

lied forth again. Again the gilded youth stepped up with smiles, and the thick sticks and Jacobin heads renewed their acquaintance. Then the Jacobin Club got some tried soldiers to head its forces, and went again to battle; but it was of no use; as you may suppose, the gilded youth had more grit and pluck than murderers and brawlers, and the Jacobins went howling back to their club, with cracked crowns and bloody noses. Once they put a lot of horrid women at their head and marched into the Assembly Chamber, to threaten and bully and swagger in their old way. These were the same women who had marched to Versailles, and had afterward sat round the guillotine. When the gilded youth heard that the Jacobins had invaded the Assembly, they quickly turned out and marched at the double-quick, sticks in hand. The Jacobins, who by this time knew those sticks very well, did not stop to argue, but scurried out as fast as the doors would let them; the ladies were disposed to linger, but for them the gilded youth had brought whips which they plied steadily and smartly, till the sweet creatures ran out, crying that a man must be a brute to strike a woman. Then the Assembly abolished the Jacobin Club, and there was an end of that nuisance.

But the sections remained. There were forty-eight of them, and all agreed to follow the lead of the Lepelletier section. They had forty thousand men in arms under their orders, and it was simply impossible for the Assembly to carry on the business of governing France, so long as they continued to dictate to it and threaten it and defy its authority. One of the two—either the sections or the Assembly—must go to the wall.

The Assembly sent for Barras, who had commanded the troops when Robespierre was arrested, and asked him would he undertake to put down the sections? He said he would, if he might choose his second in command.

The man he chose was a captain of artillery, twenty-five years of age—a small, thin man with long black hair and an olive complexion. He had made a name for himself by showing the French how to take Toulon from the English. But he had not made a fortune. He was very poor and knew hardly anybody. He used to walk the streets of Paris in a gray overcoat buttoned to his chin, a round hat pulled over his eyes, and a black cravat badly tied. There was something in his face which made people turn round to look at him; for he was Napoleon Bonaparte.

He made his plans swiftly. He secured all the field guns near Paris, and planted them so as to command the long St. Honoré street, the cross-streets, the quays, and the bridges. His infantry he distributed so that at the point of conflict they could pour in two shots to the section's one, besides raking the cross-streets. When his men were all in place, and all his guns were just where he wanted them, at half-past four in the afternoon he mounted his horse, and gave orders to open fire upon the troops of the sections, who were on the steps of the church of St. Roch.

His fire was so straight and so rapid that the section men could not stand it. They began to drop one by one, then they broke and ran down the streets toward the river. At every crossing infantry poured volleys into them; at the squares, quays, and bridges cannon opened on them with grape, mowing them down by scores. By six o'clock every member of the section's army was either dead or wounded or hiding in his house. All that night the big guns thundered with blank cartridge, and the section men shivered. Napoleon had resolved they should not forget that night. And they did not. The sections followed the Jacobins into history.

Thus freed from its enemies, the Assembly adopted a new constitution, under which France was to be governed by a house of ancients, like our Senate of the United States,

NAPOLEON BONAPARTE

an assembly, like our House of Representatives, and five directors, who were to do the work of our President. Which done, the Assembly adjourned, not to meet again, having done well for its country and laid the foundation for a French republic.

Paris again had peace, and became once more the liveliest city in Europe. There never were such gay parties or such joyous society as in the winter of 1795–96. Charming women swarmed. Among them was Madame de Staël, who was not a beauty, to be sure, but who was clever and witty and knew everything from high politics to millinery; Madame Tallien, who had the face of an angel and the figure of a nymph; Madame Récamier, who had feet and hands so small and white and finely shaped that they were the talk of the town; Madame Beauharnais, who could turn any man's head, though she had to keep her mouth shut, because her teeth were bad, and false teeth had not then been invented; and others whose bright eyes and rosy cheeks and merry laughter—you may be sure they had forgotten all about the guillotine—made life in their society a dream of Paradise. At the feet of these beauties knelt "incredibles," many of whom afterward proved that they had good stuff in them—among others brave young Hoche, who had risen in one year from private to general, and who was handsome as a young Apollo; and the young man with an olive complexion, piercing eyes, and a grave face, who began to be known as General Bonaparte.

You remember that when the States-General undertook to mend the laws of France, they found it could not be done. Almost everything was bad, and it was necessary to build anew from the ground up. The several assemblies which met one after another had done their best to pull down and build up afresh. And some of the changes must have been puzzling.

They changed the names of the years. Instead of dating from the birth of Christ, as Christian nations do, they dated from the foundation of the republic, as the Romans had from the foundation of Rome; thus the year 1793 became year 1. Then they changed the names of the months. The 21st of September became New Year's Day,

MADAME DE STAËL

and the thirty days following were called the Vintage Month. Then followed a month which was called Chilly Month, one called Frosty Month, then in succession months called Snowy, Showery, Windy, the month of Buds, of Flowers, of Meadows, of Harvests, of Heat, and of Fruits. Sunday was abolished; and instead, every tenth day was observed as a day of rest, when people went to the country with their families for a holiday. I need not tell you that these changes did not last, and that the old names and the old divisions of time were soon restored.

Chapter XLVI

BONAPARTE

A.D. 1796–1799

You remember that when Louis the Sixteenth was guillotined, all Europe declared war on France to punish her. Austria—of which country Marie Antoinette was a native—Prussia, Italy, Sardinia, Holland, England, and Spain—all joined forces to crush the nation which believed in freedom and did not believe in kings. You might suppose that such a combination of enemies, falling upon France when she was distracted by dissensions and troubles of all kinds at home, would have made short work of her. But a brave nation, when driven to the wall, is capable of tremendous efforts, and is apt to produce great men.

The army of Emigrants, Prussians, and Austrians which gathered at Coblentz just after the death of Louis the Sixteenth actually got into France, and was on the high road to Paris when it was attacked by Dumouriez and beaten back at Valmy and Jemappes. Dumouriez soon afterward quarrelled with the government at Paris and left his army. It fell under the command of General Pichegru, who not only pushed the enemy farther back, but entered Holland, conquered it, and established a republic there; but he also fell out with the Paris government, left his army, and was succeeded by Moreau, who made himself famous by planning the most skilful retreats that had ever been known.

On the other side of the country the Bretons, who were then commonly called Vendeans, and who were wrong-headed and obstinate, took up arms to put down the republic and restore the monarchy. They got help from England, and, as they had some exceedingly brave and intelligent leaders, they gave a great deal of trouble. Against them the government sent a soldier who was more famous for attacking than retreating—the General Hoche of whom I have told you. He penned up the Vendeans with a circle of troops that was like an iron chain, and beat the English till they were very glad to get on board their ships and go home again.

The wars of France were managed by a war minister whose name was Carnot; he was an ancestor of the present President of France. He resolved not to wait to be attacked, but to attack the enemy in their own countries. The army on the Rhine was ordered to strike into Germany; General Hoche was told to invade Ireland; to carry on the war in Italy against the King of Sardinia and the Emperor of Austria, Carnot chose General Bonaparte.

The trouble with all these wars was that France had nothing to carry them on with but pluck and skill: she had no money, no trained troops, no supplies. When Bonaparte crossed the Alps, in March, 1796, his soldiers were in rags and barefoot; the army chest was empty; he had not a week's provisions with him; some regiments had twice as many men as muskets. He stirred their courage with a little speech he made them:

"Soldiers, you are ill-fed and almost naked! I am going to lead you into the most fertile plains in the world, where you will find large cities and rich provinces, honor, glory, and wealth."

Fifteen days afterward he again addressed them:

"Soldiers, in a fortnight you have gained six victories, taken twenty-one flags, fifty-five cannon, several forts, and fifteen thousand prisoners. You have gained victories without cannon, crossed rivers without bridges, made forced marches without shoes, bivouacked without bread!"

Fancy how words like these stirred the troops' souls! It was actually true that in less than three weeks he had overrun all Piedmont, and the Italians were at his feet. But he had the Austrians still to deal with. They were more numerous than the French; they had strong forts to cover their rear; they had experienced generals. The trouble with these generals was that they were slow and methodical and fought strictly according to the rules of war, while Bonaparte cared nothing for rules, but dashed here and there, as his genius prompted him, fell upon the enemy's right when he should have fallen on his left, marched so swiftly that he always turned up before he was expected, and, though his force was inferior to that of Austria, he so managed that at the point of battle he always had more troops than his enemy. As an old Austrian general said, "Here is an absolute boy who knows nothing of the military art; now he is on our front, now on our flank, now in our rear. Such violations of plain rules cannot be justified."

Justified or not, they led to victory. In a single campaign he swept the Austrians out of Italy; Genoa, Milan, Parma, Leghorn, Mantua, Bologna, Ferrara, and ever so many other strong places fell into French hands; and every place which Bonaparte took had to pay him a sum of money, to send him a quantity of supplies, and to yield to Paris a certain number of fine pictures. The Duke of Modena had to pay ten millions of francs, Milan twenty millions, the pope twenty-one millions, and other cities and potentates in proportion; so that Bonaparte was able not only to feed and clothe his own army, but to send to the government at home large sums of money, besides some of the finest works of art in Italy.

This was not accomplished without desperate battles. At a place named Lodi, on the river Adda, the French were on one side of the river, the Austrians on the other. There was a little bridge, one end of which the Austrians held with sixteen thousand troops and twenty guns, which were trained on the bridge. Bonaparte took six thousand grenadiers, and led them himself on a quick run to the bridge. The Austrian cannon opened fire and mowed down the front ranks. But Bonaparte, waving a flag over his head, called on the rear ranks to follow him. Mad with excitement, they sprang forward in the teeth of the grape-shot, crossed the bridge, bayonetted the gunners at their guns, and scattered the sixteen thousand Austrians. In this battle alone forty-five hundred men perished—twenty-five hundred Austrians and two thousand Frenchmen. At the siege of Mantua the Austrians lost thirty thousand men, ten thousand of whom were killed. Pretty bloody work! But this was only the beginning.

Sometimes Bonaparte won victories at less cost. One dark night an Austrian general met his forces at a place called Lonato. The Austrian, feeling confident that he was the stronger, summoned the French general to surrender. Bonaparte replied that he gave the Austrians just eight minutes to lay down their arms; and they, fancying they had run up against the whole French army, did so at once.

After having made peace with Austria and planted the Cisalpine Republic—as he called northern Italy—on a firm foundation, Bonaparte was eager to get home to Paris. He had been twenty months away. He had marched so many miles, fought so many battles, and borne so much fatigue that he was worn out. He was so weak that he could not sit on horseback. His cheeks were hollow; if it had not been for the fire in his eyes, he would have looked like a dying man. Before leaving Paris he had married Josephine Beauharnais, a beautiful widow of thirty-three, who was six years older than himself. He loved her passionately. Just before leaving Italy he wrote to her:

"Soon thy husband will fold thee in his arms. Adieu for the present, adorable Josephine. Think of me often. When your heart grows cold toward me, you will be very cruel, very unjust. But I am sure you will always be faithful. A thousand and a thousand kisses."

Three months afterward Bonaparte was in France. He had a splendid reception. All Paris turned out to meet him. The directors, who for some queer reason wore Roman togas, welcomed him from a raised dais, and all round, on seats arranged as they are at a circus, the greatest people in France sat and applauded. Bonaparte was plainly dressed and was modest in his manner. He said,

"I bring you a treaty with Austria which insures the liberty, prosperity, and glory of the republic."

THE DIRECTORY. FROM A PRINT OF THE TIME

Then he sat down, while the sky re-echoed the shouts of the people, and bands played triumphal airs, and batteries of artillery fired salutes. He was so shy and retiring, so small and unobtrusive, that no one would have taken him for a great conqueror who had just won sixty-seven battles, subdued a whole country, and taken a hundred and fifty thousand prisoners and six hundred heavy guns.

But the brain of this shy and retiring soldier was full of great projects. He wanted to conquer Egypt. He said he wanted to do so in order to humble England. But as the English did not own Egypt, and as it was no manner of consequence to them who did, I think that Bonaparte was not sincere, and that his real object was to acquire glory for himself. He had read that Alexander the Great and Cæsar had won glory in Egypt; he wanted to couple his name with theirs. So, in May, 1798, he set sail from Toulon, with a large army and a fine fleet, picked up Malta by the way, landed at Alexandria, and marched up to Cairo. There a battle was fought with the Egyptians, and the French won. Bonaparte worked his men up to enthusiasm by telling them that, from the top of the pyramids—which they could see from the battle-field—forty centuries were looking down upon them.

In order to please the Egyptians, Bonaparte put on a Turkish dress, went to the mosque or church, seated himself, as the Turks do, cross-legged, and said prayers in the Arabic tongue, rocking his body to and fro, as the followers of Mohammed do.

But I do not observe that the Egyptians were much touched by his conversion; and when the English, under Nelson, fell upon his fleet at Aboukir and destroyed it, they were more suspicious than ever. It didn't matter what they believed. Bonaparte held Egypt with a grip of iron, and when some of the chiefs annoyed him by hanging round his camps on their fleet Arab horses and killing Frenchmen, he sent a flying squadron to punish them, and every night a dozen asses were driven into Cairo with sacks on their backs. When they reached the market-place the contents of the sacks were dumped, and they proved to be heads of Arab horsemen. Bonaparte invaded Palestine, and beat the Turks there; he took no rest until the French were masters of the country from the Holy Land to the cataracts of the Nile.

You will be surprised to hear that he received no news from France for a whole year. The Mediterranean was patrolled by English fleets, and it was only by pure accident that, after being fifteen months in Egypt, Bonaparte heard that the French had been driven out of Italy, and that the greatest confusion reigned in Paris. He said nothing to his officers, but took ship, and landed at Frejus, in France, in October, 1799.

He found everything in frightful disorder at Paris. The

five directors were quarrelling among themselves and were despised by the people. Bonaparte called them to task.

"What have you done with the France I left you? I left you peace; I find war. I left you victories; I find defeats. I left you millions; I find starvation. What have you done with my brothers in arms? They are dead."

Three directors were cowed and resigned; the other two Bonaparte locked up. Then, on a day which the French always remember by the name of the eighteenth Brumaire, he sent a company of grenadiers with fixed bayonets into the hall of the Assembly, drove the members out, locked the doors, put to death the Republic of France, and replaced it by a one-man government—the man being Bonaparte.

He called his government a consulate, there being three Consuls—he the first and Sieyès and Ducos the second and third. You will understand that the second and third Consuls were for show, and that the First Consul was the government. Bonaparte said he had been compelled to make himself Consul by the intrigues of members of Assembly to restore the monarchy, and by the endeavors of the English to bribe the assemblymen to betray their country. I dare say there were a few assemblymen who would have liked to see the king back; and it is possible that Mr. Pitt, who hated France and the French Republic, may have given a few pieces of gold to knaves to create trouble. But the real secret was that neither the Directory nor the Assembly knew enough of the business of governing to hold France well in hand; and that by their side there stood an ambitious young man, who not only knew how to master France, but was resolved to do so.

THE THREE CONSULS. FROM A MEDAL

Chapter XLVII

THE FIRST CONSUL

A.D. 1799–1804

When Bonaparte became First Consul he set himself two tasks—first to restore order, and then to make France the first power in Europe. At the same time he purposed to become the absolute ruler of France. It was to be great and orderly, but it was not to be trusted with freedom. Whether or no he believed in his heart the French were not fit to be free, he resolved to be on the safe side and to keep in his own hands supreme power in great things and small. He purposed to do a good and useful thing, and to do it in such a way that it should turn to his personal advantage.

There was no money in the treasury, and the Directory had been unable to raise any. Bonaparte levied wise taxes, which were cheerfully paid. He put the government credit on a sound basis and started up trade and industry. He taught people to throw the wretched old assignats into the fire and to do business with real money. He reformed and boiled down the laws into one code, which is in force to-day and has been copied in a dozen countries—among others, in our own State of Louisiana. He kept as good order in the French cities as he had in his camps; if any one, Jacobin or other, disturbed the peace, the police quickly laid him by the heels and taught him a lesson. He founded a number of colleges, which are flourishing to-day. He reopened the churches and paid the priests for preaching and celebrating mass. You must keep these good works in mind when you blame him, as you cannot help doing, for making himself a military despot.

To give France time to recover after ten years of warfare, he made peace with the rest of the world. Spain, Portugal, the pope, Naples, Turkey, Bavaria, Russia, were quite willing to sign treaties of peace. Austria hung back until Bonaparte beat her armies terribly at Marengo, and Moreau did the same thing at Hohenlinden—then she laid down her arms; and last of all England agreed to live in friendship with her old enemy.

Then the First Consul tried to reform the morals of the French, which needed mending. You can easily understand that, under the example of the Regent Orleans and Louis the Fifteenth, men and women had learned to lead bad lives. Things got worse during the dreadful confusion of the early years of the Revolution, when there were no more marriages, and the leading men boasted that they respected nothing. Bonaparte now set an example of leading a clean life. He and his wife lived at the Tuileries when they were in town, and at Malmaison when they went to the country.

Josephine, her daughter, and their guests and friends rose when they pleased. They breakfasted together at eleven, and spent the afternoon in chat, reading, or driving. Bonaparte got up at five or six, went at once into his office, and spent the day there—when there was no review—receiving visits, reading despatches, and giving directions to his ministers and officers. At six in the afternoon he dined with his family, who had not seen him till then; the evening they spent together. He gave a dinner-party every ten days, to which two hundred people were invited, and he was careful to invite no one of bad reputation. When he took a holiday he made up a small party, consisting of his wife, her daughter Hortense, and a few of his favorite officers and their wives. The grand ladies of the old nobility would not call on Josephine, and kept away from the Tuileries. In the country he amused himself by playing boys' games; at the Tuileries he played chess or cards, but never for money.

He was faithful to his old soldiers, and by little acts of kindness he won their hearts. Recognizing a drummer-boy at a review, he asked,

"Was it you who played the drum at Zurich?"

"Yes, General," said the boy.

"And was it you who saved your commander's life at the Weser?"

"Yes, General," answered the boy, flushing.

"Then," said the First Consul, "the country owes you a debt. I make you a sergeant."

Another day, as he was mounting his horse, a young man fell at his feet and handed him a paper. He was ghastly pale and trembled. The First Consul looked curiously at him and read his paper. Then, turning to the youth, he said gently,

"You will tell your mother that she can draw a pension from the government as long as she lives; and you, if you choose, can enter my army as an officer."

The boy was the son of poor General Delaunay, who was Governor of the Bastile when it was taken; as you remember, he had been murdered by the mob.

But the brood of assassins of whom I have been sorry to tell you so much was not extinct. One night, as the First Consul was leaving the opera, an attempt was made to stab him. On another occasion a barrel full of bombs was set on a cart, and drawn by an old horse toward the opera which Bonaparte was to attend. The intention was to explode the bombs as the First Consul passed. But the old horse got in the way of the escort. One of the troopers struck it a blow with the flat of his sabre, and it shied and put the machinery out of order; by the time this was rearranged the First Consul had passed, and the explosion killed no one but a few bystanders, among others a poor woman who kept a store and had run to her door to see the consul pass.

A more serious attempt was made by Pichegru, Cadoudal, and others, who, I am afraid, were set on by noble Emigrants. I suspect that General Moreau, who was so gallant a soldier that he should have shrunk from such a plot, and several members of high families were more or less concerned in it. The police intercepted their letters and caught one of the conspirators, who betrayed the others. Moreau was exiled to this country. Pichegru was put in prison, and was found one morning dead in his cell, with marks showing that he had been strangled. Cadoudal was guillotined.

Bonaparte was convinced that the Duke of Enghien, of the great house of Condé, who was an Emigrant, was in the plot. He seized him, in violation of law, on the territory of Baden and had him conveyed to Vincennes; in that fortress he was put on his trial at two in the morning of the day after his arrival. He was sentenced to death. Without an hour's delay he was led by General Savary to the castle moat, where a platoon of gendarmes were posted and a grave had just been dug. He stood erect and intrepid, his back against the wall of the fortress, with a lantern on his breast to guide the soldiers' aim in that gloomy moat, which was like a still cavern in the sombre night. When his sentence had been read, he begged an officer to cut off a lock of his hair and send it to his wife. Then the command, "Fire!" and the brave young man fell forward on his face.

There was no reason why England and France should not have remained at peace, except that the two peoples had been educated to hate each other by their governments. Bonaparte felt that so long as England flourished there would always be one nation to oppose his dream of supreme power in Europe; the English regent and the English nobility felt that if their people had no foreign foe to fight they would want to reduce the power of the throne and the privileges of the nobility. A pretext for more fighting having been found, the war broke out in the old way. Bonaparte was master not only of France, but also of all Belgium, Holland, a slice of Germany, and all Italy north of Naples; Spain was his ally; the English had with them Russia, Austria, Naples, and Sweden. The whole continent was in the war on one side or the other.

Before beginning it in earnest Bonaparte changed his title. Some time before he had been made consul for life. He now declared he would be Emperor of France and King of Italy, and the Senate—as the council of ancients

EXECUTION OF THE DUKE OF ENGHIEN

was called—and the Assembly swiftly answered so he should. The pope was brought from Italy to crown him.

It was done in the old church of Notre Dame. The church was splendidly draped in velvet, with B's all over it. The pope sat on a throne, with sixty bishops, as many generals, and judges, senators, assemblymen, and foreign ministers all around him. Bonaparte approached, with his marshals escorting him, and knelt at the altar. At a signal the pope took a phial of sacred oil and anointed the new emperor on the forehead, on the arms, and on the hands; he girded the sword of state round his waist and placed the sceptre in his hand. The emperor, who had appeared to be uneasy lest the sacred oil should drip on his imperial mantle, seizing the crown, placed it on his head without stopping to observe a small stone which just then dropped from the ceiling on his shoulder, and would have been regarded as an evil omen by a Roman; then, taking another crown, he placed it on the head of Josephine, who knelt before him and burst out crying. The pope blessed them both, and the whole audience broke out with the cry, "Long live the emperor!" while cannon outside thundered deafening salutes.

Six months afterward he was again crowned, at Milan in Italy. This time the crown which he set on his head was an old iron crown, which was said to have been used by the emperors of the ancient empire of the West; all the great church dignitaries and civil officers of Italy, with a swarm of French officers and foreign ministers, watched the ceremony. When it was over Napoleon touched the crown and said in Italian, "God has given it to me; let him beware who touches it."

You may perhaps think that this soldier, who made himself emperor by war, was impious in imputing his usurpations to God. He had two crowns set on his head—one in Paris and one in Milan; whoever put them on, you will not find they stuck there when the time came for them to fall off.

CHURCH OF NOTRE DAME, AT PARIS

Chapter XLVIII

THE EMPEROR NAPOLEON

A.D. 1804–1807

In choosing which of his foes to attack first Napoleon selected England, because it was the richest among his enemies and had the smallest army. He collected his troops on the coast of the Channel, round the town of Boulogne. There were so many of them that he is said to have placed one hundred thousand in line at one review.

THE COAST OF BOULOGNE

There is no doubt that he had a large force of infantry, cavalry, and gunners, all veteran soldiers, and some three thousand broad boats to ferry them over to England. You know that there were no steam-boats in those days; Napoleon's boats were sail-boats, and they could not defend themselves against frigates. To cross the Channel in safety it was necessary for him to get control of it, and hold control at least for one whole day. To accomplish this he ordered his naval captains to entice as many British ships as they could away from the coast of England; and he directed his best admiral, Villeneuve, to attack and beat and sink the remainder.

Unluckily for him the English fleet was commanded by an exceedingly skilful and daring sailor, whose name was Nelson. He saw through Napoleon's plans, left ships enough near home to hold the Channel, and with the rest went in sharp pursuit of the French fleet. One day, near a point on the Spanish coast called Trafalgar, he came up with it, cut it in two, and sank and battered out of shape so many French ships that at the end of the fight it was no good for anything. So the English kept their mastery of the Channel, and Napoleon did not dare to put to sea with his three thousand boats.

While he was grinding his teeth with rage news came that the Austrian army, eighty thousand strong, had marched from Vienna to invade France, and that a hundred thousand Russians were only two or three marches behind them. Like lightning he turned his back to England and made for the new foes. He seized every carriage and every horse in northern France; and the troops, in coaches, wagons, carriages, trucks, phaetons, hay-carts, and on horseback, were hurried to the valley of the Danube, before the slow, lumbering Austrians imagined they had left the Channel. Napoleon seemed to need neither sleep nor rest. He was everywhere at once. So swiftly did he move that he wrapped his men round the first Austrian army corps of thirty thousand men before they knew he was near and made them all prisoners; then he shut up the next army corps of thirty-six thousand men in Ulm and, by threatening to open fire, forced them to surrender in order to save their lives. In a month he made an end of the Austrian army without firing a shot.

Another army rose up at Vienna and joined the advance corps of the Russians. He marched to meet them at a little Moravian village called Austerlitz. They were more numerous than the French, but they had no general who knew his business. The Emperor of Russia was in command, and he placed his men so that Napoleon cut his army in two—as Nelson had done to Villeneuve's fleet—and overcame each half separately. It was the 2d of December and bitter winter weather. The ground was covered with snow and ice. In retreating, the Russians crossed some frozen ponds. Napoleon fired his big guns in the air so that the balls fell on the ice and broke it, and thousands of poor soldiers, overloaded with their guns and their knapsacks, were drowned.

This was enough for the Russians this time. Those who survived the battle hurried home as fast as they could. And with Francis of Austria, whom he received at an open bivouac, protected from the wind by an old mill-shed, Napoleon made peace, on condition of getting a large slice of territory and a great deal of money.

There is a story—I hope it is true—that on his return to Vienna he met a convoy of wounded Austrians, immediately alighted from his carriage, took off his hat, and called to his officers,

"Honor the brave!"

He was not always so thoughtful for the wounded and the dying.

What was passing in his mind you may perhaps guess from his private letters to the Empress Josephine. He wrote to her after Austerlitz:

"I have beaten the Russian and Austrian armies commanded by the two emperors. I am a little fatigued. I have slept eight days in the open air, though the nights are severely cold. To-night I shall get two or three hours' sleep in a castle. Adieu, my love. I am pretty well and eager to kiss you. Not one letter from you since you left Strasburg."

He had no sooner got back to Paris than he showed what his real purpose was in carrying on the wars to which he had been invited by the kings of Europe. Some years before, you remember, France had helped to establish a republic in Holland; this Napoleon now overthrew, and planted in its place a monarchy with his brother as king. Louis was a silent, morose man, whom the Dutch hated.

Then he made his wife's son, Eugène Beauharnais, viceroy of northern Italy, and, to round out his dominions, he took Venice from Austria and put it under Eugène.

Finally he sent an army to Naples to drive out the worthless king who reigned there. He was a miserable creature, who was always making treaties and breaking them, and I am not sorry he was upset. But it startled Europe when Napoleon made his brother Joseph King of Naples in his stead. People began to say that the Bonaparte family were covering a good deal of ground—especially when another of them, Jerome, was made King of Westphalia.

Prussia became so uneasy that she agreed to join the Russians in another effort to put down the "Corsican upstart," as Napoleon was called. He met their armies at a place called Jena, and the Prussians lost 12,000 men killed and wounded, 15,000 prisoners, and 1200 cannon. This was ten months after the battle of Austerlitz, and was quite enough for the Prussians. Those of them who could made the best of their way home. The King of Prussia ran away, and Napoleon entered Berlin in October, 1806.

Then he turned on the Russians and fought a number of battles with them in the spring of 1807, at Eylau, Friedland, and other places, and his good fortune was such that he won all the battles, and at each one Russia lost men and guns and glory which she could not spare. At last the Emperor Alexander got tired of this business and sent to Napoleon to see if they could not arrange a peace.

The two emperors met on a big raft, anchored exactly in the middle of the river Niemen, near the little town of Tilsit. On the raft a small pavilion had been built with a table and chairs and maps for the two emperors. The officers of their suites stood outside or rowed about in their boats. To decorate the pavilion the shops of Tilsit had been stripped of all their fine silks and cloths. Here the two monarchs, with the King of Prussia, met day after day from the 25th of June to the 7th of July, 1807, and they finally agreed on a treaty, by which Russia got nothing, Prussia lost half her subjects and nearly one half of her territory, and Napoleon got everything that he wanted. You will probably think that he was as skilful at making treaties as he was at fighting battles.

The Emperor of Russia dined with him every day, and you may be sure that Napoleon did not spare expense to give him fine dinners and rich wines. The Russian did not see till long afterward how he had been hoodwinked; but the poor stupid King of Prussia saw plainly enough what was to be his fate, and he sent for his wife, Louise of Prussia, who was the most beautiful woman in Europe, to try to get better terms from Napoleon. The emperor was struck with her marvellous beauty and could not take his eyes off her; he told her she was the queen of loveliness; but when she tried to get him to be more forbearing with Prussia, his face grew hard as stone, and he said "No" in a way which showed that he meant it.

He had made himself ruler of France, Italy, Belgium, Holland, and nearly half of Germany; and he did not propose to let a pretty woman talk him out of a foot of land.

I need not tell you that this great empire had not been won without hard fighting and much hardship. You have heard of the battles; now hear how Napoleon lived during these campaigns. He wrote to his brother Joseph,

"The officers of my staff have not undressed for two

months, and some not for four months. I myself have not had my boots off for a fortnight. We live in snow and mud, without wine or brandy or bread, on meat and potatoes, making long marches and counter-marches without ceasing. Our wounded have to be carried a hundred and fifty miles in sleighs, through the bitter cold, before they reach a hospital."

But neither the fatigues of his marches nor the privations he endured were enough to occupy his mind. When he was fighting battle after battle he was constantly planning some new thing for Paris. He laid down new rules for the collection of taxes. He gave points for articles in the newspapers. He sent directions to Paris for the manufacture of boots and shoes, saddles and baggage-wagons. He directed the theatres what pieces to play and what actors and actresses they should engage. He read all the principal books and sent money to the authors of good ones. He started a number of schools and directed what they should teach. One of his schools was for the daughters of soldiers killed in the service. About this one he was very particular. He wrote:

"Women have weak minds, therefore they should be taught religion. I want the pupils of this school to be virtuous rather than agreeable. They should learn a little medicine, dancing (but not ballet-dancing), reading, writing, ciphering, and needle-work. They must make their own chemises, stockings, dresses, and caps, and also know how to make clothes for their children when they come to have any."

MEDAL OF NAPOLEON, KING OF ITALY

CHAPTER XLIX

FRANCE UNDER NAPOLEON

A.D. 1807–1809

AFTER the treaty of Tilsit, Napoleon soon found himself back in France once more, with no wars to carry on for the moment, for the French and the English could not get at each other. He then bent his whole mind to improving the condition of Paris and France; when you see how well he succeeded you will feel sorry that he wasted so much genius in fighting and angering foreigners by setting his relations over them as kings. France had never been as prosperous nor the people as well off as he made them.

He put into his schemes of public improvement the same energy that he had put into his campaigns. Under his orders ten canals were dug to connect rivers. He cut roads over the Alps and through Brittany. He opened seaports and built wharves. He gave splendid rewards to silk weavers, woollen spinners, and makers of beet-sugar. He established all manner of schools—art, military, and naval schools, ten law schools, six schools of medicine, twenty-nine colleges, and common schools in every town. He managed his money-affairs so well that there was always plenty of money in the treasury, though people did not complain of being overtaxed; there was always work for every one who wanted work, and no boy grew up in ignorance if he cared to learn. You will not be surprised to hear that the French were contented; and, though good men deplored the want of freedom, the masses of the people thought the empire a fine thing.

He made Paris more splendid than ever. He built the Madeleine, and the Vendôme column out of cannon taken from the Austrians and Russians (it was pulled down by the Commune in 1870, but has since been rebuilt); he finished the Louvre and the Pantheon; he built the Arch of Triumph and the Arch of the Star. He supplied Paris with water, put the streets into good repair, and established a police force which made it safe for every one to go where he would at any time of night. He put a stop to street begging and established poor-houses all over France. His system of laws was the best in Europe, and he saw to it that his laws were obeyed.

Notwithstanding these services to France the members of the old nobility, who had emigrated when the republic was declared, and who had since come creeping back to pick up some remnant of their old estates, would not have anything to say to him. They kept away from the court, and their wives and daughters would not call on the empress. Napoleon laughed at them and their titles; and, partly to spite them and partly to reward his old soldiers, he began to create dukes very fast indeed. Almost every general who had done good service in the wars was made a duke or a prince, or at least a marshal of France, and had a fat salary given him to enable him to sustain his rank.

These changes of titles were embarrassing. A man who had been a marquis under Louis the Sixteenth became a plain citizen under the republic; now any one who happened to distinguish himself in the army ran risk of being made a duke. Most of the new dukes were of humble birth and had won their titles by gallant deeds in war under Napoleon's eye.

PARIS FROM NOTRE DAME

All these people had to dress splendidly in order to encourage industry. The court dress for men was a coat of red watered silk embroidered in gold; the embroidery was in imitation of branches of olive, oak, and laurel. They wore black cravats and boots coming up to the knee. The ladies wore round their necks tulle ruffs, with gold or silver points. The dress was embroidered in gold, but no one but a princess could wear embroidery all over her dress; on ordinary ladies' dresses the embroidery was limited to four inches at the bottom of the skirt. On common occasions ladies wore dresses of cambric and muslin, which were then very expensive; white cambrics were not made in France, but were smuggled from England, and the emperor was angry when he saw one of the ladies of his court dressed in them. Much time was spent by ladies in dressing their hair: on the day of the coronation some ladies had their hair dressed at two in the morning, and sat in their chairs until the ceremony began at nine. The court ladies wore splendid diamonds, and with these it was the fashion to dress in black or dark-colored velvet. When Napoleon's sister, the Princess Borghese, was presented at court after her marriage, her head, her neck, her ears, and arms were loaded with diamonds.

As the English had command of the sea France could get few goods from foreign countries. Napoleon told the ladies to drink Swiss tea instead of tea from China, and French chicory instead of coffee from Java or Brazil. He paid so much attention to beet-sugar that to this day the French use more of it than they do of cane-sugar.

He was very friendly with the clergy and saw to it that they were not molested. But when a priest was intolerant he had no pity for him. A ballet-dancer happening to die, the priest of her parish refused to give her Christian burial. A couple of days afterward Napoleon put in his newspaper the following little notice, which he wrote with his own hand,

"The curate of St. Roch, in temporary forgetfulness of

reason, has refused to pray for Mademoiselle Chameroy, and to admit her remains within the church. The Archbishop of Paris has suspended the curé of St. Roch for three months, to remind him that Jesus Christ commands us to pray even for our enemies, and to teach him that superstitious practices, begotten in times of ignorance, or created by overheated zealots, degrade religion by their foolery."

When his work was over the emperor was always ready for a frolic. He went to balls, parties, and masquerades, and loved to intrigue the guests. He used to dress up some one in domino and mask, and give out that this was the emperor. His double used to go through the rooms, copying the emperor's walk and manners, and the real emperor would take delight in treating him with a familiarity which shocked the guests. For Napoleon was a stickler for dignity. No one ever joked with him. When he entered a room, every one rose, and no one, not even ladies, could sit down in his presence. He was playful himself, and was fond of pinching the ears and noses of the ladies he liked; but no one could venture to be playful in return.

I am sorry to add that he was cruel to those who ventured to criticise his actions. Madame de Staël, who, I think, was rather a tiresome person, found some fault with him; upon which he exiled her from France and kept her in exile for ten years. She had a friend, Madame Récamier, who called to see her before she left. For this Madame Récamier was also sent into exile, though she was the most beautiful woman in France, and had been the idol of Paris in the days of the republic. For the benefit of men who talked so as to give him uneasiness, Napoleon revived the old system of the Bastile, and locked them up for long periods of time without giving them a trial. He was the most suspicious person in France. He kept swarms of police spying on people, and then, fancying that he was not being faithfully served, he set others to spy on the spies.

These wretches, in order to earn their pay, made a practice of revealing to the emperor plots which they made up; he was thus kept in constant alarm.

An enormous athlete, armed to the teeth, slept across the door of his bedroom, and he would rarely eat anything that had not been cooked in his own kitchen. On one occasion, when he accepted an invitation to dinner, he suddenly called his body-servant as the soup was being served, and bade him fetch a loaf of white bread and a bottle of wine; he would touch nothing else.

With all his common-sense he was superstitious, and used to consult fortune-tellers. He believed in destiny. At a battle he saw a soldier duck his head as a round shot came flying that way.

"My friend," said Napoleon, "you are putting yourself to needless trouble. If that shot is not intended for you, you may just as well stand up straight. If it is destined for you, it will find you out though you should bury yourself a hundred feet below the surface of the earth."

Though he had been constantly under fire throughout his wars, Napoleon had never been hit until the skirmish of Ratisbon, some time after the battle of Austerlitz. There a spent ball struck his heel and flattened itself against the boot. If it had struck four feet higher, the emperor's career might have ended then and there. The accident impressed him painfully. He said that his star must be setting.

Chapter L

JOSEPHINE

A.D. 1809-1810

Napoleon was in the middle of his work in France, when, once more, war broke out between France and Austria. He had to call out his old soldiers again, tear down the Danube valley, and fight battle after battle with the Austrians, until he finally overcame them at a place called Wagram. He entered Vienna, pulled down its walls, and once more made peace. But he then saw plainly enough that the kings intended to give him no peace, partly because he was not of them, but was a mere man of the people, and partly because they saw there were no bounds to his greed for power. There was one way in which he might get them to accept him as one of themselves—that was by marrying into a royal family; then, perhaps, he thought they might bear with him.

He had a wife already, as you know—a loving and affectionate wife—the Empress Josephine, who was then forty-six years old. She had two children by her first husband, General Beauharnais; none by Napoleon. She had been by turns happy and miserable as Napoleon's wife. He was sometimes loving; then he neglected her for some lady of the court, and she endured agonies from jealousy. When she scolded and cried he explained that he was not like other men, and was not subject to the same laws as they. He told Josephine that, being an emperor, no one could question his actions. In reality, he despised women. He thought they were inferior creatures, who were put into the world for the pleasure of men.

Josephine was warm-hearted and tender, but not very

JOSEPHINE, WIFE OF NAPOLEON I

wise. She was passionately attached to her husband, but she never became friendly with his family. The emperor's sisters hated her and tattled to their brother about her weakness for jewels and her willingness to take presents. Her chief sorrow was that she had given her husband no son. She said to a friend,

"You can have little idea how much I have suffered when any one of you has brought a child to me. Heaven knows that I am not envious, but in this one case I have felt as if a deadly poison were creeping through my veins when I have looked upon the fresh and rosy cheeks of a beautiful child, the joy of its mother and the hope of its father. I know, I know, that I, who have given my husband no child, shall be driven in disgrace from him whom I love more than my life."

Napoleon took time to consider the matter. He argued that if he got rid of Josephine he might marry the daughter or the sister of a king and be received at once into kingly society; he might get a young and blooming wife, instead of a lady of forty-six; and, above all, he might get a son of his own to succeed him when he died. I don't think he troubled himself about how Josephine would feel at parting from him, or whether he might not break her heart. Other people's hearts did not concern him much.

Having thought it all over, he sent for Josephine, and told her bluntly that the interests of France required him to turn her out. She was not surprised. She had read her fate in the faces of the people at court, who knew what the emperor intended to do. She meekly bowed her head and answered,

"I was prepared for this, but the blow is none the less mortal."

No time was lost. On December 15th, 1809, the Council of State was informed by Napoleon that he intended to divorce his wife. He had no complaint to make of her. She had done nothing wrong. He professed to love her with all his heart. But he pretended to think that France required a lineal heir to the throne, and his courtiers pretended to believe him—as though the country would go to ruin if the Bonaparte dynasty expired, and as though he had no nephews to carry it on.

On the day after, Napoleon with all his court assembled at the Tuileries. They were all splendidly dressed. Napoleon entered wearing a hat with drooping plumes; he folded his arms across his chest, as one who has nerved himself to a great sacrifice. All the great officers of state stood round the room. By a side-door, Josephine, all in white and with a face as white as her gown, came in with

MARIE LOUISE OF AUSTRIA, SECOND WIFE OF NAPOLEON I

her son Eugène and her daughter Hortense. In the centre of the room stood a small table, on which there was an inkstand of gold and a gold pen. In front of the table had been set an arm-chair in which the empress took her seat. A court official read a deed of separation; Josephine took an oath that it was her free act and deed, then, removing her handkerchief from her eyes and dipping the gold pen into the golden inkstand, she signed her name. Leaning on her daughter's arm, she left the room. Next morning, in a closed carriage drawn by six horses, she left the Tuileries forever and drove to Malmaison.

Napoleon cried a good deal in public after she was gone.

He said she was the best woman in France. He did not know what he should do without her. But he soon found out. For while the people of Paris, who loved Josephine for her kindness to the poor and for her grace and sweet temper, were murmuring over her disgrace, the emperor despatched a confidential officer to St. Petersburg to ask for the hand of a Russian princess. The Romanoffs are a proud family; they declined the honor politely, but very firmly. Then the officer went to Vienna and asked the emperor would he accept Napoleon as a son-in-law? Francis was not so particular. He replied,

"With all my heart."

And accordingly, on March 10th, 1810, not three months after he had turned Josephine out of the Tuileries, Napoleon was married by proxy to Marie Louise of Austria, whose great-grandfather was the brother of the Marie Antoinette who had been guillotined in Paris.

She was nineteen years old—amiable, sweet, and stupid. Her hair was light, her eyes blue, her hands and feet small, her figure graceful. She had never seen Napoleon till he met her on her way to Paris. The only remark she made was that he was better looking than she had expected. But she had been told that it was her duty to love him, and she was ready to do her duty as a well-bred girl should.

On April 1st, 1810, the French marriage took place; and on the 20th of March following the emperor's son was born, in a room in which there were twenty-two people present to serve as witnesses. Never was a baby so grandly welcomed into the world. It had been arranged that if the child was a girl, twenty-one guns were to be fired; if a boy, one hundred. When the twenty-second gun went off, all Paris burst into shouts, and the men threw their hats in the air for joy. That night every house in Paris was illuminated. At street corners bands played joyous music, bonfires were lit, rockets rose in the air, and fireworks were set off in the squares. The Parisian women laughed and cried in the ecstasy of their delight, and the men drank bottle after bottle of wine, as if a great happiness had befallen them.

If they could only have foreseen! That poor little boy was made King of Rome while he was still in long clothes. When he was five years old he was taken to the court of his grandfather, the Emperor of Austria, to live, and there

THE PALACE OF FONTAINEBLEAU

he grew up—a sad, silent, sickly boy. He was not called King of Rome any more, but Duke of Reichstadt; king or duke, he was always in low spirits, and with the brand of fate stamped on his face. He had no intimate friends; he loved to sit by himself and brood and mope, or to ride alone through the dark woods of Schönbrunn. Kind people at the court at Vienna tried to amuse him and to put a little life into him. Beautiful girls shot tender glances at him out of bright eyes. But nothing interested him. And at last, at the age of twenty-one, he died, having had as sad a life as the beginning of it was joyful.

When he was a child he had a curious dislike for his mother, who, on her side, rarely cared to see him. There was one woman who pined in secret for a sight of his face, and who offered to humble herself before Marie Louise if she might be allowed to fondle Napoleon's son—that was Josephine.

CHAPTER LI

THE WAR IN SPAIN

A.D. 1807–1813

I THINK you will suspect that Napoleon began to lose his head some time before his divorce from Josephine. His mind became less clear than it had been; he grew subject to gusts of passion, in which he made blunder after blunder.

England and France were at war without fighting. England declared that no nation should trade with France, under penalty of having its goods seized by English cruisers. France declared that no nation should trade with England, under the like penalty. As England had a large foreign trade, and France had none, this arrangement was hard on England's customers, and some of them, Portugal in particular, refused to stop their trade with England to please Napoleon. On this Napoleon put a little notice in his paper:

"The house of Braganza [which was the reigning house of Portugal] has ceased to reign."

And he sent an army under Junot into Portugal to drive out the king and occupy the country.

In the neighboring kingdom of Spain, which had been an ally to France, confusion prevailed. King Charles the Fourth, who was an imbecile, was ruled by his wife, and she was ruled by an adventurer, whose name was Manuel Godoy. The eldest son of the king, Ferdinand, was as bad as his father, and was always quarrelling with him. One day the old king would disinherit his son, and Ferdinand would threaten to take up arms; the next day Charles would forgive him, and would swear that it was Godoy he wanted to get rid of. Among them all Spain was horribly governed. Under pretence of taking one side or the other, and also of supporting Junot, Napoleon sent an army into Spain.

Then on false pretexts, and by making promises which he did not intend to keep, he entrapped King Charles and his wife and their son Ferdinand into going to meet him at Bayonne in France. When he got them there, he bullied Ferdinand, who was a weak creature, into resigning his claim on the Spanish throne, in exchange for a castle in France and a salary of a million francs a year; then turning on the old king, he frightened him so terribly, by threats of what he was going to do, that Charles abdicated and made over his throne to Napoleon. So now the ground was clear.

Napoleon made his brother Joseph, who was King of Naples, King of Spain, and to replace him as King of Naples he chose Marshal Murat, who had been a waiter in a café, but who, by way of reward for turning out the Assembly on the eighteenth Brumaire, had been made a marshal of France and allowed to marry Napoleon's sister Caroline. Thus, you perceive, all western Europe, from the borders of Prussia and Austria, was to be ruled by a member of the Bonaparte family, which meant Napoleon himself.

But the emperor forgot that no people likes to be ruled by a foreigner. Above all others, the Spaniards, who are a high-spirited people, deeply attached to their own country, were sure to rebel. They despised Charles and Ferdinand; but, after all, these were Spaniards, and they thought the worst Spaniard had a better right to govern Spain than the best Frenchman. All over Spain, from the Pyrenees to the Mediterranean, the people rose, with such poor arms and such poor leaders as they could get, and swore on their crucifixes that they would fight the French as long as their ancestors had fought the Moors. And they got help. On the 25th of October, 1808, an English army, under the command of a general of whom you will hear more—he was then Sir Arthur Wellesley—landed at Oporto in Portugal.

The Spanish and Portuguese then began to fight in earnest. Junot's army was forced to surrender. And the

PORT OF HAVRE

French army, at Baylen, was attacked, beaten, and many of the prisoners murdered. Such was the rage of the Spaniards, that when the French General Dupont was marching on Cordova he came across the bodies of two hundred Frenchmen—some hanged or crucified on trees, some who had been half buried alive, some sawn in two between planks. Four hundred French merchants at Valencia were slaughtered by a mob. When Spaniards' blood is roused they are very cruel.

All over Spain a new catechism was scattered; I give you a short extract:

Q. Child, what art thou?

A. A Spaniard, by the grace of God.

Q. Who is our enemy?

A. The Emperor of the French.

Q. What is the Emperor of the French?

A. A wicked being, the source of all evils, and the centre of all vice.

Q. How many natures has he?

A. Two, the human and the diabolical.

Q. What are the French?

A. Apostate Christians turned heretics.

Q. Is it a sin to kill a Frenchman?

A. No, my father; heaven is gained by killing one of the heretical dogs.

Maddened by the obstinacy of the Spaniards in defending their country, Napoleon entered Spain himself, with three hundred thousand men and some of his best generals, and defeated the Spanish armies wherever he met them. But, as in the old times, they fled to the mountains when they were beaten, and after a breathing-spell began to fight again as fiercely as ever. There was one walled town named Saragossa. The French besieged it under Lannes and Junot, and at last broke into it. But every house was defended, as if it had been a fortress. It was necessary to blow up each building separately, and the men with their wives kept up the fight after they saw the mine was going to be sprung. At last, at the end of a battle which lasted thirty-one days, after the French had got into the city, it surrendered, fifty-four thousand people out of a population of a hundred thousand having been killed. The corpses which the garrison had not had time to bury poisoned the air.

The war lasted four years more, but Napoleon was not with his troops, and his generals lost as many battles as they won. It is difficult to conquer a country where every man, woman, and child is resisting the conquest. The French were led by one French marshal after another—Lannes, Junot, Ney, Murat, Soult, Masséna, Suchet; the

Spaniards and their allies, the English, by Sir Arthur Wellesley—who afterward became the Duke of Wellington—Sir John Moore, and others. In the war splendid deeds of bravery were done on both sides and glorious victories won. But you will not remember any of them as well as the lines on the death of Sir John Moore, who was killed as his army was retreating to Corunna. I dare say you learned them at school:

"Not a drum was heard, nor a funeral note,
As his corpse to the rampart we hurried;
Not a soldier discharged his farewell shot
O'er the grave where our hero was buried.
We buried him darkly at dead of night,
The sods with our bayonets turning;
By the straggling moonbeams' misty light,
And the lantern dimly burning.
No useless coffin enclosed his breast,
Nor in sheet nor in shroud we wound him;
But he lay like a warrior taking his rest,
With his martial cloak around him."

The end of the war in Spain was that the French were driven out by the combined Spaniards and English, and were followed in pursuit as far as Toulouse in France, where they were badly beaten. They lost thousands of brave soldiers, who were sacrificed to Napoleon's greed for empire; and the war filled the hearts of Spaniards with a hatred for the French name which has not yet been quenched.

ST. CLOUD

Chapter LII

DOWNFALL OF NAPOLEON

A.D. 1812–1814

Napoleon's attempt to make his brother Joseph King of Spain convinced the kings of Europe that there could be no peace for them so long as the emperor reigned. They were still so much afraid of him that none of them declared war, but he could see that they meant it all the same. He prepared for it accordingly, and as the first step he raised the number of his army to a million men, twice as many soldiers as the Union armies ever counted at any one time in our civil war. To raise this enormous force he had to press young men into the ranks long before their beards had grown; in many villages not one young man or half-grown boy was left, and the woods were full of boys trying to escape the draft. He also drew soldiers from the countries he had overrun, Italy, Bavaria, Westphalia, and even parts of Austria and Prussia.

In the first spring days of 1812 the emperor reviewed four hundred thousand men in the Field of Mars at Paris; they made so grand a show that it looked as though under such a leader they could conquer all Europe. He had resolved to attack Russia first; not that he had any particular ground of quarrel with her, but that she was the head of the combination against him and the only nation in Europe, except England, which he had not humbled. Pretexts for a war were easily found, and in March, 1812, he ordered his army to move. It numbered six hundred and fifty thousand men, sixty thousand horses, and twelve hundred cannon.

The Russians lay waiting for them on the Dwina and the Dnieper rivers, with something over three hundred thousand men. They were commanded by a wise old general named Barclay de Tolly, who knew how hard it was to beat Napoleon in battle. When the French came up he retreated, burning towns and villages, grain, fruit-trees, and food of all kinds. Napoleon pushed on; Barclay kept falling back before him. Every day the French gained a few miles, and every day the Russians retreated as many. Thus Barclay kept drawing the French farther and farther from their home, and into a country where a field-mouse would have starved. The Emperor of Russia could not understand this wise policy; he removed Barclay and put in his place General Kutusoff, who gave battle to the French at a place called Borodino.

This was one of the most terrible battles of these terrible times. The Russians lost sixty thousand men killed and wounded, the French thirty thousand. The French won the day, but they could not prevent the survivors of the Russian army from retreating into Moscow. There the French followed them.

You will be surprised to hear that just before entering Moscow, Napoleon wrote to the Russian emperor,

"Whatever may be the fortunes of war, nothing can weaken my regard for my friend of Tilsit."

You see, Napoleon could not be honest. He was always playing a part and making believe.

Moscow was a city as large as Baltimore or San Francisco; it was the ancient capital of Russia, and was full of wealth and splendor. When the French saw from a hill-top, under the rays of the setting sun, the ancient city with its gilded domes and Asiatic spires, its roofs glittering with many-colored tiles, and its gorgeous Kremlin, the citadel of the czars, they burst into shouts of joy. They felt that here were rest and plenty, and glory and triumph, such as they had found in the Italian cities. But when they entered Moscow they found it as empty as a desert and as silent as a grave. There was no one in the streets. The houses were all shut up. The only sound that caught their ear was the occasional howl of a deserted dog. By orders of the Russian emperor every one had quitted the city, leaving only the ghost of Moscow behind. The French officers galloped from quarter to quarter, but could find no enemy and no people. They were disappointed, but they made the best of it: the weary troopers camped in gorgeous palaces and stretched themselves under silken canopies; bearded grenadiers set their muddy boots on laced linen sheets and tried to forget their bleeding wounds.

That night, fire broke out in twenty different places at once. The prisoners had been released from the jails on condition that they would burn Moscow from end to end. They had cut off the supply of water and disabled the fire-engines. A fierce equinoctial gale swept over the city, and the houses, which were built of wood, burned like tinder. In fifty different places barrels of powder, with their heads staved in, had been set in cellars. Explosion followed explosion; the night air was lit up with burning sticks and sparks; the Russian jail-birds crowed with fiendish glee. In wild confusion the French soldiers rushed from their beds, groped their way through smoke and flame, and ran into the suburbs and thence into the country. Those who had served in Spain said to each other that the Russian blood was up, as the Spanish blood had been up.

Napoleon made the best of his way to a castle three

miles from Moscow, and as he watched the sea of flames, which rose and fell, he said,

"This forebodes no common calamity."

In which prediction he was more nearly right than he had been of late in his prophecies.

The fire lasted five days. At the end of that time there was no shelter for the troops, nor food for them to live on. So thoroughly had the work been done that fifteen thousand Russians who had been left in the hospitals were all burned to death.

It was then the 19th of September, and the terrible Russian winter was near at hand. If Napoleon had been wise, he would have ordered an immediate retreat. But he was too proud to avow himself beaten, and he wasted six precious weeks in skirmishing round Moscow, while his men were dying of hunger and privations and wounds from an unseen foe. At last, on November 1st, he gave orders to march homeward. But now the Russians got their innings. They set their teeth in their stolid way, and vowed to each other that not one of these prowling Frenchmen who had come to conquer their Russia should be allowed to return home. They dogged their footsteps, hung on their rear, worried their flanks, popped up in front of them. Every morning, when the sun rose over the glittering stretches of the snow-fields, the French saw between them and the horizon clouds of Cossacks, riding with their sharp lances in air, waiting for a chance to dash in and stab tired troopers who stopped to rest; every little hill and clump of bushes hid a party of sharp-shooters who took aim at the weary fugitives as they passed. From morning till night the crack of the Russian musket never ceased, and the French could be followed by their bloody trail.

As the season advanced terribly cold weather set in, with heavy snow-storms and icy winds. The French had lost their tents and their overcoats. They lived on the flesh of the horses which died and a little flour soaked in water. The wounded had to be left behind for want of means to move them. Frost and sickness reduced the emperor's guard from thirty-seven thousand to ten thousand, though it had not been in battle. The famous first corps, which had counted seventy-five thousand bayonets and sabres at the beginning of the campaign, could only muster eight thousand at the end. Suffering made the troops torpid; they just lay down and died where they were. On the bank of the Berezina, where large bonfires had been lit and supplies of food gathered, they crouched round the fires, and did not stir when the Russian bullets came crashing among them. When they were warmed and fed, they made a rush for the bridges, and pushed one another into the freezing river in their haste to escape the Cossack lances.

On that retreat from Moscow, Napoleon had lost his wits as well as his men. While his troops were starving, he burned up provisions for fear the Russians should use them, and he left his generals to get out of the scrape into which he had led them. On December the 5th, without saying a word to any one, he deserted his army and ran away to Paris. He left Murat in command, and this general managed to draw off the small remnant of the army, who fought their way through Cossacks and struggled through snow-drifts to Wilna, where the Russian pursuit ceased.

There were at this time not over twenty-five thousand troops left. Of the great army which Napoleon had led forth to conquer Russia, three hundred thousand were dead, and one hundred thousand were prisoners. The rest had been left in garrison on the line of march.

Napoleon reached Paris on December the 18th. You might suppose that after such an awful defeat he would try to make peace with his enemies. Nothing of the kind. By gathering the soldiers he had left in France, scooping up all the boys he could find, and adding them to the remnant of his Russian army and his garrisons in Germany, Italy, and Spain, he figured that he could still put five hundred thousand men in the field, and he set about doing it. Human life was never anything to him.

But his luck was gone. By tremendous efforts he succeeded in gathering two hundred and fifty thousand men —enough perhaps to hold his own against Russia and Prussia, which had now joined Russia. He counted that Austria would be neutral, because he had married the Austrian emperor's daughter, and here is where his calculations failed. There was a meeting between him and the prime-

RETREAT OF THE FRENCH

minister of Austria, Metternich, at Dresden, on June 28th, 1813. Metternich, who was more far-sighted and more cool-headed than Napoleon, told him frankly that Europe wanted peace, that the emperor must give up some of his conquests and stop making war on his neighbors. Napoleon flew into one of his rages, dashed a priceless porcelain vase to pieces, threw his hat on the ground and stamped on it, and said he would never, never surrender a foot of land he had won; whereupon Metternich, with a sneering smile, observed,

"Sire, you are done for."

And as soon as the Austrian got back to Vienna, Austria joined Russia and Prussia against France and agreed to put a quarter of a million men in the field. Meanwhile, Bernadotte, King of Sweden, one of Napoleon's old generals, joined the coalition, Wellington, with his English troops, came marching up from Spain, and another English army landed at Hamburg. With his old dash and boldness, Napoleon invaded Germany and fought several battles which decided nothing; but the enemy were two to one, and at last, at Leipsic, on October 18th, 1813, he fought a battle in opposition to the advice of his wisest generals. Here his Saxon troops deserted him as soon as fire was opened. Napoleon claimed that he was not beaten, but in fact the result of the fight was that he had to retreat to France.

Even then he would not agree to the terms of peace which Metternich pressed on him. He insisted on levying more boy-soldiers. There was no reasoning with him, and on December 21st Schwartzenberg, at the head of his Austrians, entered France, and Blücher, at the head of his Prussians, followed ten days afterward. Both armies headed for Paris. Napoleon fell upon them again and again on the march and sometimes won small victories; but the great swell of the foreign armies was too mighty to be resisted, and on the last day of March, 1814, the allies, under the command of the Emperor Alexander of Russia, entered the French capital. On the day following the French Senate—ah! how it had crawled at his feet in past days!—decreed that Napoleon had ceased to reign.

He had been some days in Paris, listening to the muttering of the coming storm. He knew that the members of the Legislative Assembly were tired of him; he called them together and dismissed them with these words:

"Your object is to humble me. My life may be sacrificed, but my honor, never. I was not born in the rank of kings. I do not depend on the throne. What is a throne? A few deal boards covered with velvet. Must I sacrifice my pride to obtain peace? I am proud, because I am brave. I am proud, because I have done great things for France. France needs me more than I need her. In three months we shall have peace, or I will be dead. Now go to your homes."

He was at Fontainebleau when the Senate deposed him, and even then he proposed to go on with the fight in the streets of Paris. But his officers flatly told him they would be guilty of no such folly. Then he said he would abdicate in favor of his son. This was proposed to the allied generals, and Alexander of Russia, who was tender-hearted and liked Napoleon, was for accepting it. But the other generals would not listen to it for a moment, and after spending a whole night in vain pleadings, at six in the morning, on April 2d, he signed a paper, renouncing the French throne for himself and his heirs.

It read as follows:

"The allied powers having proclaimed the Emperor Napoleon to be the only obstacle to the restoration of peace in Europe, the Emperor Napoleon, faithful to his oath, declares that he renounces for himself and his heirs the thrones of France and Italy, and that there is no sacrifice, even that of life, which he is not ready to make for the interests of France.

"Given at the palace of Fontainebleau, April 2d, 1814."

It was arranged that he should have the island of Elba in the Mediterranean for a dominion. He was to start for his new empire on April 20th. His wife and his son were not to go with him. Her father, the Emperor of Austria, thought she would be safer at Vienna, and in her dull, passive way she thought so too. Napoleon did not care to have her, and she had long before let every one see that she did not care for him. There was one woman whose heart was aching with painful longing to be with him in his hour of sorrow. That was Josephine. She offered to go to take care of him, and to be his handmaid and his nurse, if Marie Louise kept out of the way. But all parties said it was out of the question.

In one of the magnificent galleries of paintings in Paris you will see a fine picture of Napoleon taking leave of his marshals and generals.

Perhaps you may think it a trifle theatrical. For two or three years the emperor had been grossly unjust to his generals, blaming them for the results of his own blunders. Many of them were tired of him and of his endless wars, in which they had seen their brothers in arms give up their lives for his ambition. Some of them had for some time been secretly treating with the enemy. I don't think that those who knew him best were sorriest to get rid of him.

When he parted from them he threw his eyes to heaven and cried,

"Soldiers, I have but one mission left in life—to recount to posterity the glorious deeds we have done together."

I do not find that that history was begun till long afterward, when Napoleon had nothing else to do; and I suspect that, even when he uttered these words, he was thinking how near Elba was to France.

On his way south the people of Avignon and Orgon mobbed his escort, and shouted that the tyrant should be hanged or thrown into the Rhone. At Orgon, the first object which struck his eye was an effigy of himself, hanging by a rope round its neck and swinging in the air. When the gate of the court-yard where his carriage stopped was closed, a butcher chopped it in pieces with an axe, and the yard quickly filled with a seething, shouting crowd of men and women.

"Where are my two sons, whom I lost in Russia?" cried one woman.

"Where," cried another, "is my husband, who fell at Wagram?"

"Give me my father, who was killed in Italy," screamed a third.

The escort had to bestir themselves to get their prisoner off safely. Napoleon put on a disguise and drove away by a back gate. Thus he got through, embarked on an English frigate, and landed at Porto Ferrayo in Elba on May 4th, 1814.

AVIGNON

LOUIS XVIII

CHAPTER LIII

WATERLOO

A.D. 1814–1815

WHEN Napoleon was overthrown the government of France fell into the hands of the Emperor of Russia, the Emperor of Austria, and an exceedingly adroit Frenchman whose name was Talleyrand. These three decided that Louis, the brother of Louis the Sixteenth, was the proper person to succeed the emperor; he was to be known as Louis the Eighteenth, because the poor little dauphin, who had died in the Temple and had never reigned at all, must be counted among the kings of France, as Louis the Seventeenth. It was agreed that the conquests of Napoleon should be given up, and that, under her new king, France, with her old boundaries, should make such laws for herself as she saw fit, without foreign interference.

Louis the Eighteenth was a fat man of sixty, who had spent the last twenty-five years in England and had become very English indeed. He had never had any experience in public affairs or in the wars of the day. He

TALLEYRAND

was a quiet old gentleman, who loved his ease and his books; he was fond of the Latin poets; he was also fond of English roast beef and plum pudding; in the middle of a good dinner he would eat half a dozen lamb chops just by way of whetting his appetite. You will not be surprised to hear that he was gouty and walked with difficulty. He wore a blue coat with epaulets, an English hat, and red velvet gaiters which hid his swollen legs. He had neither wife nor children, but the daughter of Louis the Sixteenth, who was called the Duchess of Angoulême, lived with him and took care of him. Another lady, who was beautiful and gifted, and whose name was Madame

Du Cayla, also took care of him and bandaged his gouty legs. He was so sluggish that, when he was told he was wanted in Paris to reign over France, he was loath to leave his quiet English home. But he came, landed at Calais on April 24th, 1814, and travelling by easy stages, for fear of making his gout worse, entered Paris on the 3d of May, in a coach drawn by eight horses, with the Duchess of Angoulême by his side.

He soon showed that he had learned nothing in his long exile. He made a speech in which he said that he owed his throne to the English, which could not have been pleasant to the French. He ordered the old French flag, which was white with lilies on it, to be restored, and forbade the flying of the tricolor, under which the French soldiers had won so much glory. He said that he wanted to put things back just where they had been before the Revolution. Now, the French had learned a great deal during the twenty-five years that he had spent abroad; and though some of the things they had learned were not good, others were, and the people did not take kindly to the idea of having all the lessons of those years, bitter as some of them had been, wiped out altogether. They began by treating their new king with indifference, then they got to despising him, and finally they hated him.

There were in France thousands of old soldiers who had grown to love the excitement and the glory and the spoil of war. Many of them forgave Napoleon his selfishness and the reckless way in which he had led his troops to death, for the sake of the fame and the rewards he showered on them when they won battles. Under him every private expected to become a general and to live in a palace. They now grumbled at the idea of leading humdrum lives of peace. After Napoleon had gone, these old growlers compared him to the dull, gouty, fat man who had taken his place — not much to the advantage of Louis.

Meanwhile, their hero was chafing in his little island—

which was not much larger than the District of Columbia and was chiefly crag and bog and wild forest. He could ride round it in a day. In clear, bright weather he used to sit on the top of a mountain and gaze wistfully at the coast of Italy, where he had won his first victories. After a time his longing to get out of his narrow prison, in which he could hardly breathe, and back into the great world once more became too strong to be resisted. He had renounced the crown of France for himself and his heirs. But I dare say you remember he had broken his word before. It was no new thing.

On February 26th, 1815, after less than ten months' captivity, he stole out of Elba, with eleven hundred men and a little fleet of small vessels, and steered for France. Three days afterward he landed near Cannes, in Provence. Without losing an hour he climbed the foot-hills of the Alps and took the road for Grenoble. He had provided himself with proclamations, in which he said,

"Frenchmen! in my exile I heard your prayers. I have crossed the sea to assert my rights, which are yours. Come and take your place under the standard of your chief! Victory will advance with full gallop, and the eagle with the national colors will fly from steeple to steeple, even to the towers of Notre Dame."

The appeal had the old ring. The people of Dauphiné, through which he passed, forgot all about their sufferings and his mad rage for war, and met him with shouts of "Long live the emperor!" Some joined his little band; others brought him horses and provisions. At Grenoble, a royal regiment tried to stop him; he stepped forth in his old gray overcoat and, with his cocked hat on, marched straight up to the front rank and cried,

"Soldiers, do you know me?"

"Yes, yes," answered hundreds of voices.

Then he threw open his overcoat, and, baring his breast, he shouted,

"Which among you will fire on your emperor?"

A roar of "Long live the emperor!" rose to heaven, and big men cried for joy at seeing him again.

In Paris all was commotion. The fat old king, wheezing and whining, began to pack his trunk, and his courtiers bought tickets for Belgium. A few of the generals were for fighting it out. One of these was Ney, who had been an especial favorite of the emperor's and was the bravest of the brave; he told Louis that if he would give him an army corps he would march against Napoleon and "bring him back in an iron cage." He got his army corps and did march, but he no sooner met the emperor than he proclaimed him the only rightful ruler of France and joined him in the march to Paris.

Napoleon reached the Tuileries on March 20th and was nearly stifled by the crowds which filled the rooms and the passages to get a sight of him, and wring his hands, and fall on his neck, in the excitable way the French have. He had not fired a shot on his three weeks' journey. Every one seemed as glad to see him as he was to be back. From the wild joy of the people he might have imagined that his troubles were over. But he was too wise for that.

He knew that in two months all Europe would be in arms against him again, with forces so much larger than his that nothing short of a miracle would enable him to hold his own against them. He tried to conciliate every one. His old harshness and his imperious manner were gone. He submitted to rebuke quite meekly and let his officers scold him, even when he was right and they were wrong. He was ready, he said, to give up his foreign conquests, and to let France have a real instead of a sham Assembly to make laws for her. Ah! if his word could only have been trusted!

In public he was cheerful and even gay, but this was only acting; in private he was bowed down by sadness. He spent days and nights in thinking over the past and brooding over the future. In his inmost soul he felt that his sun was set. His chief companion in those days was

Hortense, Josephine's daughter—Josephine herself had died when he was at Elba. With Hortense he spent long hours at Malmaison, wondering what strange lot fortune had yet in store for him.

He knew that his only chance was to strike the first blow at the Russians and Austrians and Prussians and English and Belgians who were gathering beyond the Rhine, and with what soldiers he could gather he left Paris in June. Before he left he appointed a council to rule France while he was with the army. His last words to them were mournful. He said,

"If I am victorious we shall build up a new régime. If I am conquered God alone knows what will become of you and of me. It is our fate, and nothing can avert it. All will be decided in twenty or thirty days. For the present let us do what we can and see what the future will bring. But let the friends of liberty look well to it; if the game is lost they will have to deal with the Bourbons, who will be worse than I have been."

He set out for Belgium with a hundred and eighty-two thousand soldiers. Waiting for him near the city of Brussels were a hundred and twenty-four thousand Prussians, under Blücher, and ninety-five thousand English and Dutch, under Wellington. Three hundred thousand Austrians and a hundred and seventy-five thousand Russians were on the march, and would join the English and Prussians in July. On June 15th, Napoleon crossed the Sambre with a hundred and twenty-four thousand men and three hundred and fifty cannon.

On the 16th he beat the Prussians at Ligny; on the 17th it rained all day, and artillery could not be used; on the 18th the battle of Waterloo was fought.

This was one of the most bloody battles of modern times, and it changed the face of Europe. The battle began at eleven in the morning, as soon as the fog had lifted from the wet fields; it did not end till near nine in the evening, when the faces of the dead and the wounded could no longer be seen for the darkness. All that day the cannon thundered with an endless roar, and the French cuirassiers, with their shining steel breastplates and on their big horses, charged and charged and charged again upon the squares which the English infantry formed on a hill. On a hill on one side of the battle-field Napoleon sat on his horse, with his spyglass in his hand; on the other side of the battle-field, also on a hill, stood Wellington, in his red uniform, silent, stern, and cold. Between the two the face of the plain was often hidden from view by clouds of smoke through which red flames flashed.

When the French cuirassiers again and again charged up the hill to the spot where Wellington stood, he threw himself into an infantry square, and said quietly,

"Hard pounding this, gentlemen."

When the Scotch Grays, an English cavalry regiment, charged the French lancers and actually rode through them, Napoleon, who was watching with his spyglass, said to the Belgian who held his horse,

"Look at those gray horses—how they work! They are all mixed up with my lancers."

It was the French, led by Ney, who forced the fighting. The English stood stubbornly in their squares, or lay down on their faces on the ground to avoid the hail of round shot and grape and bullets.

Both generals kept gazing from time to time into the distance. Napoleon expected Grouchy to arrive with thirty-four thousand fresh men; but he never came, nor even sent to say he was coming. Wellington expected Blücher with his Prussians; he did come, early in the evening, and when he came the battle was won. He launched his troopers against the tired French, and, Wellington hurling his English guards against them at the same time, the emperor's army broke and fled.

One battalion of the Imperial Guard formed a square, and when the English summoned it to surrender, its commander, old Cambronne, replied,

"The guard may die, but it will not surrender."

The English pulled trigger, and not one man escaped.

When darkness fell the French army had ceased to exist. Through all the dark hours of that summer night fierce old Blücher, with his heavy cavalry and his flying artillery, galloped after the flying French, taking prisoners and slaughtering. In all his life Blücher never spared a beaten enemy. The pursuit only stopped when the swords

TOMB OF NAPOLEON AT ST. HELENA

of the troopers were dripping with blood, and they were falling from their horses from weariness. At that hour Napoleon, curled up at the bottom of a carriage, was being driven swiftly to Paris, gazing with wide-open eyes into the darkness.

When he reached the city he still planned further resistance. But the Assembly plucked up courage enough to demand his abdication, and when he proposed to abdicate in favor of his son they would not even answer him. So he took horse and started with a few old friends for the sea-coast, whence he said he would sail to the United States. While he was riding the English and Prussians entered Paris, and sent word to Louis the Eighteenth that he might come back.

Napoleon left Paris on June the 29th. For three days he never spoke a word. On July the 3d he arrived at Rochefort, which was blockaded by an English battle-ship called the *Bellerophon.* On board this vessel the emperor took refuge, saying that he cast himself on the hospitality of the English and claimed the protection of their laws. The *Bellerophon* weighed anchor and sailed to England.

Napoleon did not receive from the English the hospitality he expected. The government decided to send him to the little sultry, barren rock of St. Helena, in the tropics, off the coast of Africa, and to hold him there as a prisoner. St. Helena is surrounded by so stormy a sea that it is not easy to land on it, or to leave it, except in very fair weather.

If a ship-of-war mounted guard near the island Napoleon could not escape from the place, as he had escaped from Elba. That was what the powers wanted to make sure of. The fallen emperor was allowed to take with him three of his old generals, a personal friend, a doctor, and twelve servants. He had a plantation in the centre of the island for his residence, horses to ride, and a good table. But to keep sure watch of him an English officer was required to see him twice every day, and when he rode off his plantation he was followed by this officer on horseback.

Over him was set the Governor of St. Helena, Sir Hudson Lowe. I suppose that no one in such a station could have pleased his prisoner, and that Napoleon, who grew irritable in his captivity, could not have been friendly with his jailer, even though the latter had been an angel. But Sir Hudson Lowe was a small-minded, mean man, who seemed to take pleasure in annoying Napoleon and making him feel that he was fallen indeed. The British government, to which he had given so much trouble, did not go out of its way to make life pleasant for one who had cost England so many lives and so much money. It was constantly laying down rules which wounded the emperor's proud spirit and threw him into rages.

One source of quarrel was the title by which he was to be addressed. He insisted on being called the Emperor Napoleon. To this Sir Hudson Lowe replied that he was not emperor any more, and that his right title was General

LUXEMBOURG

Bonaparte. Napoleon would not receive letters addressed to General Bonaparte; Sir Hudson would not deliver any to the Emperor Napoleon. Finally it was settled that the latter should be called plain Napoleon Bonaparte, without the title of emperor or general or even mister.

He was not allowed to write sealed letters to any one. When he wrote to his friends Sir Hudson opened the letters and read them. He could not receive money from his own family.

He was in bad health when he arrived at St. Helena.

His constitution had been broken down by work and anxiety. Under the fierce rays of the blazing sun of that treeless, scorched island he grew worse, and cancer set in. The dreadful disease grew gradually worse, and the pain it caused became frightful. In April, 1821, when he was fifty-two years old, he knew that he was dying. He called his friends round him and told them.

"You," he said, "will return to Europe. I am going to meet Kleber, Desaix, Lannes, and my other dead comrades. They will come to meet me. We shall speak together of what we have done. We shall talk of our profession."

The agony grew worse, and he became delirious. In his delirium he cried, "My son! The army! Desaix! The head of the army!"

As the sun was setting that night in waves of light over the rolling ocean, and just as an English cannon fired the evening gun, an attendant stepped to his bedside and found that he was dead. His body was straight, and there was a tranquil smile on his face. It was the 5th of May, the anniversary of his first day at Elba, seven years before.

When Louis the Eighteenth got back on his throne, under the protection of English and Prussian bayonets, he determined to make an example of some officers who had been false to him when Napoleon returned from Elba. He chose Marshal Ney to begin with.

The marshal, as you remember, had been one of Napoleon's favorite generals. When Louis the Eighteenth came to the throne, after the retreat from Moscow, Ney offered him his services and was given a high command. When Napoleon returned from Elba it was Ney who volunteered to meet his old commander, and he went out of his way to say that he would bring him back to Paris in an iron cage. When he did meet him he deserted his king, joined Napoleon, marched with him to Paris, and fought gallantly at the battle of Waterloo. I think you will have to conclude that if any man had been guilty of treason, Ney was the man.

MARSHAL NEY

He was arrested, put on his trial before the Chamber of Peers, found guilty, and sentenced to be shot. The king refused to pardon him, though some of his best friends begged Ney's life on their knees.

He was taken into the Luxembourg Gardens and set with his back against the wall. You can see the spot if you go to Paris; a statue of Ney has lately been erected there. A file of veteran troops stood in front of him. He took off his hat and waved it, crying, "Long live France!" then, raising his left hand to his breast, he called,

"Soldiers, aim at my heart."

The officer gave the command; and Ney fell on his face, dead, with ten bullets in his breast.

CHAPTER LIV

THE BOURBONS

A.D. 1815–1830

LOUIS THE EIGHTEENTH had studied politics in England, and his idea of governing a country was to have a parliament elected by the people and to let it make the laws. He arranged accordingly for the election of a Chamber to act with a House of Peers, and appointed a ministry that was expected to be agreeable to both. But the persons who composed the Chamber were a small, select class, and they were not born with the faculty of self-government. People must be educated up to that business, and very often the education takes time. The Chamber which met became as hot a scene of strife as the old Assembly and the Convention had been; nobody was willing to yield anything to anybody else, and instead of healing the wounds of France the Chamber seemed to make them worse.

The people were divided into two parties. One consisted of those who wanted to make the best of the situation, to forget the past, and try to get the government working again in an orderly way; the other was led by the Emigrants and the old nobles, who wanted to take vengeance on the men of the Revolution and the followers of Napoleon and to put things back on their old footing. Between these two parties Louis wavered, now this way, now that. He could not prevent the exile and execution of a number of Napoleon's friends, though he tried to do so. But he adhered to the old notion that kings were kings by the grace of God, and that the will of the people had nothing to do with the case. He never quite understood that there had been a revolution in France, and that men's opinions had changed in the past twenty-five years.

He was old, too, and lazy, and his gout troubled him a great deal; so, when the nobles and Madame du Cayla bullied him, telling him that the party of order would guillotine him as they had guillotined his brother, he shivered and let them lead him. They brought the Jesuits back; they proposed to restore the old privileges of the nobility and the clergy; they would not allow any one to vote unless he had property worth at least sixty dollars; they put a gag in the mouth of newspapers; they filled the offices with men of title. Finally, the wretched King of Spain—the same man who had sold his birthright to Napoleon for a castle in France and a million francs a year—having fallen out with his people, they gave Louis no rest till he sent an army into Spain, under his nephew, to put the Spaniards down and hold the king up.

This angered the French, who said, very truthfully, that the Spaniards had as good a right to govern themselves as the French had, and plots began to be concocted for the murder of Louis. I am afraid that one of them would have accomplished its purpose, but that, in September, 1824, after a reign of nine years, he one day died in his bed.

He was succeeded by his brother Charles, who had borne the title of Count of Artois, and after his coronation was known as King Charles the Tenth.

He was sixty-seven years old. In his youth he had been wild—he had led the same vile life as Louis the Fifteenth and the Regent Orleans. In his old age he fell into the hands of the priests and became very pious. Still he began well—he took the gag out of the mouth of the newspapers, asked some of Napoleon's generals to court, and invited liberal men to help him with their counsels. But this did not last long. People noticed that Charles went to mass every morning, which perhaps was not such a bad thing; but he also walked through the streets in religious processions, was anointed by an archbishop, and pretended to cure people who had scrofula by touching them. He had newspapers indicted for speaking ill of the Jesuits, and he was surprised when they were acquitted by the juries.

He began to be very obstinate indeed. He revived the nunneries, which the Republic had abolished, and he set at defiance a decree of court declaring that Jesuitism was illegal in France. When he appeared at a review, and the people shouted, "Down with the ministers! Down with the Jesuits!" he replied haughtily, "I came to France to receive homage, not a lecture."

Which so exasperated the mob that they followed the carriage containing the ladies of the king's family, shouting, "Down with the she-Jesuits!"

Determined to crush those who objected to the power of the priests, Charles dissolved the Chamber. A riot following, he sent troops against the rioters and killed numbers of them. Béranger, the song-writer, who was the idol of Paris, wrote a song quizzing Charles; he was sent to prison for nine months and was fined ten thousand francs, which was ten times more than he had. On October 9th, 1829, the king appointed a new ministry, consisting of men who were hateful to the French. Prince Polignac, of the Holy Roman empire, was at their head.

Then loomed up in the midst of the confusion the man of all others whom the French loved—old, white-haired Lafayette, the hero of the beginning of the Revolution. He was afraid of nothing, and he said that France ought not to submit to a bigoted tyrant, and that the new prime-minister, Polignac, must go. The French hung round him when he appeared in the streets and cheered him as loudly as they cursed Polignac. Charles was not shaken. When the Chamber met he said,

"Should obstacles arise in my path, I will find strength to surmount them."

The Chamber sent a petition requesting the king to dismiss Polignac. He replied,

"I have announced to you my intentions. My resolves

are not to be shaken. My ministers will explain my purposes to you."

On July 25th, by royal ordinance, Charles suspended the liberty of the press, dissolved the Chamber, and reduced the number of citizens who could vote to a mere handful. Then he went out hunting. Lafayette started from his country place for Paris, and the people of the stout old city got ready for another tussle with a despot.

MARQUIS DE LAFAYETTE

At five in the morning of the 28th the people turned out with such weapons as they could get, and filled the streets. They tore down pictures of the king from the signs, threw down the white flag, pole and all, from the City Hall, and hoisted the tricolor to the highest steeple of Notre Dame.

They seized a powder magazine, and the women made cartridges. General Marmont, Governor of Paris, warned the king that a revolution was impending. Charles waved his white, jewelled hand in his grand way, and bade him brush away all that rabble with his troops. Polignac ordered him to open fire at once. The fighting did indeed begin, under a sweltering sun, and several thousand people were killed. By night crowds of countrymen came trooping into Paris, armed with old muskets and scythes and pitchforks.

Marmont advised the king to give way, but he only laughed his high-bred laugh and sat down to his usual game of whist, while the cannon which were being fired at the people shook the windows of the room in which he sat.

On the next day several of Marmont's regiments passed over to the side of the revolutionists. The mob took the Tuileries, and hoisted the tricolor over it. They set guards over the Treasury and the Louvre, and when a man was found stealing he was promptly shot. At evening Lafayette came in and took command of the national guards. Late that night Charles wrote that he would dismiss his ministry and revoke his ordinances. Then he sat down to his whist-table and began leading trumps.

It was too late. On July 30th one of the leaders of the movement asked Lafayette,

"Are you willing to be president of a new French republic?"

The answer came quick and clear,

"Certainly not."

"Then you must help us to make the Duke of Orleans king."

The duke went to the City Hall to meet him, and said to the people,

"You see before you an old national guardsman of 1789, who has come to see his general."

People were not quite satisfied. The Orleans family had a bad name. General Dubourg said to him,

"If you make promises and break them, we shall know how to deal with you."

"Sir," said the duke, "I am an honest man, and do not need to be reminded of my promises."

By this time the king, who was still at Rambouillet, was having trouble with his digestion, and was beginning to think that it was about time to stop leading trumps. He sent for Odilon Barrot, and asked him in a trembling voice,

"What am I to do?"

Said Odilon Barrot: "Your majesty must get out of France as fast as you can. And, by-the-bye, I happen to have with me a regiment of cavalry, which will escort your majesty to the frontier, for fear any one should be rude to you."

It was so done. Charles was escorted to Cherbourg, where he took ship for England. He settled at Edinburgh, and there spent the rest of his life, going to mass and leading trumps.

Meanwhile things settled down at Paris. When some one wanted to set up the republic once more, old, white-haired Lafayette, who, as you remember, had seen a good deal of republics in France, answered that the Duke of Orleans was the best possible republic.

Paris being of this mind, and France being of the mind of Paris, the Duke of Orleans became king, under the title of Louis Philippe the First. But there were two changes in the kingship. It was stated, and affirmed on the coins which were issued from the mint, that Louis Philippe was king, not of France, but of the French; and that he was not king by the grace of God, but by the will of the French people.

Chapter LV

A CITIZEN KING

A.D. 1830–1848

Louis Philippe was the son of that bad Philippe Equality who had so disgusted the Parisians by his shamelessness that nobody was sorry when the Jacobins sent him to the guillotine. Equality's son was severely brought up by a strong-minded woman named Madame de Genlis. She made him get up at six, winter and summer; trained him to sleep on bare boards, and would not allow him to eat anything but roast meat, bread, and milk. He was never allowed to play, but was taught carpenter-work, mason-work, and the management of horses. When he grew a tall lad, he went to the armies, and under Dumouriez fought for the republic gallantly and faithfully. When the Jacobins, after executing his father, ordered his arrest, he fled from France, and for twenty-one years he wandered over the world an exile, without home or country or money, supporting himself at times by teaching school. He was fifty-seven years old when he became King of the French, and was thought by those who knew him to be an honest, brave, and well-meaning man.

He took an oath to govern in conformity with a bill of rights which the French called a charter It had been first put forth by Louis the Eighteenth, and afterward accepted by Charles the Tenth; but as neither of them had paid attention to it after he was crowned, I have not thought it worth while to mention it. Louis Philippe did try to live up to it. And on the whole, though he reigned through troublous times, and not long ago it was customary to speak ill of him, I think myself that he was a fair king, as kings go.

He called himself a citizen king, dressed like an old grocer, and walked the streets with an old umbrella, talking to every one he knew. He took a rough common-sense view of his duties. When some one urged him to dismiss his ministers (you will find that, even in our day, the French no sooner set up a ministry than they try to pull it down) he replied,

"The policy of my ministers! I don't know what you mean. There is but one policy, and that is my policy. Convince me that I am wrong and I will change it; until then I will stick to it though you bray me in a mortar."

THE BOULEVARDS FIFTY YEARS AGO

The best men in France—old General Lafayette, the banker Lafitte, Guizot, and Thiers, and others of equal note—thought he gave France a very good government indeed.

But the old fermentation still continued. Every few months discontented people tried to get up a revolution, mostly without knowing what they really wanted, and the king had his hands full to maintain peace and order.

A horrible villain named Fieschi, and two or three others,

made an infernal machine of a number of gun-barrels set side by side, and fired them off simultaneously at the king, who was passing at the head of a procession. Forty persnos were killed, but the king was not hit, and when the explosion was over he said quietly,

"Let us go on, gentlemen."

Fieschi was arrested and betrayed his accomplices. He had been a thief and bandit; he was consumed with vanity, and gloried in his deed. After he had turned state's evidence against Pepin, his partner in crime, he was told that it was dinner-time.

"Dinner!" he cried. "I have dined already. I have dined off Pepin's head."

He laughed while the judge was pronouncing his sentence. When he got a chance he struck an attitude and declaimed,

"In a few days my head will be severed from my body. I shall be dead, and my body will rot in the earth. Yet I have rendered a service. After me, no more assassinations, no more disturbances."

He was a poor prophet. Louis Philippe was always being shot at by cranks to the end of his reign.

It was under his reign that France conquered Algeria. And it was while he was king that the remains of Napoleon were brought back from St. Helena, which, as you will see by and by, was not quite so grand a thing as people thought at the time. It was also while he was beginning his management of France that two of the famous Frenchmen of the revolutionary era came to their end—Lafayette and Talleyrand.

I suppose that Lafayette was the most beautiful character of that time. He began life as an officer in Washington's army in 1777, and ended it as a private adviser of Louis Philippe in 1834. During all those fifty-seven years, he never did or said anything that was not wise and manly and loyal and unselfish. When the brutality of the Jacobins forced him to leave his army, he went to

Austria, whose emperor shut him up in a dark and damp dungeon at Olmütz. For a long time no one knew what had become of him. The Austrians would not tell where he was. When his plight was discovered President Washington wrote personally to the Emperor of Austria begging for his release, and Mr. Fox, the famous member of Parliament in England, wrote also; the emperor would not listen to either. But one day Napoleon took the matter in hand, and in his short, sharp, stern way sent his compliments to the emperor, and would he be so kind as to set Lafayette at liberty, and pretty quickly too? Whereupon the prison doors flew open, and the captive walked out into the open air after five years of dungeon life. He was grateful to his liberator, but his principle was so high that he refused to serve in the imperial army.

Talleyrand was very different. He was a lame man, and was a prince, a priest, a wit, and in his private life a reprobate. Queen Marie Antoinette, Mirabeau, Robespierre, Napoleon, the Emperor of Russia, Louis the Eighteenth, Charles the Tenth, Louis Philippe, and Thiers, in their turn, all leaned on him for advice. He knew everybody and everything, cared for nobody, respected nobody; but was feared by everybody, and was prodigiously wise and far-seeing. There is a curious story about his last end. When he died it was resolved to embalm him, and to do so, as you know, it was necessary to remove the soft parts of the body, including the brain. When this had been done, the embalmer carried off the shell of Talleyrand, and his assistants buried the inside, which had been taken out. By some oversight, the brain was left where it had been placed. A servant who entered the room found this grewsome and bloody object on the table, and, not dreaming what it was, swept it into a bucket, carried it downstairs, and threw it into a gutter. Thus the brain which had swayed Europe and moulded politics for fifty years finally fetched up in the slops of a filthy drain.

After Louis Philippe had been some years on the throne

the people began to clamor for a larger share in the government, while the king thought they had too large a share already. He said,

"I will not be caught as Charles the Tenth was; I will take precautions and defend myself better."

On February 22d, 1848, the streets of Paris filled with people, and barricades began to lift their heads. The king had thirty thousand soldiers at his command, and in the afternoon he called out the national guards or militia. They refused to stir. The king offered to sacrifice his ministry; the leader of the people said it was too late for that. At about nine in the evening a regiment opened fire on the crowd and killed a hundred men. The spark kindled a blaze. From eleven o'clock till midnight every church-bell rang the alarm.

When next morning dawned fifteen hundred barricades, made of paving-stones, had been erected, some of them as high as the second story of the houses, and every regiment was besieged where it stood.

Thoroughly frightened at last, the king agreed to abdicate. But it was too late even for that. Musketry fire all round the Tuileries drowned the sound of voices. The mob was drawing nearer and nearer. Through the crowd, Crémieux, a lawyer, forced his way, and said to the king,

"Sire, you must leave Paris!"

Without answering a word, Louis Philippe threw off his uniform and his general's hat, put on a frock-coat and a round hat, and hurried through the Tuileries to a gate where four carriages should have been waiting. They were not there; the mob had seized and burned them. A carriage coming up with the king's daughters-in-law and their children in it, Louis Philippe stepped up and called,

"Get out, all of you!"

He got in himself with his wife, and bade the coachman drive to Versailles. On the way he threw off his wig, and put on a skull-cap which came down to his eyes. At Versailles he got another carriage, and drove on through the night; toward morning he stopped at a farm-house. A fire was lit for him in the kitchen. He said,

"I am very cold; I am very hungry."

Said the farmer, "Would you like some onion soup?"

"Very much indeed."

And he ate heartily.

He was in an agony lest the revolutionists should catch him. They were in an equal agony lest he should be caught. They sent trusty messengers to guard him without his knowledge; they sent him money. They never let him out of the sight of their men until they got him safely on board a steamer, which hoisted anchor at once (the captain had his instructions) and landed him next morning in England. The men who had overthrown him breathed more freely when they knew that he was safe.

Chapter LVI

ANOTHER REPUBLIC

A.D. 1848–1852

When Louis Philippe left there was no government in France. To carry on the public business a few of the leading republicans formed themselves into a provisional government; they were the poet Lamartine, Étienne Arago, Garnier-Pagès, Marie, who were reasonable republicans; Ledru-Rollin and Louis Blanc, who were inclined to socialism; and a labor-agitator named Albert. The chief talker of the party was Lamartine, who delivered beautiful speeches which meant nothing; the work of restoring order out of the prevailing confusion fell chiefly to Arago, Garnier-Pagès, and Marie.

The trouble of the hour was the vast number of men who had been thrown out of work by the disturbances at the close of Louis Philippe's reign and by the revolution which ensued. These people threatened to set the guillotine going again if they could not find work, and Louis Blanc, the man Albert, and others pretended to have discovered that the government owed every man work, as though any state could live by taking money out of one pocket and putting it into another. The provisional government, however, did not feel strong enough to engage in a conflict with this vast, noisy mob; it enrolled several thousand of them in a guard called the Guard Mobile, and it opened government factories at which other thousands were employed in making things which were not wanted.

This plan, of course, could not work long. The government itself was in straits for money, and was in no position to support people by charity. In a short while the government factories had to be closed, and the workmen were thrown on the street. They declared that they would start another revolution, and that property should be taken from those who owned it and divided among those who had nothing, in order that all should be equal. When this nonsense began to be talked openly, the provisional government knew that it must fight or surrender. And, at the same time, the workmen were as good as their word; they made ready for the fray.

The government appointed to the command of its army a tried and valiant soldier named Cavaignac, who was a sincere republican and a man of sense and honor. The workmen were led by Louis Blanc, who was a visionary; Barbès, who was a murderer; Raspail, who was a crank druggist; and Blanqui, who had spent his life in prison and had become paralyzed in his legs. These people did not know what they wanted; they said that there were a hundred thousand men in Paris who had no work and no bread, and that when such was the case something must be wrong.

You know that it is no part of the business of any government to feed its people, and that when riots and disturbances occur daily, industry stops and workmen go hungry. The Paris workmen were complaining of the consequences of their own acts. If they had been less disorderly, they would have more easily found work. But the poor, hungry fellows were in an angry mood, and demagogues—who wanted to pull everything down in the hope of finding plunder in the ruins—persuaded them that they would gain by rising in arms. Accordingly, on June 23d and 24th, four months after the establishment of the provisional government, they began to build barricades once more. Cavaignac sadly but resolutely ordered out his troops.

On June the 26th the battle was over, and the insurgents were crushed. It had not been done without sacrifice of life. About two thousand of the workmen had been killed, as many wounded, and some eleven thousand made prisoners; and they on their side had killed a number of generals and leading men, and worse than all, the Archbishop of Paris, who had not an enemy in the world, and was beloved by every one in Paris. The good old priest had gone to a barricade to appeal to the workmen; some felon hand aimed a shot at him from a window, and he fell with his gray hair dabbled with blood.

When the rebellion was ended Cavaignac laid down his power and proposed to return to private life, but the provisional government insisted on his retaining control of affairs for a time. An Assembly had been elected, and it was engaged in framing a new constitution for France. When the work was completed, it was submitted to the people and accepted.

An election for president was held on December 11th, and, by a large majority, Louis Napoleon Bonaparte was elected president over Cavaignac, whom the workmen could not forgive for his victory over their "brothers." Of Louis Napoleon you will hear much in the next chapter; here it may be enough to say that when he was sworn in he offered his hand to Cavaignac, who turned his back and walked away. Cavaignac was a good judge of men.

Before you pass to the reign of Louis Napoleon, you must give credit to the kings who governed France between 1815 and 1850 for the eminent writers who flourished in their reigns. First among these was Victor Hugo, equally famous as a poet, philosopher, and writer of novels; then, when you learn French, you will read with delight the poems of Lamartine and Alfred de Musset; among historians, you will enjoy Guizot, Thiers, Thierry; among philosophers, Comte, St. Simon, Lamennais; among novel-writers, Balzac, Dumas the elder, Cherbuliez, Alfred de Vigny, Octave Feuillet, Zola, and others; among men of science, Ampère, Gay de Lussac, Biot, Champollion, Poisson. At no time in French history was the French mind more active or more fertile than during the reign of Louis Philippe, and I cannot think that a reign is inglorious of which so much can be said.

LOUIS NAPOLEON AS A YOUNG OFFICER

CHAPTER LVII

THE SECOND EMPIRE

A.D. 1852–1871

LOUIS NAPOLEON BONAPARTE was the son of Louis Bonaparte, at one time King of Holland, and of his wife Hortense Beauharnais, daughter of the Empress Josephine. He was born in 1808.

After he reached manhood he lived much in England, where people thought meanly of him. He was regarded as a dreamer and a crank. He used to say that he was predestined to succeed his uncle as emperor of the French, and, as at the time he could not pay his tailor, people laughed at him. They laughed the more when he tried to get up an insurrection at Strasburg, and was promptly arrested and sent out of France in contemptuous pity; and when he repeated his attempt at Boulogne—where he landed with a tame eagle in his hand, to remind people of the eagle which Napoleon's soldiers carried on their standard —he was caught again and locked up in a prison at Ham.

Even when he made his escape in the disguise of a carpenter and turned up at Paris, after the overthrow of Louis Philippe, nobody took him seriously. It was proposed to expel him from France, but when he made a speech in his own defence, the deputy who had proposed the expulsion withdrew his motion, saying that he had once imagined the gentleman to be dangerous, but now, having heard him, he felt satisfied he was harmless.

This was the man who, on December 11th, 1848, became President of France. He had risen to that rank through the power of money and intrigue, and through a lingering fondness among the French for the memory of Napoleon, which the importation of his remains from St. Helena had helped to foster.

The new president had hardly got seated in the presidential chair when he began a duel with the Chamber, which was evidently to be a fight to a finish. Each side accused the other of plotting treason. On one side was Louis Napoleon, cold, calculating, silent as the grave, bent on treading in his uncle's footsteps; on the other were the members of the Chamber, loyal, honest, unselfish, loud-spoken, and boisterous, having nothing to conceal. Napoleon began by dismissing from his cabinet three ministers who were known to be loyal to the republic, and replacing them by General St. Arnaud, De Morny, and Maupas, three unprincipled and resolute knaves, upon whom he could rely for any deed of darkness. St. Arnaud was set over the army; he told the soldiers that the new Napoleon would be as liberal to them as the old Napoleon had been; Maupas was set over the police, and De Morny looked out for things generally. Other friends of Napoleon went about calling the Assembly a nest of demagogues who were plotting a new revolution. This frightened business-men and working-men.

On the evening of December 1st, 1851, a party was given at the palace of the Elysée, where the president lived. All Paris was there in diamonds and laces and

CLEARING THE PARIS STREETS

smiles. One lady, who stole away for an hour to visit the opera, met De Morny there, and said to him,

"I hear that there is to be a clean sweep pretty soon."

"Indeed, madame?" replied De Morny; "if there is any sweeping done, I hope I will be on the side of the broom-handle."

At midnight, after the guests had gone home, Louis Napoleon, De Morny, St. Arnaud, and Maupas met in an inner room of the palace. The president sat close to the fire, with his elbows on his knees and his face in his hands. He said never a word. The others talked violently and loudly; they only spoke to the president when they wanted money from him to buy the colonels of certain regiments.

At two that morning the printers of the *Moniteur*, each printer with two policemen standing over him, set up a proclamation from Louis Napoleon, abolishing the constitution, dissolving the Chambers, declaring martial law, and proposing to the people to elect their chief magistrate for ten years. When the winter day broke, this proclamation was found posted all over the walls of Paris. At four that morning, Thiers, Cavaignac, Changarnier, Lamoricière, and eighteen other leading republicans whom the people trusted, were seized in their beds and carried off to prison. With the first glimmer of daylight the other members of the Chamber met, and declared that Louis Napoleon had broken his oath and forfeited his office; whereupon they were all arrested by soldiers, and locked up with Thiers and his friends. This is called the Coup d'Etat.

On the following morning the people—including most of those who had voted for Louis Napoleon in preference to Cavaignac—fell to building barricades in the old way. This was what Louis Napoleon wanted. He gathered fifty thousand soldiers, flung them on the barricaders, and slaughtered them mercilessly. The work of slaughter went on all night. When day broke on the 5th, the pavements of Paris were soaked in blood, corpses lay stretched out in rows, and in one cemetery, where three hundred and fifty unknown men were buried, their heads were left sticking out of the ground, so that their friends could recognize them. What was done in Paris was done in every town in France where the Coup d'Etat was opposed.

France, cowed and trembling, quickly voted that the Coup d'Etat was a divine blessing, and prepared for the next act in the drama. It was not long delayed.

In October, 1852, Louis Napoleon spoke as follows at Bordeaux:

"France seems to be returning to the empire. That is because the empire is peace, and France desires peace."

One month afterward the Senate, which Louis Napoleon had appointed, drew up an address proposing to abolish the republic and restore the empire; the question being submitted to the people, they voted by a large majority for the empire; and on December 2d, 1852, Louis Napoleon was crowned emperor with the title of Napoleon the Third, the poor boy who had died at Vienna being accounted Napoleon the Second.

In order to found a dynasty, he married; his wife was beautiful and bright, a Spanish lady, whose name was Eugenie of Montijo. Next year this lady gave him a son, who grew up to be a fine, manly lad. He was educated in England, and when the English went to war with the Zulus of South Africa, he joined their army and was killed just as his manhood was beginning.

During the early years of his reign Napoleon the Third labored faithfully to make France prosperous and Paris beautiful. Millions were spent in pulling down the old rookeries where revolutions had been hatched, and cutting splendid boulevards through their sites. Industries of all kinds were encouraged, and, as he was a wise statesman, he established free trade with England and tried to establish it with other countries. He promoted enterprise, and under him speculation became active. Vast fortunes were made, and spent lavishly; everybody in France appeared to be well off; and, though the national and city debts were growing, everybody was satisfied, and the empire was pronounced to be an excellent thing.

Being a Bonaparte, however, and owing much to the army, he could not help plunging into wars. His first war was with Russia and was undertaken jointly with England. There was no reasonable ground for the war; but it lasted a couple of years, cost numbers of lives, and ended in the capture and destruction of the chief seaport and arsenal of south Russia—Sebastopol.

Then he made war upon Austria—perhaps to redeem a promise he had made to Mazzini, when he was at Ham, to establish a kingdom for Italy; he took the command of his armies himself, won two splendid victories at Magenta and Solferino, and freed all Italy, except Venice, from the Austrian yoke. So here was more glory, and people began to say that the Third Napoleon was as brilliant a soldier as the First.

Then he turned on China, which he invaded jointly with the English, marched to Pekin, looted and burned the emperor's palace, and the French again said that wherever his eagles went victory perched upon their crest.

But this was rather a mistake, as they found out when, shortly afterward, the emperor made war upon Mexico. Our civil war was drawing to a close, and Mr. Lincoln and the people of the North had no love for Napoleon, because they knew that he had been in his heart in favor of the rebels, and that if it had depended on him the Union would have been destroyed. When Richmond fell Mr. Seward wrote a short, sharp letter to Paris, advising the emperor to take his troops out of Mexico by the shortest available road; and, by way of giving point to the letter, Mr. Lincoln ordered General Sherman to move with fifty thousand men to the bank of the Rio Grande. Marshal Bazaine, who commanded the French in Mexico, did not wait to be introduced to General Sherman; he re-embarked his army at once and returned to France. His return gave a shock to the French; they began to ask whether it was possible the emperor was not the all-conquering hero they had accounted him. The very men who had shouted loudest in praise of the empire now began to find a good deal of fault with it.

The emperor bowed to the storm and began to make concessions to the people. He let them have a little share in managing the government and let the press speak a little more freely. He said that he had been much misunderstood—that he had been all along in favor of giving the fullest liberty to the French, and that he had merely taken power into his own hands to distribute it to the people in the right doses and at the right time.

But he soon had other concerns to occupy his mind. France and Prussia were drifting into war. There was a shallow pretext—a dispute about the selection of a prince of the Hohenzollern family to be King of Spain. France protested against the Hohenzollern, and the King of Prus-

NAPOLEON III

sia required him to decline the throne, but France was not satisfied. The fact was, the people of both countries hated each other and were eager for the fray—the French, because they thought they saw in the future visions of glory and conquest; the Prussians, because they remembered their defeats sixty years before and had forgotten the vengeance they took for them. Chancellor Bismarck, prime-minister of Prussia, had foreseen the war for two years or more and had been preparing for it. In France, I am sorry to say that the mad rage of the people for an unprovoked war was fanned by a woman—the Empress Eugenie.

She went about saying,

"It is my war!"

And when mobs passed her windows shouting "On to

Berlin !" she clapped her hands. She was a good woman, but she did France a terrible mischief. What she did not know was, that Germany was ready and France was not. The army on which she and the emperor had counted existed only on paper. The generals had drawn pay for troops who did not exist in the flesh.

War was declared on July 19th, 1870. By July 31st Prussia had half a million of men on the Rhine. The Emperor Napoleon never had half as many in one spot. He issued a proclamation in which he said:

"Soldiers! I am about to place myself at your head, to defend the honor and soil of the country. Whatever road we take beyond our frontiers, we shall find glorious traces of our fathers. The fate of liberty and civilization depends upon our success."

Von Moltke, the German general, issued no proclamation, but he said to the King of Prussia,

"If Napoleon does not cross the Rhine in a fortnight he will never cross it, except as a prisoner."

There was a fight early in August at Weissenberg, another at Worth, another at Saarbruch, another at Forbach; at each of these the Germans were two to one, and the French were beaten. The latter fell back, and were again attacked at Gravelotte, and one of their two armies, under Bazaine, was driven into Metz, where it was bottled up and took no further part in the war. The other army, which was commanded by MacMahon and with which the emperor was serving, was pushed into Sedan, was surrounded there and compelled to surrender.

On September 2d an officer brought a letter from the emperor to the King of Prussia, which began with the words,

"Having been unable to die at the head of my troops, I give up my sword to your majesty."

Every man of MacMahon's army, including the emperor himself, became a prisoner and was sent into Germany. I think that, while you must blame the emperor for having undertaken an unjust war, and while you must regard him as insincere and an enemy of freedom, you would have been sorry for him then. He had never liked the war. He had been driven into it by the empress and the Paris mob. He had never felt sure of victory. He was suffering from a dreadful disease, which gave him constant and acute agony and of which he afterward died. There is a picture of his meeting with the King of Prussia, in which the German, tall and erect, with his fierce moustache and his scowling eyes, frowns upon the emperor, who looks like a shrunken old man, bent from pain and grief, and with a face distorted by suffering. I think it is a very sad picture.

When the news of the capture of the emperor reached Paris the republic was again proclaimed; but the German armies besieged the place, and took it after a four months' siege, during which the people endured such misery from famine that they not only ate all the horses in the city, but also the wild animals in the Garden of Plants. Peace was made at last, the Germans went home, and after a long struggle a new republic was founded which lasts to this day. May it be enduring, peaceful, and prosperous!

INDEX

THE END

www.ingramcontent.com/pod-product-compliance
Lightning Source LLC
LaVergne TN
LVHW012206040326
832903LV00003B/159